REAL LACE REVISITED

REAL LACE REVISITED

JAMES P. MACGUIRE

Guilford, Connecticut

*For Michelle, half-Kiwi, half-Californian,
daughter of the Sacred Heart*

An imprint of The Rowman & Littlefield Publishing Group, Inc.
4501 Forbes Blvd., Ste. 200
Lanham, MD 20706
www.rowman.com

Distributed by NATIONAL BOOK NETWORK

British Library Cataloguing in Publication Information available

Library of Congress Cataloging-in-Publication Data:
Names: MacGuire, James P., author.
Title: Real lace revisited / by James P. MacGuire.
Description: Guilford, Connecticut : Lyons Press, [2017] | Includes bibliographical references.
Identifiers: LCCN 2016042840 (print) | LCCN 2016044377 (ebook) | ISBN 9781493024902
    (hardback : alkaline paper) | ISBN 9781493037346 (pbk) | ISBN 9781493024926 (e-book)
Subjects: LCSH: Birmingham, Stephen. Real lace. | Irish Americans—Biography. | Upper class—
    United States—Biography. | Rich people—United States—Biography. | United States—Social
    life and customs. | United States—Ethnic relations.
Classification: LCC E184.I6 B573 2017 (print) | LCC E184.I6 (ebook) | DDC
    305.8916/2073—dc23
LC record available at https://lccn.loc.gov/2016042840

∞™ The paper used in this publication meets the minimum requirements of American National
Standard for Information Sciences—Permanence of Paper for Printed Library Materials, ANSI/
NISO Z39.48-1992.

Printed in the United States of America

CONTENTS

CONTENTS

Acknowledgments

It goes without saying that my first thanks go to Stephen Birmingham, who conceived and wrote the original *Real Lace*. We had met many years ago at Saratoga Race Course in Mary Lou Whitney's box, and when I approached him in late 2014 to inquire about updating and expanding *Real Lace*, Mr. Birmingham was kind and accommodating. His agent, Henry Thayer, of Brandt & Brandt, has been a pleasure to work with, as has my old friend and agent, the venerable Jacques de Spoelberch. None of this would have been possible without the interest and encouragement of Jed Lyons and his team at Rowman & Littlefield, including first and foremost Eugene Brissie, Emily Tyler, and Alex Singer, who shepherded the book into being patiently and professionally. I am grateful to all of them for the contributions they have made to *Real Lace Revisited* and to all those family, friends, and other associates whom I called upon for assistance in the research and writing. They responded generously and wisely.

Ronald Hoffman and Sally D. Mason's *Princes of Ireland, Planters of Maryland* was an invaluable resource in writing on the Carroll family. Jean Stein's *West of Eden* provided fresh perspectives on the Doheny family. The speakers at the first Portsmouth Institute in 2009 on *The Catholic William F. Buckley Jr.* also provided me with many insights I would not otherwise have had, and I am grateful to them. Jim Forest's talk on Dorothy Day at the 2013 Portsmouth Institute was equally valuable in writing about her. Finally, George Weigel's and Peter Steinfels' competing visions of the future of the American church, delivered at the 2013 Institute on *Catholicism and the American Experience*, were thought-provoking and deserved to be summarized here. J.O. Tobin II's encyclopedic knowledge of San Franciscan genealogies was essential.

Finally, I would be remiss not to thank my old English teacher, the late Father Damian Kearney, O.S.B., for suggesting to Mr. Frank Pagliaro, then a student at our mutual alma mater, Portsmouth Abbey School, that he might ask me for help in writing a story on the original *Real Lace* for the school newspaper in 2010. Out of that kernel came this book. All of those mentioned above share in whatever merits this book may have, while I alone am responsible for any errors or other shortcomings.

Preface

In Praise of Stephen Birmingham

Stephen Birmingham died in December of 2015 at his home in Manhattan after a brief struggle with cancer. He was eighty-six.

Mr. Birmingham made more than a dozen literary excursions into what his *New York Times* obituary termed "pop sociology," including the best-selling *Our Crowd*, which chronicled the rise of the first wealthy German-Jewish families in America; a group portrait of the Dakota, the exclusive Manhattan apartment building on the Upper West Side; and explorations of the African-American and Irish-American elites. *Real Lace: America's Irish Rich* was the title of his book on this last group, published in 1973.

When I approached him in late 2014 to inquire about updating and expanding *Real Lace*, Steve immediately offered his cooperation. I am grateful for his encouragement and regret we did not have the chance to spend more time together as I got down to writing. I would have enjoyed his wry sense of humor and profited from his vast experience in chronicling America's moneyed classes.

At the same time, the fact that Stephen Birmingham was not available to guide me on this revisitation of the subject may, in fact, have forced me to look at the subject afresh and enabled me to make my own judgments. For one thing, neither my family nor any of the other *Real Lace* families would have ever dreamed of referring to themselves as First Irish Families, or "FIFs," in Mr. Birmingham's phrase. The audacity of such pretension would have appalled them. In fact, I can remember the delight my father took when a rather stuffy aunt who had married into the family let it be known that she had hired a professional genealogist to establish the American branch of the Butlers' (from whom we were descended) precise relation to the Butler Dukes of Ormond. Needless to say, despite this gentleman's best efforts, the answer came back . . . well, let's just say no answer came back. Our Butlers were apparently, to use the late C.D.B. Bryan's delicious phrase, "more felonious than thou."

My father hoped that at a bare minimum an ample strain of horse thievery would show up in the bloodlines, but in the end his dear and very determined aunt simply stopped alluding to the great research project, the professional genealogist doubtless suffered her withering scorn, and we were joyfully liberated to hazard our own, not always printable, improvisations about his findings.

Nor was it true that the so-called First Irish Families all knew each other, though some did, of course, if they grew up in the same city (New York or San Francisco), went to the same schools (the Priory, Canterbury, or Sacred Heart), or worked in related industries, such as Wall Street.

Furthermore, the families Birmingham profiled are only a small subset of those Irish Americans who attained significant wealth in the latter nineteenth and first half of the twentieth centuries, and an even smaller subset of those who have achieved it since. So it took some editorial discrimination to decide exactly how and whom to focus on nearly half a century on. Some families have declined, of course. Others have held their own or thrived. And many new fortunes have been made.

I have taken the liberty of adding a few profiles, such as that of the *real* First Irish Family in America, the Carrolls of Maryland, whom Stephen Birmingham ignored because of his focus, as with his previous best-seller *Our Crowd*, on those families whose wealth originated in the late nineteenth and twentieth centuries, more than two hundred years after Charles Carroll ("the Settler") arrived on these shores.

I have also given fuller consideration to the Kennedys, a family that Birmingham mentioned only to *exclude* from the ranks of the FIFs (try pronouncing that twenty times in a row if you want a troublesome little tongue-twister) for their arriviste boorishness, immorality, and social climbing. Whatever the snobbery of the Murrays and McDonnells in another generation, the Kennedy achievements in business and public service, as well as their tragedies and highly publicized shortcomings, deserve recognition here. Hilariously enough, in fact, if you were to buy the e-book edition of the original *Real Lace* today, you would find the cover photo is of the Kennedys! One hopes Mr. Birmingham is not turning over in his grave. I doubt it, because, as an ad agency copywriter in the *Mad Men* era, he had a keen eye for marketing opportunities, which, after the success of *Our Crowd*, is probably what led him to write *Real Lace* in the first place.

Real Lace Revisited, then, is not a revision of *Real Lace*. I hope, however, it pays tribute to Stephen Birmingham's book and is an entertaining portrait in its own right of some colorful characters and families. It is most certainly not a definitive study, nor is it the last word on this very broad subject. Ultimately, there are many ways of being Irish in America and many variations of success, geography, and community. All of them should be celebrated for what they are.

J.M., New York City
St. Patrick's Day

FOREWORD

The Real *First Irish Family*

THROUGHOUT *REAL LACE*, STEPHEN BIRMINGHAM REFERRED TO HIS subjects as "FIFs," an abbreviation for First Irish Families, who became prominent in the late nineteenth and early twentieth centuries. This was a term he appears to have coined himself. I have never heard or seen it used by others, and, in fact, if there is such a thing as a First Irish Family in America, we have to look for it many years before. According to the *Encyclopedia of the Irish in America*, one Richard Butler from Tipperary was the first documented Irishman to arrive in the Americas, in the year 1584. But in terms of familial preeminence, it is best to look to the late eighteenth century, when the first Charles Carroll, called the Settler, emigrated to Maryland, in large part because of its reputation for religious toleration, especially of Catholics.

The Slieve Bloom Mountains along the southeastern border of County Offaly were from Tudor times until the seventeenth century a battleground in the fierce struggle between the Gaelic Irish and the English for control of the destiny of Ireland. Ely O'Carroll, the territory over which the O'Carrolls held sway, originally lay in Munster (along with Leinster, Ulster, and Connacht, one of the four ancient provinces—"the Four Green Fields" of the rebel song—of Ireland). In medieval times Ely O'Carroll encompassed parts of the modern counties of Offaly, northern Tipperary, and Laois. The chief of Ely was named Daniel O'Carroll, who had by the end of the twelfth century settled in Litterluna. In due course the O'Carroll lands included twenty-three castles in the Clonlisk and Ballybritt regions.

The O'Carrolls were not, however, the preeminent of clans. That designation would go to the most powerful of the Anglo-Norman clans (descended from forces who invaded with the approval of Henry II in 1169 to establish English claims but who in subsequent generations became Gaelicized and began calling themselves "Anglo-Irish"). This family were the Fitzgeralds, the mighty Earls of Kildare. By the end of the fifteenth century, a second great Anglo-Irish family, the Butlers, Earls of Ormond with their seat at Kilkenny Castle, had risen to rival the Fitzgeralds' dominance. The houses of Kildare and Ormond struggled over large portions of Leinster and Munster, drawing less powerful Anglo-Irish and Gaelic families into their orbits. Among these Irish clans were the O'Carrolls, who shifted allegiances with the times as they strived to gain advantage and security for themselves.

Before 1513 the O'Carrolls generally regarded the Fitzgeralds as the greater threat and thus nurtured their ties to the Butlers. With the accession of Henry VIII, however, who sought to break the Fitzgeralds' control via a policy of surrender and regrant (surrendering lands to the English Crown to have them officially regranted), the balance shifted. While the Gaelic chiefs such as the O'Carrolls saw the policy as an abrogation of their ancient birthrights that belonged to them by tradition and custom, they also saw the possibility of manipulating the Crown's program to serve their immediate interests. For Ely O'Carroll and many others, taking this step would ultimately bring destruction for the family's succeeding generations.

Unlike the English practice of primogeniture, in the old Gaelic tradition, when the lord died, "the strongest succeeds: and the son seldom succeeds the father. They get many children beside their lawfully begotten, whereof all be gentlemen." As in many developing countries today, fecundity was considered a virtue and many children an insurance policy against an impoverished and enfeebled old age.

Clan leaders like Teige O'Carroll (d. 1533), Sir William O'Carroll, and Sir Charles O'Carroll worked to maintain lands even as the Ormonds bore down on them and the Tudor government under Queen Mary became more assertive beyond the Pale of Settlement (the area of

British control surrounding Dublin). Sir Charles made repeated trips to London to pledge his loyalty to the Crown. In July of 1597 an anonymous royal official grasped his strategy:

> *Sir Charles O'Carroll and Sir John Mac Coghlan are both lords of great countries; both have been rebels, and more rebellious minds are not in Ireland, yet both are subjects; but why? They have rivals. There be others who have more right to their lands than themselves. Their surrender to Her Majesty (now, of course, Queen Elizabeth I) is their only security.*

In 1594 Sir Charles chose to remain loyal to the Crown when Hugh O'Neill, Earl of Tyrone, raised his banner in Ulster and sought to drive the English from Ireland in the Nine Years' War (1594–1603). Many Gaelic chiefs rallied to the cause, but others, who suspected Tyrone's true intention was to make himself overlord of Ireland, held back. O'Carroll maintained a company of Irish foot in royal service, and when he attacked a force of Tyrone mercenaries that threatened Ely O'Carroll, Tyrone was enraged and ordered the entire O'Carroll territory destroyed. Tyrone then set up a rival O'Carroll chief, who arranged Sir Charles's murder in July of 1600.

John O'Carroll, the four-year-old great-nephew of Sir Charles, was recognized by the Crown as the legitimate successor, supplied with a Protestant guardian, and in due course married to the Earl of Ormond's great niece, Eleanor. These events marked the death of the O'Carroll lordship and the end of the era of Ely chieftains.

The Carrolls paid dearly for their devout Catholicism, not only in Ireland but also in America.

"The Carrolls' position as Catholic outsiders in Protestant Maryland and their conscious memory of their family's long, bitter, and ultimately futile struggle against conquest and dispossession in Ireland provide more than a different perspective on early American society," Ronald Hoffman writes in his invaluable 2001 study *Princes of Ireland, Planters of Maryland: A Carroll Saga, 1500–1782*, upon which much of this chapter relies.

Threatened relentlessly between 1500 and 1782, first by the territorial ambitions of rival clans, then because of their stubborn attachment to their Gaelic heritage, and finally for their defiant adherence to Catholicism—both in Ireland and in Maryland—the Carrolls consistently developed strategies comparable to those used by their ancestors, confronting each peril with compromise, cunning, implacable will, and a tenacious determination to survive.

By 1642, however, the crisis between King Charles I and Parliament deepened and spilled over into Ireland and the colonies, in Maryland especially. The struggle between the King's Cavaliers and the Parliamentarian Roundheads produced chaos in civil society. Once they had executed the king and consolidated their power at home, the Parliamentarians turned their attention to Ireland. On August 15, 1649, Oliver Cromwell and an army of three thousand men landed in Dublin. They received a welcome with great fanfare from the city's Protestants, whereupon Cromwell laid waste to the country's Catholic centers, massacred the population in two cities, and confiscated much of the remaining Catholic lands. When it was over, Catholic-held lands in Ireland had been reduced from 60 percent of the total to 25 percent. All of these events had their impact on Maryland life as well, where Catholic toleration suffered. Even the restoration of the Stuart line in 1660 did not erase the tensions that had surfaced among Protestants and Catholics in the colonies.

Throughout this period in Ireland, the O'Carrolls suffered grievous loss of lands. With the help of Richard Grace, some of Daniel Carroll of Ballymooney's tracts were restored, where his grandson Daniel inherited a 136-acre townland called Aghagurty and styled himself Daniel Carroll of Aghagurty, which translates from Gaelic as "field of hunger or starvation." Later generations of his family preferred to style him as Charles Carroll of Litterluna. Of his four sons, two came to Maryland—John, who died a man of modest means, and Charles. Educated at St. Omer's, Lille, and University of Douai in France and called to the Inner Temple in London, Charles secured the post of attorney general in Maryland before emigrating there on October 1, 1688, and used his offices to good effect, amassing considerable power and influence as an ally to the mighty Lord Baltimore. These he passed on to his son, Charles Carroll of Annapolis, and to his grandson, Charles Carroll of Carrollton, the only Catholic signer of the Declaration of Independence.

Maryland had a long tradition of religious tolerance, which was forged by the Catholic Calvert family. It was Sir George Calvert who, in 1635, had successfully petitioned King Charles I to establish a colony called the Province of Maryland where Catholics could live freely. Throughout the seventeenth century, as Protestants and Catholics across the British Empire battled for supremacy, Maryland was a relatively safe haven for Catholics in the American colonies.

As it turned out, Charles Carroll (the Settler) was named the colony's attorney general (serving under the third Lord Baltimore). However, England's so-called Glorious Revolution of 1688 ushered in yet another era of Catholic subservience and Protestant ascendancy, which made its way to the colonies as well. Charles Carroll threw himself into his official and private duties with energy and even changed his family motto from *In fide et in bello fortis* ("Strong in faith and war") to *Ubicumque cum libertate* ("Anywhere so long as there be freedom"). However, he still had to fight many battles for his rights and those of other Catholics against the Elizabethan-era penal laws barring Catholics from public office and other injustices, and in the event he was sentenced to two terms in jail for his intemperate refusal to accept these iniquities.

Founded in 1729, Baltimore was named after a port town in West Cork. The name Baltimore is derived from the Gaelic *baile an tigh mór*, meaning "the village near the big house." By that time the Carrolls had already established themselves as an influential family with extensive landholdings on Maryland's Western Shore.

Though Catholics were disenfranchised, the Baltimore region remained a relatively good place for Irish Catholics, as evidenced by the landholdings and fortunes established by Charles Carroll and his two sons, Charles Carroll of Annapolis (born in 1702) and Daniel (born in 1707).

Indeed, despite the swirling religious acrimony of the era, Baltimore's diverse blend of Irish and English Catholics, not to mention Irish and English (and Scottish) Protestants, suggests that some people did manage to get along and establish a certain level of civil peace in the New

World. This comity was roiled from time to time by events overseas, such as the Fifteen Rebellion (1715) when John, Viscount Bolingbroke, and James Butler, Duke of Ormond, tried to install the Stuart "Old Pretender," James III, on the throne. When they failed, both fled to France, but the Jacobite and anti-Jacobite passions they unleashed caused political disturbances as far away as Maryland.

Along with the tradition of religious tolerance established by Cecil Calvert (Sir George's son), Baltimore's geographical location, a substantial distance from the Northeast and bordering on the American South, helped the city avoid some of the problems of New England, where a more rigid form of puritanism held sway (1688, the year Charles the Settler came to America, was the same year a devout Catholic and Gaelic-speaking Irish woman named Goody Glover was hanged as a witch in Boston).

Ultimately Charles Carroll the Settler would amass a huge estate of many properties totaling 47,700 acres. In 1771 his grandson, Charles Carroll of Carrollton, recounted the circumstances of his grandfather's coming to Maryland from Ireland:

The family estate being greatly impaired by the iniquity of the times, which had stripped the most ancient Irish families of their property, he resolved to seek his fortune far distant from the scene of such oppressions. Being a Roman Catholick he pitched on Mryd where the free exercise of that religion & its equal privileges were granted to its professors by a Royal Charter, and afterwards confirmed by a perpetual law of this province.

Like other early Chesapeake entrepreneurs, Carroll built his fortune by combining favorable marriages with high public office and private dealings in planting, banking, legal, and mercantile activities. As with many of his contemporaries, he held many slaves, 112 at his death.

Among his properties was Elk Ridge, seven thousand acres on the border of Baltimore and Anne Arundel Counties, the nucleus of what would become Doughoregan Manor, the family's principal dwelling plantation. Another was Clinmalira, patented by the Settler in 1711, a five-thousand-acre parcel adjoining My Lady's Manor, the ten-thousand-acre tract north of Baltimore given by Charles Calvert, third Lord Baltimore, to his wife, Margaret. Carroll's proximity to and favor with the great lord (who, it should be said, had left Maryland to reside permanently in England in 1684) was advantageous and one he pushed, in the end, too far for his own good.

In advancing relentlessly his and other Catholics' claims, Carroll became an enemy of the governor, a Protestant named John Hart, who called him "a stubborn Irish Catholic Jacobite." On February 20, 1717, after intense lobbying from all sides, the proprietor, Lord Baltimore, revoked Carroll's commission and cast him aside, bestowing the office on a Protestant Calvert relative. Though Carroll never ceased to struggle for his and his coreligionists' rights, the tide turned against them as Hart passed two acts repealing the Catholic right to vote and making religious observance more difficult. At his death Carroll had greatly complicated the estate that fell to his son, Charles Carroll of Annapolis, but left an enduring legacy of fierce tribal loyalty and a tenacious memory—*Marylando-Hibernus*.

Or, in a favorite phrase of my old history teacher, Bill Crimmins, another Anglo-Irishman raised in Maryland: "The Irish, they never learn, but they never forget." Another variant on which is: "Irish Alzheimer's: Forget everything except the grudges."

CHARLES CARROLL OF ANNAPOLIS

It took the Settler's son, Charles Carroll of Annapolis, thirty-seven years to settle fully his father's will, which he accomplished after much effort in 1857. His younger brother Daniel returned from his European education and married a wealthy woman named Ann Rozer, who bought him a 1,326-acre tract called Duddington Manor. Thereafter Daniel styled himself as Daniel Carroll of Duddington.

Charles was happy to let his brother take on more social activities while he concentrated on managing the family's complex business affairs. When he failed to get his way to raise tobacco prices, he challenged his adversary in the matter, James Hollyday, to a duel and was duly reprimanded by the House of Delegates, in which they both sat. He began to install a system of tenantry on some of his lands and brought the tenants from Ireland, seeing it as a more beneficial long-term solution than slavery. His land development schemes succeeded well, but at various times his management of his relatives' affairs, and the commission he charged for so doing (5 percent), were challenged by them and their representatives, enraging him. In his mind the services he had provided and the results obtained were far superior than others could have achieved, and the fees he requested were cheap at the price.

Perhaps the largest and longest-lasting controversy surrounding Charles Carroll of Annapolis was the birth of his son, Charles Carroll of Carrollton, on September 19, 1737, to the older Carroll's first cousin and longtime companion, Elizabeth Brooke. They had long lived in the same household and she was an intimate friend of Charles's sisters, but not his legal wife. Carroll did not marry Elizabeth until twenty years later, on February 15, 1757, when a Jesuit priest named Mathias Maners joined them in holy matrimony. Whereas common-law marriages were common, and we have seen in the past that Irish heads of families often produced recognized sons out of wedlock, this unusual state of affairs was considered an assault against propriety in the colony. Technically young Charley remained a bastard until 1788, when the Act to Direct Descents passed, which applied to him. But Charles Carroll of Carrollton's illegitimacy in civil and canon law at birth would remain controversial well into the twentieth century.

Charles Carroll of Annapolis would remain a diligent father to young Charley, sending him off to the Jesuits at St. Omer's in France, founded by Father Ralph Persons there in 1614 as a haven for English Catholic gentlemen, who could not then be educated in their religion in their own country (the school returned to Stonyhurst in the north of England after the relaxation of the Penal Laws in the nineteenth century). Afterwards Charley continued his European education at Douai (1748–54), Rheims (1755), and Paris (1756–57) and in law at Bourges and common law at London's Inner Temple (1759–64). Charles Carroll of Annapolis advised Charley on his studies, on his clothing, and on his comportment, including the society of acceptable English Catholics whose company he could keep on his allowance of three hundred pounds a year, in an endless stream of correspondence that today is faintly reminiscent of the letters in Bulwer-Lytton's once well-known nineteenth-century novel, *Pelham*. His aim was clear: to train and equip his heir to carry out the Carroll family's leadership and high social status into the next and succeeding generations. By the time Charley had returned from Europe in 1765 and begun to work with his father on family and public affairs, it was clear he had served the necessary apprenticeship and possessed the native ability to succeed in these tasks, as his leadership in the Continental Congress and Revolution would later prove. When Charles Carroll of Annapolis died in 1782, he had reason to be well pleased in his son and the tenacity of his paternal stewardship, which had produced the sole Catholic signer of the Declaration of Independence.

When Charley first returned in 1765, there were approximately eighteen Carroll estates on the Western Shore of Maryland and the Baltimore Iron Works to oversee and steward. These included such storied properties as Doughoregan, Annapolis, White Hall, Bashford Manor, St. Clement's Manor, Baltimore Town, St. Mary's City, Mellwood, Rock Creek (today a park in the District of Columbia), Berkeley Springs, Poplar Island (just off the Eastern Shore), and Duddington Manor.

He also set about the important task of finding a suitable wife. Having been spurned by an English girl named Louisa Baker, Charley set upon an Eastern Shore cousin named Rachel Cooke, but she fell ill and died just weeks before their planned wedding in November of 1766. Ultimately he would marry Molly Darnall, another cousin, whose mother had long been a part of the Carroll household. They were wed on June 5, 1768.

Charley pressed on with his business affairs, which often meant travel away from home. He faced resistance from Protestant tenants over back rents and began importing slaves from Virginia into Maryland. His and Molly's first child was born ten months later but died in infancy. Following a miscarriage, Mary Carroll ("Little Pol") was born on September 2, 1770. By September 1772 Charley had joined the Maryland Jockey Club. In that same year his dinner guests included one George Washington. And on March 2, 1775, a boy, Charles, later to become Charles Carroll of Homewood, was born.

Doughoregan Manor had expanded from 7,000 to 12,500 acres and was split into ten operating quarters, four of which were managed by a white overseer. Three hundred eighty-six slaves provided the brunt of the labor to care for livestock, grow wheat and corn, and raise a wide assortment of cabbages, lettuces, green onions, and endives. The Carroll orchards produced an equally varied crop of apples, pears, peaches, cherries, currants, gooseberries, and strawberries. Wherever possible the place was self-sufficient. Doughoragen contained tobacco barns, a prize house (for packing tobacco), flour and grist mills, a workhouse for weaving, a cobbler shop, a blacksmith shop, a fulling mill (for cleansing and thickening cloth), a tanyard, a cider house, a brickyard, a repair yard, and a quarry.

In their correspondence the Carrolls show an affection for many of their long-held slaves, referring mournfully to the deaths of "Aunt Sally" or "Old Fanny," but they showed no compunction about continuing the trade in human chattel, nor did the other members of their landowning class. They continued their moneylending and, on a modest scale, land speculation activities. As the 1770s began, however, they saw new opportunity in the public arena, where shifts in the provincial power structure offered the chance to regain rights, entitlements, and lands that had been lost at the end of the Settler's era half a century before.

CHARLES CARROLL OF CARROLLTON

Although it was impossible to foresee at the time, George Grenville's Stamp Act, enacted on November 1, 1765, just eight and a half months after Charley's homecoming, set into motion a series of protests that ultimately led to rebellion and revolution in 1776. Charley had grown up in the relatively tolerant atmosphere of England and Catholic France, far different than his father's memories of anti-Catholic persecution in the early 1700s and his grandfather's memories of Catholic suffering in Ireland.

His father's long memory of the oppression in the family past and his own experience of injustice convinced him that a Catholic in a Protestant society might best protect himself by building a bastion of economic security. This was not so very different than the attitude that would impel the *Real Lace* Irish Americans to build their fortunes in the late nineteenth and early twentieth centuries.

By the 1750s Maryland's Roman Catholics accounted for approximately 16,000 of the province's total population of 160,000. Anti-Catholic measures continued to be enacted, such as the Maryland council's direction in 1744 that Catholics no longer be enrolled in the militia. The Jacobite rising in 1745 for the "Young Pretender," Bonnie Prince Charlie, increased Protestant suspicion of the province's Catholics. At one point the threat of increasing oppression became so severe that Papa Carroll seriously considered removing his estates and family to Louisiana, but Charley, trusting in the English tradition of civil liberty more than continental tyranny, talked him out of it.

Both men were devout, doctrinally orthodox Catholics, and yet their most powerful impulse was to the betterment of their estates and the furtherance of their families in this and the generations to come.

With the imposition of the tea tax imposed by Parliament in 1767, and the subsequent Boston Tea Party on December 16, 1773, when a party of men disguised as Mohawks boarded the tea ships and broke up 342 cases of tea before heaving the contents into Boston Harbor, the stage was set for secession from the Crown. The imposition of the Intolerable Acts only accelerated the clamor for rebellion. Charley accompanied the Maryland delegation to the First Continental Congress in September of 1774 and in November became a member of the Committee of Correspondence for Anne Arundel County and Annapolis, gaining election to the second of the provincial conventions. In February of 1776 his public duties expanded when the Continental Congress asked him to participate in a diplomatic mission to Canada for the purpose of engaging support for the American cause. Ironically, in this case his religion and familiarity with French were considered assets for the job. He performed well, and shortly after his return to Maryland in June 1776, the convention chose him as a delegate to the Second Continental Congress.

The dangers of independence, especially to the landowning classes, were clear, and on May 21 the convention voted unanimously against it, only to reverse itself five weeks later on June 28. Charley campaigned vigorously for independence, so much so he missed the vote on it, but was present for the signing on August 2. He and his family had now moved once again to the center of the political whirlwind encompassing the colonies, and would have no recourse but to face the opportunities and challenges of revolution. Writing half a century later, Charley stated that he, as the only Roman Catholic signer, had struck a blow "not only for our independence of England but for the toleration of all sects professing the Christian religion and communicating to them all equal rights."

He had thus begun to move beyond his own kith and kin and to form a broader alliance with a diverse company of men and women determined to create a republic. In such circumstances, as debate raged over the course of future governance, it was only natural that Charley would alternate between hope and extreme anxiety. "God knows," he wrote his father, "what sort of a govt. we shall get." They quarreled over the Legal Tender Act, with the elder Carroll taking a narrow view, worried it would negatively impact their family fortunes, and Charley, peering farther into the future, seeing compromise and some diminution of capital as necessary sacrifices to future prosperity and posterity.

This proved the wiser course. By aligning his family with the broader Maryland gentry and submitting, however painfully, to the concessions necessary for the propertied classes to solidify their hold over society, the younger Carroll had brought his family through the Revolution fiercely determined that the Carroll wealth would never again be placed in jeopardy. In the world made by the American Revolution, the interests of men of substantial property transcended their differences, an attitude for good or ill that persists in American society even unto today.

Sadly, the events that propelled Charley and the Carrolls back into public life cost him much happiness in his private affairs. He was often traveling on public business and spent long periods away from his young family. Molly endured multiple pregnancies, but her health suffered and at different times she became addicted to laudanum, an opiate painkiller. The death of her mother in 1781 was a cruel blow that reduced her spirits further. The following May 30 "Papa" Carroll, Charles Carroll of Annapolis, died after hitting his head in a fall from the porch of his Annapolis home. Molly took to bed from the shock and began a decline that ended with her own death only days later, on June 10.

Charles Carroll of Carrollton remained a widower for fifty years. When he died on November 14, 1832, the nation mourned the passing of the last symbol of its Revolutionary birth. President Jackson ordered the United States government closed. Only one other Revolutionary hero had been accorded this honor—his former dinner guest and friend George Washington.

Charley's personal life continued to be marred by tragedy. A year after Molly's death, her youngest child, three-year-old Eliza, died. His son and heir, Charles Carroll of Homewood, today the site of Johns Hopkins University, turned into a troubled alcoholic, a great disappointment to his father who wanted nothing more than a strong male heir to succeed him. He was survived by four daughters and another son, Charles of Doughoregan, who became his heir.

Papa's "Little Pol" led a happier life. She and her husband, Richard Caton, a merchant, raised four daughters, three of whom—Mary Ann, Elizabeth, and Eliza—gained entrée to the highest levels of English society. Eliza married first Sir Felton Hervey-Bathurst, first Baronet Bathhurst, and later Francis Godolphin D'Arcy Osborne, Marquess of Carmarthen, the future seventh Duke of Leeds; Mary Ann married first Robert Patterson, brother of Elizabeth Patterson, the first wife of Napoleon's younger brother Jérôme Bonaparte, and second Richard Wellesley, first Marquess Wellesley and lord lieutenant of Ireland, older brother of the Duke of Wellington; and "Bess" married Sir George William Jerningham, eighth Baron Stafford and seventh Baronet of Costessey Hall in Norfolk, England.

More than half a century before the Gilded Age marriages of rich Americans to British peers that formed the basis for *Downton Abbey*, it was Mary Ann's that was the most brilliant of these matches. Richard Colley Wellesley, second Earl of Mornington and Marquess Wellesley, was the elder brother of the Duke of Wellington. A former governor-general of India and foreign secretary during the Peninsular War, Wellesley was made viceroy of Ireland, and Mary Ann returned with him there in triumph, as viceraine, where despite the Catholic Disability Statutes she went openly to Mass and, to the scandal of English society, undertook to complete and verify the pedigree of the Carroll family. Thus, like other Carrolls before her, Mary Ann affirmed a Gaelic past and defiant heritage.

In his waning years Charley used Wellington's attachment to his sister-in-law to impress upon Mary Ann his disappointment with England's policies toward Roman Catholics in England and Ireland. Although Wellington, as prime minister, personally opposed Roman Catholic emancipation, political reasons induced him to ram that measure through Parliament in 1829. Mary Ann became lady of the bedchamber to Queen Adelaide, wife of William IV, after Wellesley died in 1842. She died in 1853, in her grace-and-favor apartment in Hampton Court.

None of Charles Carroll of Carrollton's children could manage money. He capitalized their marriages generously and lent them additional sums when necessary, but never hesitating to secure collateral. When Charley finally surrendered power of attorney at the age of ninety-four, he insisted on imposing a clause that could reverse such a stipulation if he became displeased. He died the following year, very much in his father's mold.

The story of Carroll's illegitimacy lived far beyond him, perpetuated by such ladies as Rosalie E. Stier Calvert, whose own husband, George Calvert (1768–1838), was the illegitimate but acknowledged son of Charles Calvert, fifth Lord Baltimore. (George Calvert, in fact, began an alliance with a slave mistress in the 1780s that had produced several children by the time he married Rosalie in 1799, and he took open responsibility for them, so Mrs. Calvert came by her interest in the subject honestly.)

Another version of the Carroll story, told by Anna Hanson McKenzie Dorsey, a prominent Roman Catholic author, in a letter to Notre Dame University's Father Daniel Hudson in 1892, claimed that Charles Carroll of Carrollton refused to return home from Europe until his father "legitimize my birth by marrying my mother, wiping dishonor from her as well as myself."

However fanciful that version may be, the fact remains that even into the early decades of the twentieth century the presence of the bar sinister (a symbol of bastardy in heraldic coats of arms) in the Carroll past led a prominent patriotic society to refuse membership to women who claimed descent through Charles Carroll of Carrollton.

Another prominent Carroll descendant was John Lee Carroll (1830–1911). Carroll was born in Baltimore, Maryland, the son of Col. Charles Carroll (b. 1801) and Mary Diggs Lee (b. 1800). Col. Charles Carroll was the great-grandson of Charles Carroll of Carrollton. John Lee Carroll was also a great-grandson of Maryland's second (and seventh) governor, Thomas Sim Lee (1745–1819).

After his legal studies in Baltimore and at Harvard, he practiced law in New York and served as a United States Commissioner in the office of the clerk of the United States District Court. At the outbreak of the Civil War, he returned to Maryland, where he then remained the rest of his life. When he returned to Maryland, Carroll purchased the Doughoregan Manor, the historic family estate in Howard County, near Ellicott City, from his older brother, Charles Carroll.

In 1875 Carroll became the Democratic Party nominee for governor of Maryland, opposed by James Morrison Harris. He won by a ten-thousand-vote majority and was inaugurated as governor on January 12, 1876.

John Lee Carroll was married twice, first to Anita Phelps (1838–1873), daughter of Royal Phelps of New York, on April 24, 1856. His son by his second marriage, Philip Acosta Carroll (1879–1957), was married to Nina Ryan (1897–1989) of the *Real Lace* Ryans.

Doughoregan Manor has survived into the twenty-first century. It was a hub for munitions for Southern supporters in the Civil War. It had its own post office from 1876 to 1907. The annual Howard County horse show attracted thousands of spectators through the 1930s, keeping up a Thoroughbred tradition that went back to Charles Carroll of Annapolis's horse being beaten in the first Annapolis Subscription Plate by George Hume Steuart's Dungannon in 1743. As recently as 1971 Doughoregan was still 2,800 acres. "Only God, the Indians and the Carrolls have owned this land," a family member said. Today it is the only home of a signer still in family hands.

For much of the twentieth century, Doughoregan was presided over by Philip Carroll, born in New York City on August 9, 1924, to Nina Ryan and Philip Acosta Carroll. He attended Brooks and Harvard and the University of Pennsylvania Law School after serving as a combat engineer in World War II. He married the former Clellia Delafield LeBoutillier in 1957. Carroll was remembered as gentlemanly and kind. He opened the family chapel to neighbors as a place to worship for years. Later in life he worked to keep the place private. Yetta Goelet, the wife of one of his Brooks School schoolmates, remembers going to dinner at Doughoregan early in the twenty-first century when Philip Carroll ordered the meal off a takeout menu from a nearby Chinese restaurant. He placed easements on much of the land and received development credits for other parts of it until, at his death in 2010, the estate had been reduced to about nine hundred acres. His daughter, Camilla Carroll, lives at Doughoregan with her family and operates a farm-to-table stand that sells beef, pork, and poultry grown on Carroll land. They also rent out six-hundred-plus acres for the farming of corn and soy. Her brother, Philip Delafield Carroll, and his two sons, Philip and Harper, are also heirs to the manor.

Other Carroll descendants include Charles Carroll Carter, a former publisher, who lives in Washington with his wife Rosemary. He is a direct descendent of Daniel Carroll II of Rock Creek, who donated the land on which stands the Capitol of the United States. They remain active in Catholic causes, especially the Knights of Malta, as do several of his sons, including Carroll Jr. and Adam, a labor lawyer in the District of Columbia. Another son, Samuel Casey Carter, studied at St. John's Annapolis and Oxford University before taking his doctorate in philosophy at Catholic University of America. He also spent several years trying his vocation for religious life at Portsmouth as Brother Augustine. Later he was the executive editor of *Crisis*, the conservative Catholic magazine founded by Ralph McInerney and Michael Novak. He has written two influential books on education, *On Purpose* and *No Excuses*; headed National Heritage Academies; and today is CEO of Faith in the Future, an independent not-for-profit partnered with the Catholic high schools of Philadelphia to stabilize and rejuvenate them for their students' benefit, which will be discussed in a later chapter. The organization's success in a few short years is a testimony to Carter's leadership and his family's lived faith after three and a half centuries in the United States.

A final Carroll cousin is Outerbridge Horsey, the seventh of his family to hold that name, the first being a U.S. senator from Maryland (1777–1842). The present Horsey's father was a career diplomat and ambassador to Czechoslovakia under President Johnson. Today's Outerbridge is a distinguished architect and is active in urban and landscape planning and conservation causes. He lives in Georgetown with his wife Georgina.

AMERICA'S FIRST BISHOP

No account of the Carroll family would be complete without mentioning another Carroll cousin, John Carroll, S.J. He was born in 1735 to Daniel Carroll I and Eleanor Darnall Carroll and grew up on the family plantation in Upper Marlboro, the county seat of Prince George's County. His older brother, Daniel Carroll II, became one of only five men to sign the Articles of Confederation and Perpetual Union (1777) and the Constitution of the United States (1787).

Like several of his cousins, John (or "Cousin Jack" as he was called in the family) Carroll was educated at the College of St. Omer in French Flanders and entered the Society of Jesus at the age of eighteen in 1753. After the fourteen years of strict Jesuit training in philosophy and theology, he was ordained to the priesthood in 1769.

He remained in Europe until he was almost forty, teaching and serving as a chaplain to a British aristocrat traveling on the continent. When Pope Clement XIV suppressed the Jesuit order in Europe in 1773, Carroll returned to America and worked as a missionary in Maryland and Virginia. With five other priests he began a series of meetings that gradually organized the Catholic church in the United States.

The priests of Maryland petitioned Rome for a bishop in the United States. At the Vatican's invitation for a candidate, Carroll was selected by twenty-four out of twenty-six voters, and Pope Pius VI approved his election on November 6, 1789. Carroll was consecrated by Bishop Charles Walmesley, O.S.B., on August 15, 1790, the Feast of the Assumption, in the chapel at Lulworth Castle in Dorset, the seat of Mr. Thomas Weld, Maria Fitzherbert's brother-in-law.

When he returned to Baltimore, he took his chair in the Church of St. Peter located at the northwest corner of North Charles and Saratoga Streets. Later he oversaw the construction of the first cathedral in the United States, the Basilica of the Assumption, designed by Benjamin Henry Latrobe, architect of the United States Capitol.

Carroll, who served as archbishop until his death in 1815, gave future American Catholic leaders a blueprint when it came to establishing a Catholic diocese. A fierce proponent of education, he pushed for the creation of what would later become Georgetown University. In 1809 he also encouraged Elizabeth Seton to establish the American Sisters of Charity for the education of girls. He was also an early supporter of a vernacular liturgy in a country where few save the upper classes were schooled in Latin.

On a recent visit to Montpelier, the home of James Madison, prime author of the United States Constitution, I asked the guide about a bust in the drawing room showing a fine, strong-featured man wearing a pectoral cross. "That's Bishop John Carroll," the guide replied, "the first Catholic bishop in America. Despite their religious differences, they were great friends."

Bishop Carroll plays a part in the little-known story of another possible First Family of America, the mystery of James Ord, the reputed son of the Prince of Wales, later King George IV, and his wife, Mrs. Fitzherbert.

Maria Smythe was born on July 26, 1756, and grew up in a fashion typical of the eighteenth century Catholic gentry. The Smythes of Shropshire held properties in several counties and had their seat at Acton Burnell Hall. Because the Penal Laws were still in existence, Catholics could not hold office and were restricted in other respects, such as in inheriting property, attending university, voting, possessing arms, or even owning a horse worth more than five pounds. In addition, until the Catholic Relief Act of 1788, their property was subjected to what often proved to be a ruinous double taxation. In spite of all of this, the Smythes had taken advantage of agricultural prosperity in the mid-eighteenth century, remained well circumstanced, enlarged their new hall, and retained their ancient family motto: *Regi semper fidelis* ("To the king ever faithful"). But their world was a somewhat retired and insular one, spent for the most part in the society of other Catholic families, with whom they had long intermarried.

In order to receive a Catholic education at the time, the sons and daughters of the English recusant families had to go abroad, and Maria for some years attended a convent school in Dunkirk. By the time of her return to England and coming out in society, she had become a great beauty. She first married Edward Weld, brother to Thomas of Lulworth Castle, where Bishop Carroll had been consecrated, but was widowed early when he fell from a horse. After a suitable mourning period, she married Mr. Fitzherbert, but after walking from London all the way west to Dorset and back, he too fell sick. Husband and wife traveled to the south of France to restore Mr. Fitzherbert's failing health, but to no avail. Tuberculosis took his life. Back in England the still-young Maria lived a country life in widow's weeds, but after an appropriate interval she was persuaded by her uncle Errington to come to town with him.

THE PRINCE

George Augustus Frederick, the Prince of Wales and Duke of Cornwall, was born in 1762 and by his early twenties had become notorious for living a bibulous and spendthrift existence. His primary pursuits were hunting, gambling, and whoring with his rather dissolute set of friends. He was well known for spending late nights arguing politics at Brooks' club. And he seemed incapable of escaping debts that grew ever larger. This was one cause of friction with his father, George III. "Perhaps you would be more productive if you got up earlier in the morning," the punctilious monarch said to him in one stiff interview. "Sir," replied the prince, "when I am given nothing to do I find that, no matter at what hour I rise, I am able to accomplish everything."

First Meeting

Now in London, Maria and her uncle Errington were one day out for a drive near Park Lane when a magnificent carriage hurtled by. "Why, it's the prince," Errington exclaimed as the handsome face of the Prince of Wales looked back with curiosity. Some nights later Errington urged Maria to accompany him to the opera. She protested that she was still in mourning, but her uncle insisted. "It will do you good, my dear." They went and enjoyed the performance hugely. On the way out they encountered the Prince of Wales. "Good evening, John," he bluffly greeted Errington. "And who the devil is this pretty girl?" "My niece, Mrs. Fitzherbert, Your Royal Highness." The prince drew Maria's veil aside to look at her and was smitten on the spot.

Courtship and Marriage

The Prince of Wales pursued Mrs. Fitzherbert in the most fervent fashion imaginable. Before long he was on his knees before her, declaring his undying love. Maria declined his advances at first but began to be swayed under the sheer force and volume of his protestations. The prince then claimed to have attempted suicide in his despair and called Maria to him in his wretchedness. Maria did go but took the Duchess of Devonshire with her as a chaperone to ensure that no scandal could arise. She then went directly abroad to avoid such a dangerous liaison, but, undeterred, the Prince of Wales pursued her still by letter, and then in person. Ultimately Maria agreed to return to England, but she made it perfectly clear to the prince that, as a Catholic, she could not possibly entertain his advances unless they were married. The prince agreed to a wedding, illegal though it was for him to do so under the Act of Settlement of 1701 and the Royal Marriage Act of 1772 without the king's permission, since he was under the age of twenty-five (he was twenty-three; Mrs. Fitzherbert was twenty-eight), which would not have been forthcoming in any case, given that Maria was a commoner and a Catholic.

The secret marriage took place at Mrs. Fitzherbert's house in Park Lane in December of 1785, an Anglican clergyman presiding and her kinsmen, including Errington, attending as witnesses. According to those present, the prince signed the marriage certificate with a flourish.

Married Life

The newlyweds retreated to Brighton, where they maintained separate establishments (said by Lady Guernsey to be connected by a private passage) but were constantly together for carriage drives, house parties, racing at Newmarket, and entertainments at the prince's lavish Pavilion.

No one acknowledged, but yet everyone considered, Mrs. Fitzherbert as "the consort to the prince."

In the background the Prince of Wales' faction voiced their late-night misgivings on the danger Mrs. Fitzherbert posed to the prince's succession to the throne. These whisperings, and the prince's natural inclinations, eventually eroded Maria's position, and the prince moved on to other lovers, including the infamous Lady Jersey, "a type of serpent, beautiful, bright and glossy in its exterior—in its interior poisonous." The prince and Maria then separated and became estranged.

Separation

To appease his father, George III, and also, not incidentally, to settle his debts, the Prince of Wales agreed to marry Princess Caroline of Brunswick. Lady Jersey led the welcoming party to meet Princess Caroline at Dover and took special care to ensure it was an hour late, after which she refused to converse with the princess in the carriage on the way to St. James. Once there, despite being apprised by Lord Malmesley of the need for impeccable personal hygiene, Caroline came to court and knelt before the prince. He gallantly lifted her up, but when she came close enough for him to smell, the prince blanched, turned sidewise, and asked an attendant to bring him a glass of brandy, pronouncing himself "unwell." At dinner Princess Caroline's remarks were hilariously crude.

The Prince of Wales was notably drunk at the April 1795 wedding ceremony in the hot chapel at St. James Palace and passed out later in the grate at Kempshot, where, as Princess Caroline later compassionately recalled, "He fell, and I left him." The marriage was a colossal failure from the first. By one account they spent no more than three nights together, and the princess expressed surprise that she could be pregnant.

Upon being notified of the marriage, Maria Fitzherbert refused to believe it could be true until Orlando Bridgeman told her, as gently as possible, that he had witnessed the ceremony. At that point Maria fainted.

Although the prince continued to woo her and they retained cordial relations, Mrs. Fitzherbert and the now prince regent (King George III having gone mad in 1810) parted after she was not included at the head table at a banquet for the royal family of France arranged by Lady

Hertford and the prince at Brighton to celebrate the regency. Maria asked for complete separation and never spoke to him again. She lived in retirement, taking pleasure in her wards, Minney Seymour, whom she had adopted, and her "niece," Marianne, said to be a daughter of her brother Jack Smythe but widely considered by many to have been the progeny of Maria and the prince.

In 1830 the king's health took a turn for the worse. His memory began playing tricks. He claimed, for example, to have led a cavalry charge at Waterloo and asked Wellington to confirm that was so, to the Iron Duke's discomfiture.

Upon learning of his illness. Mrs. Fitzherbert wrote him a moving letter of farewell, "To my King Ever Faithful" (her family's motto), though due to blindness George IV is unlikely to have read it. When King George IV died, he was wearing a locket with Maria's image around his neck, and he was buried with it.

MRS. FITZHERBERT AND THE AMERICAN CONNECTION: A ROYAL HEIR?

There is a possibility that the Prince of Wales and Maria Fitzherbert's marriage bore fruit in the form of a son, and that Bishop Carroll played a part in his story. For primarily political and dynastic reasons, these claims have been discounted by establishment chroniclers as "against British interests," but they remain well-documented traditions in the lives of those whom they touched.

The Mysterious Story of James Ord Jr.

In America in 1812 a young man in the dress of a Jesuit seminarian, James Ord Jr., rushed to his adoptive uncle's Washington bedside. A dying James Ord Sr. rose up and said, "James, I have something of the greatest importance to tell you." But then the older man fell back, unable to continue, and retreated into his final coma.

Because the Ords were well known as a staunch Catholic family in England, the elder Ord's funeral and burial were presided over by no less than Archbishop John Carroll. James Ord Jr. received a commission to the United States Navy and went to sea. When he returned and resigned his naval commission for one in the United States Army in 1816, he was welcomed by a friend of his uncle's and Archbishop Carroll's, Notley Young, at Young's Maryland plantation. During Ord's visit they discussed his naval career and his upcoming army assignment. Notley Young then handed the younger Ord a packet of papers that Young had been given by the elder James Ord before his death.

When, back in his room, James Ord Jr. looked through these documents, he found shipping records of his "uncle" and "mother" to go to Spain when he was an infant; invitations to call on the British ambassador there, a Mr. Fitzherbert; details of crossing the Atlantic to Norfolk, Virginia; and, finally, receipts for James Ord Jr.'s tuition at Georgetown, paid by "Notley Young Esq., British Agent." These papers provoked a strong reaction in James Ord Jr., and he recalled vividly various childhood memories, particularly walking by a river in Norfolk as a boy one day with his uncle James. He had heard his classmates at school discussing their birthdays, and he realized he did not know his, so he asked his uncle when it was. The elder Ord turned to him solemnly and said, "I do not know, James, if you had your rights in England you would be something very great. God forgive those who have wronged you."

The next day James bought a book in a Washington shop (Croly's *The Life of George IV*) about the marriage between Mrs. Fitzherbert and the Prince of Wales. The book contains Lady Guernsey's assertion that, soon after, Mrs. Fitzherbert became *enceinte* (pregnant). Excited, James went straight to Georgetown and sought out an old teacher, Father Matthews, S.J. Father Matthews advised him that his suspicions were correct, that James had been born of distinguished English parents, but that Father Matthews was under a pledge of silence. When James said he believed he might be the son of King George IV and Mrs. Fitzherbert, Father Matthews answered quietly, "I have heard that from another source." This would most likely have been Archbishop John Carroll. Carroll had gone abroad from Maryland to be educated at St. Omer's and there became friends with many of the English Catholic gentry. Then Father Carroll had lived with the Weld family in England after the Jesuit order was suppressed by the pope in 1773, where he would have known Mrs. Fitzherbert, then Mrs. Weld. When he was appointed the first bishop of the United States in 1789, the installation ceremony was performed at the chapel of Lulworth Castle, Dorset, the seat of Thomas Weld, Maria's brother-in-law. This would explain why James Ord spent his young life looked after by and in the company of the Brents and Youngs, Archbishop Carroll's brothers-in-law, and their families and friends.

As their meeting came to a close, Father Matthews did suggest that James write a letter to Mrs. Fitzherbert and helped him to draft it as diplomatically as possible.

Dear Madam,

Believing that there is no person living better acquainted with eminent and distinguished personages than yourself, I take the liberty of asking your assistance in an effort to find out if yet among the living are my dear and beloved parents. . . .

I have good reason to believe I was taken from the bosom of her who brought me into life as an helpless infant, carried over into Spain and thence to the United States of America by James Ord . . . The declarations and conduct of James Ord induce me to believe he was under strong obligations of secrecy as to parents and family . . . Should you think proper to honor this communication by an answer, affording me your assistance to discover if still be living my beloved Parents, please enclose to the Archbishop of Baltimore or the Reverend William Matthews under cover to Aaron Vail Esq. Charge d'Affaires of the Court of & c.—

James Ord Jr. could not be sure that the letter ever reached Mrs. Fitzherbert via Aaron Vail, the United States minister to England, but he knew it was never answered. He lived out his life in the army; married Rebecca Ruth Cresap, daughter of Col. Daniel Cresap of the Revolutionary War; and, after holding various government positions in Washington, moved to Chicago in 1837 as Indian disbursing agent, and on to Sault Ste. Marie, Michigan, as Indian agent until returning to Washington in 1850. In July 1855 he embarked to California on the steamer *George Law* and afterward went to live with his son, Maj. Gen. Edward Otho Chesap

Ord, U.S. Army, in Nebraska, where he worked on his memoirs and died at the age of about eighty-seven on January 27, 1873.

The Aftermath in America and in England

The Ord descendants in America and the Fitzherbert descendants in England searched for answers to their joint mystery for many years. In 1863 an Englishman turned California rancher named William B. Watkins wrote to Pacificus Ord, then living in Paris, to relate that two strangers had called on him for breakfast at his house in Monterey County. Upon discovering they were English, he related that he, too, was English and mentioned Mrs. Fitzherbert as having lived near his childhood home at Swynnerton. One of the guests then asked him if he was aware that a son of George IV and Mrs. Fitzherbert was living in America under the name of Ord, sent hither for "State reasons."

The Georgetown Tradition

Ord's daughter, Mary Ord Preston, compiled a pamphlet in 1896 of memoranda concerning her father's origins. One of the items is entitled "The Jesuit Tradition" and reads: "In the *Centenary History of Georgetown College* published in 1891, under the auspices of the college, on page 29 is the following statement, 'James Ord, son of King George IV, of England and his lawful wife, Mrs. Maria Fitzherbert, was enrolled among the students of the college in the year 1800.'" In 1920 historian H.W. Shoemaker commented on this, "Evidently, the parentage and legitimacy of James Ord were known to the Jesuits, as it is said that no one of unknown or illegitimate origin can be admitted to this famous order."

The mystery of James Ord remains unresolved to this day, and the discreet Archbishop Carroll never spoke publicly on the subject, but he clearly knew more than he let on.

CHAPTER I

McDonnell & Co.

The Aftermath

THE ORIGINAL *REAL LACE* (1973) OPENED WITH A CHAPTER CALLED "What Happened?" about the fall of the venerable Wall Street firm McDonnell & Co. and its then beleaguered head, T. Murray McDonnell. Indeed, the closing of a powerful and prestigious firm such as McDonnell & Co. (or Hayden Stone, which also failed in that era) was a calamitous event, just as the failure of Lehman Brothers would be in 2008, sending shock waves through the financial system. Many people lost jobs. Others lost their investments in the firm. Especially hard hit, of course, were the McDonnell family members who had inherited stakes in the company, and they were understandably bitter.

Murray McDonnell himself was the hardest hit of all, for in addition to his financial losses, he was forced to sign a consent decree that enumerated his improper activities as head of the firm, and also barred him from ever again selling shares in McDonnell or holding an executive position in another New York Stock Exchange firm. He was, however, permitted to continue as a registered securities salesman and was given a desk by his friend, Herbert Allen, at Allen & Co., the legendary investment bank.

As it happened, I knew Murray McDonnell well (our fathers knew each other, and he was the father of my boarding school classmate Michael Flanigan McDonnell). Over the next two decades, I saw him regularly at his Allen & Co. office; his home in Peapack, New Jersey; and elsewhere. Rather than being crushed or embittered by his experience, McDonnell took it as an opportunity for self-growth and redemption.

Murray McDonnell was born in 1922 to James and Anna McDonnell. His mother was the daughter of Thomas Murray, the Brooklyn-based inventor and associate of Thomas Edison. James McDonnell was the son of Peter McDonnell, an Irish immigrant, bondsman, and businessman. James McDonnell, known as "Little Caesar" to his family, started a successful stock brokerage business that specialized in the then arcane area of trading rights. He and Anna had fourteen children, whom they raised in splendid surroundings in New York and Southampton. At one point their Fifth Avenue triplex was the largest private residence in the City. I remember spending a night there after being down from boarding school and out on the town with her grandson in the late 1960s, being deeply impressed by the collection of papal skull caps and by Paul, the imperious butler who commanded Mrs. McDonnell's household.

After studying at Loyola, Aiken Prep, and Georgetown, Murray McDonnell fought in the European theater in World War II, winning two Bronze Stars. He then joined McDonnell & Co., and, upon his father's death in 1958, became its head. He was an effective salesman, and as the postwar stock market soared, McDonnell & Co. prospered. He married Peggy Flanigan, whose father Horace, or "Hap," headed the Hanover Bank and whose mother was related to the Busch brewing family. They moved to a beautiful farm in the New Jersey hunt country called Pleasant Valley and set to work on what was to be his life's greatest achievement—his family. Eventually they had nine children.

In the 1960s Murray reached for the financial stars. Alas, he overreached. An ambitious expansion program was undertaken to convert the brokerage house into "another Merrill Lynch." Twenty-six lavishly appointed offices were opened, including one in Paris. At the same time the sleepy world of Wall Street back office life was being transformed by the huge increase in trading volumes. Manual record keeping and "runners" between the firms and "the Floor" of the New York Stock Exchange could no longer keep up. Computerization was coming in.

Unfortunately, at McDonnell & Co. the computerization system never quite worked, and numerous abuses took place. Financial controls were not in place, bookkeeping was flawed, and, as it took on added expenses, the firm's capital base eroded badly. Murray was the high-profile salesman who did not concentrate on day-to-day administration. His youngest brother, Sean, oversaw the execution side of the business. In the midst of overhauling the firm's financial procedures, Sean went for a jog early one morning in 1968 near his Greenwich home and died of a heart attack. He was twenty-nine.

McDonnell & Co. never recovered. The bear market of the late 1960s, the so-called Nixon recession, finally pushed it into complete failure. Its liabilities far exceeded its assets, several questionable actions to raise additional capital provoked legal challenges, and the firm was finally declared bankrupt on March 12, 1970. The next day was Friday the thirteenth. Millions had been lost by Murray and other family members with holdings in the firm, and relations within the family remained frayed for years. After an SEC investigation, Murray McDonnell was censured and forbidden to be a principal in a Wall Street firm ever again. He was also forbidden to work on Wall Street in any capacity for a year. When that period expired, he joined Allen & Co. as vice president of international business, a position he held for the rest of his life.

That was the *New York Times* obituary version of Murray's life. But it wasn't the whole story.

The loss of his family's firm was a stunning, humiliating comedown for Murray McDonnell. It would have broken many other men and caused some to end their lives. But for Murray, in so many important ways, it was the beginning of his. Until then Murray, a smallish man with the swagger of an accomplished salesman, had been the king of the roost. Suddenly everything was gone, and he had to face his problems and live or give up and die. Murray chose to live.

He dealt as best he could with his financial problems. At one time he had been a heavy drinker, and that period of life ended. He had been dogged by asthma and a longtime tendency toward depression, and these he addressed as well. He sought to understand and come to terms with himself. After his death a few letters to his widow, Peggy, began much like this, "I first knew Murray when we were in our twenties around the New York Athletic Club. Frankly, back then, I thought he was a jerk."

He was never really a jerk, but he changed. He still tried to make big deals and made enough smaller ones to secure a good living for his huge family and him. But his focus turned to people, to healing himself and others. Whether it was at Alcoholics Anonymous; at L'Arche outside Toronto, the center for severely crippled and retarded men run by Father Henri Nouwen; or just in the course of his daily life, Murray spent the greater part of the next twenty years trying to help other people, not just in big ways, but in every way he could. One of these was Jacqueline Bouvier Kennedy, a friend from their childhoods in Southampton, when she moved her family back to New York after President Kennedy's assassination. The McDonnells carved a parcel of land from their New Jersey farm, Pleasant Valley, so that she, Caroline, and John Jr. would have a weekend foxhunting retreat.

At his memorial mass in Peapack, Murray's oldest son Michael (whom *Paris Match* had referred to years before as "Le premier boyfriend of Caroline"), by then a Hollywood producer, remembered some of the people who would miss him. In the church that day, in addition to Jacqueline Onassis, who had interrupted a holiday in the Mediterranean to be there for the man who made it his business to be a second father to her children after theirs had died, there were two ex-governors of New Jersey; former secretary of state Cyrus Vance; Treasury Secretary Nicholas Brady; and many others of power, influence, and wealth, such as Malcolm Forbes and Murray's brother-in-law, Peter Flanigan. But Michael spoke of none of them. Instead Michael related his father's daily conversation with the train conductor on the Erie Lackawanna Railroad, or with the shoeshine man at 120 Broadway, or the parking garage attendants at the NYAC. "I'd cringe when my pinstriped father would yell out, 'Yo, my main man!' to them, but far from taking offense, they delighted in this old man in a Morty Sills suit who took the time to talk to them as real people and considered them his friends."

Michael then spoke of his father's life's "paradoxes, ironies, and simple truths."

I'm going to tell you about the man I knew. Some of you knew him at a pony show in Southampton when he was five years old, or as a student who left Georgetown to fight the war in France, or a Stork Club regular, who made marrying Peggy McDonnell his one objective in life. But I didn't know that man.

The man I knew loved us and everyone in his life so much, and yet he found it so hard to accept that other people really did love him back . . .

Murray was paradoxical. He enjoyed playing the mayor of the Saratoga Race Course clubhouse and one day exclaimed loudly when his New Jersey neighbor Reese Howard, a squire almost as diminutive as he, approached our box one day, "Boys, I want you to meet a very unusual creature—a short WASP!"

He joked about friends' funerals, "Why should I go to his funeral? He isn't going to mine." And with the air of an armchair philosopher, a good cigar clenched between his teeth, "Let me tell you something Philippe Rothschild told me, 'You can marry more money in ten minutes than you can make in three lifetimes.'" Yet he made friends amongst all colors and classes, attended everyone's funeral, and was the most devoted of husbands and fathers.

"Maybe," he said to me seriously another time, referring to a son who had not yet settled down, "he has a sexuality problem. I've got a sexuality problem, and I have nine children."

He never stopped being a big shot and loved the fuss the staff at "21" made over him when he entered the bar there. After returning from Caroline Kennedy's wedding in Hyannisport, he declared infallibly from his regular table, "This 'Compound' I'd heard so much about . . . I figured it was something like we had in Southampton. The place was a dump!"

But, underneath the façade, his humility was absolute. Murray's last two decades were spent in a constant state of becoming. He knew he had to reach out beyond where he came from and what he had been, and grow. He did.

He did this in many public ways, supporting traditional good works but also new initiatives in which he believed. Most of all, he did it within his own family, calling them early and often, driving them to the airport before or picking them up after trips, circulating letters when anything of interest crossed his desk, forewarning them about Mother's Day, and then, for good measure, forewarning them about Father's Day too. Amidst much joy he and his entire family endured the singular tragedy of watching their youngest daughter, Mimi, die at the age of nineteen after a mysterious illness that was never fully diagnosed. This, too, he bore, not without great suffering, but with no complaint.

At his memorial mass his daughter, Anna Harper, read from underlined passages in the book of Flannery O'Connor's letters that Murray always kept by his bed:

We are not judged by what we are, basically. We are judged by how we use what we have been given. Success means nothing to the Lord, nor gracefulness. The violent bear it away. It is better to be young in your failures, than old in your successes.

At his funeral Murray's unabashed Irish sentimentality was celebrated with the congregation's singing of "Danny Boy" and the McDonnell family's favorite Clancy Brothers song, "Wild Mountain Thyme."

The gospel of the day was the story of the travelers on the road to Emmaus, and as successive McDonnell children approached the lectern, they too seemed to be traveling along that road, experiencing their father in the liturgy. Stephen McDonnell told the story of Murray calling him on the squawk box of his car phone, leaving a brief message, and then going on to other things, unaware that Stephen's answering machine recorded up to half an hour. When Stephen got home and checked his messages, he was treated to Murray's thirty minute recitation of the Rosary.

Father Henri Nouwen spoke of Murray's gift for vulnerability, and how his own suffering had never embittered him. Instead it became the source of his compassion for others. Recounting how Jesus had made mankind a gift of the Holy Spirit, Father Henri blew the spirit of Murray from his hands to the McDonnell family. Pope Francis would have approved.

The one thing Murray worried about most as a parent was that he might not have done all he should have to transmit spiritual values to his children. He prayed often. He frequently attended the noon mass at St.

Chapter II

The Rise of the Wealthy Irish Catholics

The Irish population grew from 4,753,000 in 1791 to over eight million in 1841, despite the fact that nearly two million had emigrated during that period, mostly to America. Forbidden to compete on equal terms in the world's trading economy by British colonial rule, the Irish were completely dependent on agriculture, and as land holdings were divided into ever tinier plots, the most efficacious crop to plant was the humble potato. It could be cooked in a variety of ways, ground into flour, and used as animal, as well as human, feed.

The potato crop had failed at intervals in the 1700s and early 1800s, but nothing had prepared the Irish for the serial failures of the 1830s and the catastrophic failure, due to blight, during what had been hoped to be a bumper year in 1845. Ironically, the potato murrain, as the disease was soon labeled, appeared to have spread from the United States and manifested itself in areas of the U.K., Belgium, and elsewhere in Europe as well.

By virtue of its dependence on the potato, Ireland was uniquely vulnerable, and the British government set about systematically to minimize the gravity of the problem. On October 6, Sir James Graham, the British home secretary, announced his "belief that the potato crop, tho' damaged, is not so much below the average as some of the exaggerated reports from Ireland have led us to apprehend."

Desperate farmers tried to rush their crops to market and sell them cheaply before the potatoes turned black and putrid. When diseased potatoes were fed to pigs and other livestock, the animals sickened and died. When starving people tried to eat the evil-smelling tubers, they too became violently ill. Disease accompanied the starvation—cholera, typhus, typhoid, and deathly high fever.

A scientific commission dispatched from London to Dublin issued recommendations for drying and storing potatoes in an unintelligible procedure which most could not understand and which failed to prevent the disease in any case. "If you do not understand this," the report concluded, "ask your landlord or parish priest to explain." The landlord, or course, was usually an absentee, riding out the famine on one of his English estates.

Other wild-eyed suggestions for dealing with the menace were no more helpful, and the terrible winter of 1845 grew into an even worse year of 1846. A population that should have normally expanded to nine million had instead dropped to 6,552,385. Relief funds came in a slow trickle, soup kitchens were set up, and yet over a ten-year period more than a million Irish died and more than another million fled to other lands. In the end, more than three million Irish came to the United States between the onset of the famine in 1846 and the death of Charles Parnell in 1891. Peter McDonnell, Murray McDonnell's grandfather and the patriarch of the American McDonnells, was one of this vast and hungry horde.

The arriving Irish were usually penniless and faced a bitter struggle to establish themselves as day laborers or housemaids for a minimal wage. They lived in appalling cellars, often slept on straw, consoled themselves with drink, and aroused nativist indignation and resentment. They were lambasted for "the dreadful sin of drunkenness," not only among the laity but also among their priests. At one time there were more than forty saloons in the Horseshoe section of Jersey City alone.

They were derided for their ignorance and superstition. A typical story was of an Irishman hired to chop wood who became frightened of "faeries in the forest." It was his first experience of fireflies.

As Irish immigration surged in the 1840s and 1850s, so did contempt for and fear of the newcomers on the part of the native Americans. The Irish, in turn, became increasingly resentful of the nativists. According to historian Thomas N. Brown, the Protestant Irish hastily disassociated themselves from the impoverished Catholics, and some Protestants became active in the Know Nothing camp. Thus battle lines were drawn: Irish Catholic against Anglo-American Protestant. It was not unusual, then, for the Irish to see nativism as primarily an extension of English hatred for the Irish. Those among them who were sick were condemned to hospitals that were soon overcrowded and suffered in unspeakable conditions. Moreover, all newly arrived Irish lived in fear of the bondsman.

The struggle for a place in the sun was arduous and long-lasting. "No Irish Need Apply" signs were ubiquitous in the early years of the Irish-American diaspora. When he was elected president of the Irish National League of the U.S., Michael Gannon, the handsome Davenport, Iowa, lawyer, complained, "We are today the least organized nationality in America, while we have the most to contend with."

Even as the Irish progressed in America, taking advantage of their natural gifts for language, sociability, and politics, they continued to face resistance. "Like the Negroes in the 1960s," Brown wrote, "the Irish in the 1880s felt a middle class backlash as they rose in the social hierarchy." William R. Grace of the Grace shipping family felt this hostility acutely when winning the race for mayor of New York in 1880—the first Irish Catholic to do so—since he ran far behind the rest of the Democratic ticket.

In fact, for many decades to come, the basis for anti–Irish-American bitterness on the part of "older Americans" was the fact that, as the historian Thomas N. Brown made clear in *Irish-American Nationalism* (1966), Irish influence in public life increased tremendously relative to their status in private life. Brown wrote memorably, "They could run the cities but could not get into the country clubs," that developed as suburban life expanded with the coming of the commuter railroads at the end of the nineteenth century.

To understand why the bondsman was so feared by the immigrating Irish, here is how the system worked: New York law required that ship owners guarantee that any arriving passengers would not become a candidate for public welfare. The unscrupulous bondsman met the arriving passenger at the pier and sold them a guaranteeing bond for anywhere from ten cents to a dollar, whatever he could extract. If the traveler did, in fact, become destitute and turn to the state for assistance, he was referred back to his bondsman, who did his best to avoid providing any assistance whatsoever, but in some cases had deals with cheap boardinghouses and "private workhouses."

The bondsmen also worked another profitable angle, serving as recruiting agents for American companies looking for cheap labor. Bonding was thus extremely profitable. Commissions could be collected at every turn, from railroad and steamship lines, from boardinghouses, from employers, and from the emigrants themselves. One firm collected eighty thousand dollars in a single year and paid out only thirty dollars in "benefits," although additional outlays to keep city and state officials bribed were also a necessary cost of doing business.

Peter McDonnell, the progenitor of the "Golden Clan" McDonnells, was described in an early Manhattan business directory as a "railroad and steamship agent." In fact, he was a bondsman, who used the considerable revenue he generated from those activities to branch out into other lucrative pursuits.

He was thus able to send his son James on to Fordham and help him establish a partnership with a man named Byrne on the New York Stock Exchange, which became the wellspring of the McDonnells' wealth and their ascent, from a rather disreputable employment, into the ranks of the so-called First Irish Families, and, increasingly, acceptance by established WASP society.

In *Real Lace*, Stephen Birmingham contrasts the Irish with Jewish immigrants to America who had been counseled by their European rabbis during the many periods of persecution to "live within the system": "Don't be too conspicuous in your demands; stay out of fights, be ready to pack up and go when the enemy threatens; don't rock the boat, for you might rock yourself right out of it."

The Irish penchant for socializing and conversation led them in a different direction—politics. A European visitor to New York in the 1870s commented that Christian and Jewish firms operated in much the same way, but that Jews did business quicker because they talked less! Cecil Woodham-Smith's wonderfully condescending phrase was "The Irish depend to an exaggerated extent on human intercourse."

It would take a *Real Lace* descendant, John Murray Cuddihy, to write a detailed study of Jewish assimilation in the nineteenth and twentieth centuries, *The Ordeal of Civility*, in which he applied an original interpretation of Marx, Freud, Levi-Strauss, and others. Cuddihy had a distinguished career as a professor of sociology at Hunter College, where he would treat one to a hot dog in the cafeteria while his more extravagant sister, Jane, insisted on lunching at the Carlyle.

Edward F. Roberts, in *Irish in America*, wrote, "It is probably true that the political machine was not invented by the Irish . . . but it is certain that it was developed to its greatest extent and has reached its highest degree of efficiency through the peculiar genius of the Irish for political organization."

Early confrontations emphasized the differences in class, such as the conflict between "Honest Dan" Bradley, a "soft" Democrat on slavery, versus "hard" Judge John J. Vanderbilt. The *Brooklyn Eagle* opined: "The contrast between the two men could hardly have been more manifest. Bradley was a mechanic, a plain, unlettered man. . . . Judge Vanderbilt was one of the finest looking men in the State of New York, a man of high culture, or commanding presence. . . ."

Of course, the Vanderbilts, though of old Dutch New Amsterdam stock, had been looked down upon by the more established Knickerbocker families until their Gilded Age wealth eclipsed all others. Within two generations, however, the two families were joined with the marriage of Alfred Vanderbilt Jr. to Bradley's granddaughter, Jeanne Murray.

Thomas Brown writes, "Wm. C. Whitney, the secretary of the Navy, was especially mindful of the need to deal with the Irish." In part, this was because his young partner was none other than the brilliant Virginian-born financier Thomas Fortune Ryan. Brown made a further point: "The revolt of the Irish-American worker forced thoughtful Catholics in responsible positions to a realization that the poor would no longer suffer the charity of the rich in an unjust society. Out of this would in time emerge new Catholic approaches to social problems. . . ." Here he refers to Al Smith, Catholic progressivism, *Commonweal* Catholicism, Michael Harrington, Peter Steinfels, et al., whose liberal social policy prescriptions were ultimately opposed in the 1980s by Michael Novak, Father Richard John Neuhaus, George Weigel, and conservative policies of the Reagan and Bush administrations, all very relevant in 2016 as the problem of inequality remains at the forefront of the American political stage.

"Thomas Edison's invention may have been more spectacular, with the incandescent light bulb," Stephen Birmingham quotes one of Thomas Murray's grandchildren.

But Granpa Murray virtually invented everything but the light bulb—the circuits, switches, dynamos, and power systems that got the electricity to the bulb. In my opinion it was a more important contribution. He had over 426 patents by the time he died, and his son, Thomas Jr., would add 200 more. After all, if there hadn't been a way to get the power into the bulbs, how would the bulbs light up?

Murray was the chief executive of the company that ran the major power plants in New York City in the early twentieth century, and he had an alarm system in his bedroom so that if there was a problem at any one of them he could jump out of bed to go deal with it.

His son, Thomas Edward Murray Jr., served on the Atomic Energy Commission and called nuclear energy "a thrilling manifestation of the power, the beauty and the providence of God." He was called "a contentious presence" at the AEC, whom President Eisenhower declined to reappoint. In 1958 he ran for the Democratic nomination for the U.S. Senate from New York but lost.

At first the Murrays and McDonnells faced social resistance. Ur-WASP Barclay Beekman was quoted by Birmingham as saying, "The Murrays and the McDonnells hadn't made the grade fifteen years ago. Their social aspirations were resented by the snooty. But they're kindly people who don't snub climbers."

The *Real Lace* families made a habit of marrying into the Vanderbilts, as it turned out. One of San Francisco Silver King James Fair's daughters married W.K. Vanderbilt Jr., and the other Herman Oelrichs of Newport, whose daughter, Bubbles, married bandleader Eddie Duchin and died shortly after giving birth to their musician and socialite son, Peter.

One of the more amusing exchanges Stephen Birmingham reports in *Real Lace* is between a proper WASP Newporter and a New York lady of Sephardic heritage:

"I do think our people are getting closer, don't you?"

"I hope so."

"Of course, we'll never accept the Catholics."

That, as it turned out, proved not to be so, when the Honorable Noreen Stonor, daughter of Lord Camoys, one of the oldest baronies in the English peerage, as well as a family that included no fewer than eight saints of the Catholic church, received papal permission to marry John Drexel of the famous Philadelphia banking family in the Episcopal church. For decades she was head of Newport, New York, and Palm Beach society. It didn't hurt that on her mother's side she was the granddaughter of Watts Sherman and descended from Roger Williams, the founder of Rhode Island, and Nicholas Brown, the founder of Brown University! "I'm a frustrated nurse," Noreen liked to say, and indeed her work for the American Red Cross and Newport Hospital was untiring. In this regard she resembled an earlier convert, Rose Hawthorne, daughter of novelist Nathaniel Hawthorne, whose order of nuns operated a center for cancer patients. After Mr. Drexel's death Noreen quietly resumed her family's ancient Catholic faith.

"Stereotypes exist because there's a nugget of truth to them," sociologist John Murray Cuddihy used to say. The Irish were successful in politics, insurance, banking, engineering, industry, and show business, as doctors, lawyers, stockbrokers, and advertising execs. Jews excelled in retailing, investment banking, dress manufacturing, and show business, too. In fact, one of the most interesting of the *Real Lace* marriages was when Clarence Mackay's daughter wed not a Vanderbilt but a young Tin Pan Alley composer named Irving Berlin. Her family was aghast, but they lived together blissfully in their Beekman Place house for over half a century.

Otherwise, the words of Daniel Patrick Moynihan generally held true: "The Irish were the one oppressed people on earth the American Protestants could never quite bring themselves wholeheartedly to sympathize with." Even of such a devout supporter of minority causes as Eleanor Roosevelt, Joseph P. Lash said, "Somewhere deep in her subconscious was an anti-Catholicism which was part of her Protestant heritage."

In *The Late George Apley*, John P. Marquand's comic novel of Boston manners, George Apley writes to his son in New York, "We have our Irish, and you have your Jews, and both of them are crosses to bear."

Woodrow Wilson, an Orangeman or northern Irishman, on the other hand, was both Presbyterian and anti-Catholic.

Jane Cuddihy MacGuire claimed to Stephen Birmingham that there was "very little" drinking among the FIFs. However, her own brother Michael, the influential editor of the literary magazine *Ironwood*, in his memoir remembers thinking how heavily his father drank at night at home, and alcoholism would take a heavy toll on many of Aunt Jane's cousins' and husband's families. Jane MacGuire herself, in fact, was a dedicated member of Alcoholics Anonymous in later life, so here she was gilding the lily to Birmingham.

She had married a grandson of James Butler. Butler, born in 1855, came from fifteen generations of farmers near Kilkenny, emigrated to America at the age of twenty-one, worked on farms and in the hotel trade, and in due course built up New York's second-largest chain of grocery stores, surpassed only by A&P.

In his spare time he amused himself by harness racing north of the City in afternoons, where even Commodore Vanderbilt was known to enjoy competing. Two of Butler's best trotters were Direct and Directum Kelly. Direct went on to become the unbeaten champion of old-style sulky racing. Driving King Direct, one of Direct's descendants, Mr. Butler himself broke the world amateur sulky racing mark by doing a mile in 2:04.75. Later Butler named one of his real estate holding companies Direct Realty and expanded his racing interests into Thoroughbreds and racetracks, at one time owning Empire City (today's Yonkers Raceway) and Laurel in Maryland. When, in 1914, racing was briefly banned in a short-lived spasm of reform, Butler joined with Colonel Matt Winn of Kentucky Derby fame and the original Harry M. Stevens, who popularized the hot dog, to launch a racetrack in Juarez, Mexico, where they found it convenient to take in a fourth partner, none other than local revolutionary Pancho Villa.

"Pray for good weather and a fast track," was one of Butler's bywords, as was "All men are equal, on the turf or under it."

All of the *Real Lace* families experienced reversals and tragedies, but most found the resilience to carry on.

THE DOHENYS

Edward L. Doheny, born in 1850, prospected around the West and in Mexico for decades before borrowing money for a lease and hitting La Brea crude in 1892 in Hancock Park, at the edge of Los Angeles.

As a rich man, Doheny, a former southwestern gunman, affected a monocle, a walrus mustache, British tailoring, and an autocratic manner. He bought a large part of what is now downtown Los Angeles, which he converted into a vast park and estate called Chester Place. He also contributed to the Irish Freedom Movement and the Democratic Party.

In 1920 Doheny contributed twenty-five thousand dollars to Warren Harding's presidential campaign for ads that featured full-page photos of his mother and father to counteract rumors he had "Negro blood." By 1925 Doheny's wealth from his Mexican and American interests was reliably reported to be even greater than that of the richest man in America, John D. Rockefeller.

But then came the Teapot Dome Scandal, in which Doheny, working through his friend, Interior Secretary Albert Fall, was able to lease U.S. government land at a favorable rate and extract oil for his personal profit. For a mere hundred thousand dollars in bribes, Doheny secured leases worth close to one hundred million dollars.

Doheny denied making the payment. It was, he said, his son, Edward Doheny Jr., who paid. After exhaustive hearings in Congress, Fall, Sinclair, Edward Doheny, and Edward (Ned) Doheny Jr. were indicted. Initially they were found guilty, but on appeal the verdict was reversed. Doheny's lawyer, Frank J. Hogan, defended him vigorously and gave a five-hour summation to the jury in which he compared his client's situation to the Crucifixion and Doheny to Jesus Christ himself. After deliberating well into the night and the following morning, Doheny was found not guilty. Pandemonium broke loose as his friends rushed to congratulate him, and four hundred people welcomed him home at the L.A. train station before a testimonial banquet to celebrate his acquittal, attended by the mayors of Los Angeles and San Francisco. However, by this time Doheny was old and in failing health. Tragedy awaited him.

Now that Doheny had been acquitted, it was Albert Fall's turn to be tried next. But just a few months before that event, young Ned Doheny was murdered by his male secretary, Hugh Plunkett, "after a spurned homosexual overture," as was widely rumored. This was impossible to verify because Plunkett, immediately after killing Doheny, had shot and killed himself.

In her 2016 book, *West of Eden*, Jean Stein, the longtime editor of *Grand Street*, brought together a number of Doheny descendants and family associates to discuss the case and its aftermath. She included the passage from Raymond Chandler's *The Big Sleep* that described Chester Place:

> *A winding driveway dropped down between retaining walls to the open iron gates. Beyond the fence the hill sloped for several miles. On this lower level faint and far off I could just barely see some of the old wooden derricks of the oilfield from which the Sternwoods had made their money . . . A little of it was still producing in groups of wells pumping five or six barrels a day. The Sternwoods, having moved up the hill, could no longer smell the stale sump water or the oil, but they could still look out of their front windows and see what had made them rich.*

Other literary treatments based on the Dohenys include Upton Sinclair's *Oil* and the Daniel Day-Lewis film *There Will Be Blood*. Of the latter, Patrick "Ned" Doheny, a musician and great-grandson of Edward L. Doheny, said, "There's not a shred of truth in it. The only true part of the film was at the beginning, with him in the mine shaft by himself: he did always say he once fell down a mine and broke his legs. But all the rest of it is utter horseshit."

Carole Wells Doheny, an actress married to Edward L. Doheny IV, revealed that Doheny's first wife, Carrie, became so despondent over Doheny remarrying that she killed herself by drinking battery fluid when young Ned was living with her. A susceptibility toward depression has been in the family ever since, which Carole traces to Carrie. Patrick "Ned" Doheny says that one of the "wild rumors" was that Ned was gay, but the family always denied it. It may have come from all the time he spent alone, away from his family, but this could have been the result of depression linked to his mother's sad end as well.

Topsy Doheny said that her late husband Tim explained the murder as resulting from Ned's secretary, Hugh Plunkett, developing mental problems, and Ned telling him he had to "go away" for a while. Psychotropic medicines were unknown and asylums at the time were grim, so Hugh became upset, pulled a gun, and shot Ned and then himself.

However, in *West of Eden*, writer and historian Richard Rayner says that Leslie White, the investigator for the L.A. District Attorney's office, believed it was Ned Doheny who shot Hugh Plunkett and that Raymond Chandler thought so as well. The fact that Ned was not buried with the very Catholic family in their plot at Calvary Cemetery suggests that he was a suicide and the family had said as much to their priest.

In one of the odder chapters of American jurisprudence, Albert Fall was convicted of *taking* the bribe that Edward Doheny had been found innocent of *giving*. Fall went away to prison for a year, lost much of his fortune, yet survived until 1943.

After Fall's conviction Doheny had to be tried again, for the fourth time, and was again found innocent thanks to Hogan's courtroom theatrics. "Ned Doheny speaks from the grave," Hogan intoned while sitting in the witness stand and repeating testimony Doheny's son Ned had given at the earlier trial. Doheny was found innocent in the same court, with the same judge, in the same building, and of the same offense Fall was convicted of!

"The ideal client," Hogan once said, "is a rich man when he is scared." After the initial flurry the story of Ned's murder/suicide was kept out of the newspapers by the powerful Dohenys.

Doheny got off, but he was a broken man. He lived on until 1935, though he was bedridden for much of his final three years. At his death he was seventy-nine, and his funeral was attended by twelve hundred people at St. Vincent's Cathedral, which he had built, while another two thousand stood outside the doors. Mrs. Doheny survived him for a number of years, living quietly and avoiding publicity on her vast estate, surrounded by guards and watchdogs. She burned all of her late husband's papers. After several years in ill health, she died, as a priest, advised he must make haste, rushed to give her last rites in a hospital, threw her door open, and skidded across the room, falling on her stomach. "With that," Stephen Birmingham wrote, "Mrs. Doheny expired."

Although much reduced, Doheny had distributed a fortune in trusts to his wife and family before his death, but the family has remained largely out of the limelight since. Yet the name lives on in Los Angeles through the Doheny Mansion, the Doheny Memorial Library at USC, Doheny Eye Institute, Doheny Drive, and Doheny State Beach.

Richard Rayner sums up in *West of Eden*:

> *Raymond Chandler famously said, "The law is where you buy it and what you pay for it." He completely saw the way that power works in Los Angeles, which along with corruption became his broadest subject. And he kept going back to the Doheny story. It's glanced at in different ways throughout his work, and it lingered with him as a paradigm for what he saw as the rotten heart of paradise.*

THE SILVER KINGS

Another unhappy *Real Lace* family was that of James Gordon Fair, who along with John William Mackay (Irving Berlin's father-in-law), James C. Flood, and William S. O'Brien was one of San Francisco's four fabulously wealthy Silver Kings. Today the Flood Mansion is the ultra-establishment Pacific Union Club (a later Jim Flood house was given to the Sacred Heart for their San Francisco school), and what was once the Fair mansion is now the site of the Fairmont Hotel. The Mackay fortune began with a huge strike on the Comstock Lode and increased thereafter. The Mackays were philanthropic, establishing Mackay School of Mines in Reno and building St. Mary's in the Mountains Church in Virginia City. In due course some of their priceless medieval stained glass was removed from their Long Island estate, Harbor Hill, and given to the monks at Portsmouth Priory, where it still adorns the church and monastery today.

The Fairs were another story. "Slippery Jim" made enemies in business and in politics, where with his Comstock millions he got himself elected to the Senate. But it was in his personal life that his misanthropy proved most tragic. After an acrimonious divorce from his wife, Theresa Rooney, she retained custody of three of their children, Tessie, Birdie, and Charles. Slippery Jim insisted on retaining custody of his eldest son, James. This unfortunate boy so hated his father that he promptly committed suicide. Charles Fair made a youthful marriage his father disapproved of and for which he promptly disinherited him. Shortly after, Charles and his young wife were killed in an automobile accident. Birdie married William K. Vanderbilt disastrously and divorced. "Vanderbilts often marry Catholics and always divorce them," says one of the Vanderbilts in *Real Lace*. It was left to young Tessie Fair to marry Herman Oelrichs in a huge San Francisco society wedding to which her father was not invited, and she presided over Newport society for many seasons thereafter, before succumbing to a mental breakdown.

The Floods still lived in Woodside, California, until Betty (Mrs. James Sr.) Flood died in 2011. Their comfortable spread there was then put on the market for seventy to eighty million dollars. She and Jim Flood had been married at the Flood Mansion on Broadway, which now houses the Sacred Heart school, and moved to Woodside in 1939. Her daughter Judy, Mrs. Brayton Wilbur, still lives in nearby Hillsborough on Irwin Drive, and Jimmy Flood lives in San Francisco. Elizabeth and John also survived her as did nine grandchildren and twenty-two great-grandchildren.

The final sad story of that era was that of Evalyn Walsh McLean. Tom Walsh struck silver at Leadville, moved on to Ouray, Colorado, and hit a huge vein of gold at Camp Bird Mine. His wife suffered from neuralgia and spent most of her time in a darkened room. Walsh moved the family to Washington and installed them in a million-dollar house on Massachusetts Avenue. At the age of twelve at dancing school, she met Edward Beale McLean, son of the *Washington Post* publisher. She put him off, but after being engaged "dozens of times" married him some years later rather suddenly in Denver. Their honeymoon was exorbitantly expensive, as both fathers of the happy couple competed to outdo the other.

Evalyn developed a fixation on jewels with help from Mrs. Potter Palmer of Chicago. She first acquired the Star of the East, and later, through the good offices of Pierre Cartier, the blue 45.52-carat Hope Diamond for $154,000. It was reputed to come with a curse that had killed previous owners. It had belonged to Marie Antoinette, a later Greek owner had leaped to his death from a cliff, and a third had gone down to his death in a ship at sea after disposing of it.

Evalyn McLean asked a priest to "lay the curse," but just as Monsignor Russell began his incantations, lightning flashed across the sky, and there was a giant clap of thunder and a great rush of wind without rain. Monsignor Russell continued and pronounced the curse removed, but was it?

At their Washington mansion, called "Friendship," she hosted extravagant parties, typically rose at 5:00 p.m. "too dazed from drinks and drugs to recognize her guests," and developed an attachment to morphine. Her husband's drinking was equally destructive. His associate at the *Post*, Alfred Friendly, wrote, "Mrs. Harding was understandably irritated when McLean urinated into the fireplace of the East Room of the White House, nor was the Belgian Ambassador pleased when Ned McLean urinated down the leg of his striped trousers."

The family suffered tragedy after tragedy. Evalyn's son Vinson and daughter Evalyn almost died at birth. Vinson was run down by an automobile and killed at twenty. Evalyn McLean's brother was also killed in an accident in which Evalyn herself was seriously injured. Her daughter Evalyn married at twenty to fifty-seven-year-old North Carolina senator Robert Reynolds. She died of an overdose of sleeping pills. Despite all, Evalyn continued to mock the legend of the diamond's curse, even lending it to army brides married at her Washington home during World War II.

In the end her body was racked by drink and drugs. Her appetite was destroyed by her addictions. She developed severe malnutrition and died, wasted, her vast fortune spent.

CHAPTER III

WASPs, Jews, and the Irish

IN HIS 1964 STUDY, *THE PROTESTANT ESTABLISHMENT: ARISTOCRACY AND Caste in America*, University of Pennsylvania sociologist E. Digby Baltzell begins his preface by recalling the fine May morning in 1910 when "representatives of some seventy nations, including nine kings, five heirs apparent, forty other imperial highnesses, seven queens, and Theodore Roosevelt of the United States, without titled rank and dressed in business clothes, the greatest assemblage of rank and royalty the world had ever seen, rode through the streets of London in the funeral cortege of Edward VII."

Baltzell goes on to frame his book by presciently noting the globalizing, multicultural nature of the world, in which "the authority of the white race, largely built up by the Anglo Saxon gentlemen of England between the ages of Francis Drake and Benjamin Disraeli, is now being called into question around the world." Baltzell posited that "white western man" must learn to share leadership as the WASP establishment gradually loses power. He believed that the establishment had been "unwilling or unable" to share its upper-class traditions by absorbing talented members of minority groups into its privileged ranks. Focusing on WASP anti-Semitism, Baltzell remarks, "The Negroes in America, are, of course, faced with equally important, and far more acute, problems, but their total situation—and the test of our moral conscience posed by it, is for the moment quite different than that of the Jews, and far too complex to be dealt with here."

How resonant those words, written in the early days of the civil rights movement, sound in 2017, after the heated controversies of Ferguson, Baltimore, and other racially charged tragedies around the country!

Baltzell continues: "Gentlemanly anti-Semitism has, I think, been closely related to the threatened security and authority of its old stock upper class."

Focusing on the generations between TR and John F. Kennedy, Baltzell's thesis is that in order for an upper class to maintain continuity of power, its membership in the long run must be representative of the composition of society as a whole.

Since Roosevelt's day, of course, America has become the most ethnically heterogeneous country on Earth. The Irish were initially fiercely resisted by the WASP aristocracy, although, interestingly enough, Teddy Roosevelt had some Irish in addition to his Dutch blood and was a founder of the American Irish Historical Society. (One of the two original tricolors hung above the General Post Office during the Easter Rising is now on display at the American Irish Historical Society's headquarters on Fifth Avenue.)

The late sociologist and novelist Father Andrew Greeley pointed out that there were in fact two Irish migrations. The first was completed before the Civil War, and its descendants tended to live in the South (think Katy Scarlett O'Hara at Tara in *Gone with the Wind*, whose father is forever extolling the value of the land). Greeley found that the descendants of these immigrants had by and large come to worship as Protestants. Grady McWhiney, in his book *Cracker Culture*, says there were counties in Mississippi where Irish was spoken in the 1820s.

The second migration, of course, was to the Northeast before and after the Civil War and well into the twentieth century. Greeley documented that 46 percent of Irish Catholics in America lived in New England. As hard as the emigrants' struggles in the new land were, the downward mobility of those they left behind was worse, so they struggled on in the New World.

As Joseph P. Kennedy, Franklin D. Roosevelt's ambassador to the Court of St. James, once said with some exasperation, "How long does our family have to be here before we are Americans rather than Irish-Americans?"

Baltzell concludes the preface of his book writing on Thanksgiving Day 1963, just a week after the assassination of old Joe Kennedy's son, President John Fitzgerald Kennedy. Baltzell casts his mind back again to the funeral of Edward VII.

> *I thought of how far the world had traveled from that gay and formal age. At the same time I could not help feeling that Theodore Roosevelt would have been far prouder to take part in the procession which was now walking from the White House to St. Matthew's Cathedral, with all the majesty of democratic dignity, behind the nervous black charger, whose absent rider symbolized so well the leadership and hopes of a new world which was so desperately trying to be born in his (President Kennedy's) generation.*
>
> *TR was a dreamer of dreams who dared to hope that America, in the long run, could conquer the values of caste and someday send a distinguished Catholic, and eventually a Jew, to the White House. I have written this book with the hope that when the American Establishment finally rejects the caste ideal of the country club set in favor of the ideas once dramatized by Camelot, the two Roosevelts and the late John Fitzgerald Kennedy, this whole dream will surely come to be.*

Digby Baltzell's book focused on what he saw as the conflict between the divisive forces of caste, on the one hand, which sought to maintain a WASP monopoly of upper-class institutions, and the cohesive forces of aristocracy that are capable of assimilating new talent and leadership regardless of ethnic or racial origins. He quotes Abraham Lincoln tellingly from an 1854 letter in support of his view that it was not only wrong but fatally shortsighted for the WASP establishment to discriminate against up-and-coming ethnic groups, such as the Irish:

> *I am not a Know Nothing. How could I be? How can anyone who abhors the oppression of Negroes be in favor of degrading classes of*

White people? Our progress in democracy appears to me pretty rapid.
As a nation we begin by declaring, "All men are created equal." We
now practically read it, "All men are created equal, except negroes."
When the Know Nothings get control it will read, "All men are
created equal except Negroes and foreigners and Catholics." When it
comes to this I should prefer emigrating to some country where they
make no pretense of loving liberty . . . to Russia, for instance, where
despotism can be taken pure, and without the base alloy of hypocrisy.

There were, of course, always exceptions, even in Digby Baltzell's Philadelphia. Gen. George Gordon Meade, of an old Irish Catholic family, turned Episcopalian after the Civil War, devoted himself to beautifying Philadelphia, and was as a result totally assimilated into the establishment.

Anti-Semitism was the next scourge to appear. In the year 1881 Czar Alexander of Russia was assassinated, and his son became Alexander III. A pogrom against Jews became part of the policy of the Russian regime. A third of Jews would be forced to emigrate, a third would accept baptism, and the remaining third would be starved to death. And on Christmas night that year, the streets of Warsaw were bathed in Jewish blood. Thus it was that, between 1882 and 1914, some two million immigrants were added to the American Jewish community from czarist lands; and so it became in America, alas, that all men were created equal, except Negroes, Catholics, *and Jews.*

The year 1882 saw the first federal statute restricting immigration passed by Congress, a precursor to the contentious legal and moral conversation that is still very much with us today.

Even in 1950 Baltzell relates how Jewish business leaders such as Goldman Sachs's Sidney Weinberg were not invited to join their WASP business equals at upper-class clubs such as the Links in New York City.

As immigrants gained a foothold and began to progress, they formed their own communities, such as the "Irish Riviera" in South Boston. Thanks to their language and political skills, the Irish tended to dominate both the hierarchy of the church and the urban political machines. That, Baltzell hypothesizes, rather fancifully, may have been a stimulus for some Italian Americans to enter organized crime.

In *The End of Ideology* (1960), Daniel Bell writes:

Early Jewish wealth—that of the German Jews in the 19th century—was made largely in banking and merchandising. To that extent the dominant group in the Jewish community was outside of and independent from the urban political machine. Later Jewish wealth, among the Eastern European immigrants, was built in the garment trades, though with some involvement of the Jewish gangster, who was typically an industrial racketeer.

However, even as the second and third generation of hyphenated Americans supplied outstanding leadership in the church, politics, and crime, many of these same groups began to come to the fore in business, entertainment, and the arts and sciences.

The establishment was uneasy with these encroachments, and Baltzell points out a rise in the 1920s of advertisements that expressly stated, "No Catholics or Jews need apply."

But progress slowly came.

The third generation of the so-called triple melting pot emigrated steadily to suburbia after World War II.

While the American electorate would not elect an obviously Irish-American Catholic (Al Smith) in 1928, they were apparently less prejudiced about the danger of a Catholic American being sent there in 1960.

And yet for a long time residual resentment remained. As late as August 1, 1960, columnist Lucius Beebe of the *San Francisco Chronicle* would write as follows in a family newspaper:

There is a fugitive feeling among Republicans and responsible people generally that it would have been a good thing for everybody had Stevenson been the Democratic nominee instead of a rich mick from the Boston Lace Curtain district . . . There is a sneaking sensation abroad that neither Nixon nor Kennedy is quite a gentleman. . . .

Hostility to Nixon on these grounds has an evasive quality. Prejudice against Kennedy is much easier to pinpoint: It is Lace Curtain Irish background in a political pigsty so liberally befouled by the late Mayor of Boston and jailbird, James M. Curley, that honest Democrats elsewhere in the land are appalled by it.

However, at the same time that arch Boston Brahmin, John P. Marquand, author of *The Late George Apley*, could in his last interview announce his intention to vote for JFK in the upcoming election. Henry Cabot Lodge also endorsed the idea of having a Catholic in the White House at that time, "perhaps guided in part by the fact by this time that some of his own grandchildren were married to them."

JFK was at ease with Jews and appointed the partly Jewish C. Douglas Dillon as his secretary of the treasury. Dillon's firm, Dillon Read, would later send two *Real Lace* partners to Washington in the Nixon and George H.W. Bush administrations, Peter M. Flanigan as Nixon's special assistant and Nicholas F. Brady as Bush's secretary of the treasury.

And yet in some quarters and regions prejudice remained, so that the 1964 Republican nominee, Barry Goldwater, of a distinguished Arizona family, being told he could not be a guest at a "restricted" golf club, joked, "I'm only half Jewish, so can I play nine holes?"

This was in a long line of prejudice going back to the 1870s, when the eminently respectable Joseph Seligman was excluded from the Grand Union Hotel in Saratoga Springs.

Wealth in America accelerated at the end of the nineteenth century. In 1891 it was estimated that 120 Americans were worth over ten million, and in 1892 that there were 4,047 millionaires. With this growing wealth, social habits evolved as well. In 1881 President Eliot of Harvard built a summer cottage at Northeast Harbor, Maine. In 1882 came the founding of the Country Club at Brookline (Massachusetts), which Samuel Eliot Morison once facetiously remarked coincided with the closing of the American frontier. The year 1883 saw the founding of the Sons of the Revolution, which led to many other genealogical societies such as the Colonial Dames, Mayflower Dames, and other anti-Irish and -Semitic groups, with the possible exceptions of the American

Jewish Historical Society (1894) and the American Irish Historical Society (1898), although even these were exclusionary of those they thought an ill fit.

The year 1884 saw the founding by Endicott Peabody of the Groton School, which catered to the old-stock families, and in 1887 came the *Social Register*. Long Branch, New Jersey, summer capital of presidents from Grant to Arthur, was filled with proper New Yorkers and Philadelphians (so much so that the Western Union company moved one of its senior executives, P.J. Casey, there during the Season to look after the heightened activity on its wires). Cape May, Spring Lake, Nahant, Bar Harbor, and the Berkshires also emerged as summer resorts.

A questionnaire devised for assessing the suitability of applicants to buy homes in Grosse Pointe, Michigan, required extra points for Italian and Jewish (but not, interestingly, Irish) to qualify.

Another St. Grottlesex school, St. George's, was founded by John Byron Diman in 1896. Diman was an Episcopal deacon, who later converted to the Catholic Church and founded Portsmouth Priory as a Benedictine foundation in 1926. It plays a part in our story, as does Canterbury School, another Catholic school founded by laymen in 1916 in New Milford, Connecticut, which, like Portsmouth, still thrives today. A third Catholic boarding school, Cranwell, was situated on the Berkshires estate of the Reverend Henry Ward Beecher, the great women's suffrage and antislavery advocate, who wrote of the site, "From here I can see the very hills of Heaven." Later Edward Cranwell purchased it in 1930 and deeded the estate to the Society of Jesus of New England in 1939. Several private donors provided generous funding for the property to be turned into the Cranwell School, a preparatory school for boys. After prospering for many years, the school slipped into decline, closing its doors in 1975.

By 1893 there were enough Catholics in Harvard Yard to support the St. Paul's Catholic Club, which acquired Newman House in 1912.

The 1920s, called the "decade of the dying Anglo-Saxon" by H.L. Mencken, produced the second great renascence in American literature. Baltzell speculates that this may have been in part because the members of the Lost Generation came to maturity in a period of transition from

Anglo-Saxon and provincial homogeneity to ethnic and cosmopolitan heterogeneity. Rather than identify with the smug attitudes of the business elite during the Harding, Coolidge, and Hoover eras, the likes of Dos Passos, Wilder, Faulkner, Hemingway, and Fitzgerald identified with Kipling's "legion of the lost."

Of these, Fitzgerald, whose Irish surname and Catholic mother made him well suited to adopt the perspective of an outsider, nonetheless left the most detailed portrait of establishment mores, including in *Gatsby* the vulgarian Tom Buchanan's admiration for Goddard's *Rise of the Colored Empires*.

> *This fellow has worked out the whole thing. It's up to us, who are the dominant race, to watch out or these other races will have control of things. . . . The idea is that we're Nordics . . . and we've produced all the things that go to make civilization—oh, science and art, and all that . . .*

Donald Trump could hardly have said it better!

Baltzell comments idiosyncratically on many aspects of social history. "Club life had been in steady decline since World War II"—and to Baltzell that decline illustrates an up-and-coming disillusion with anti-Semitism.

John F. Kennedy listed only one club—the Brook, in New York, to which, before beginning his mayoral career and resigning his club memberships, Michael Bloomberg was elected, and where Henry Kissinger still lunches frequently today. Baltzell also asserts that debutante rituals of 1964 were even more elaborate than formerly, but the celebrations have far *less* meaning for the debs concerned, who can now go to college, work, and have careers.

But Digby Baltzell remained hopeful for the future and came to see the Kennedys in particular as harbingers of a more inclusive and heterodox age.

> *The Kennedy family set the tone for a great deal of the private, informal and family-centered life of the New Frontier. It will be the*

children (and grandchildren) of this young generation of leaders—having been schooled together around the nation's capital, having gone away together to Exeter or Andover, Harvard or Radcliffe, and finally having intermarried—who will, in the long run, lay the foundations for a truly representative establishment in this country. This may be the most important, if unplanned, consequence of the composition of the generation of New Frontiersmen. For an establishment is never created by revolution or deliberate design, but only through a slow evolutionary process over several generations.

This sounds well-meaning but somewhat quaint today, since in the intervening years Christianity has been decimated in the Protestant mainline churches and severely wounded in the Catholic church, whereas the Jews, despite mixed marriage, have rebuilt the six million lost in World War II.

The influence of the Ku Klux Klan should also be mentioned. According to Philip Jenkins,

At its height it attracted several million followers in the US, most of whom were at least as concerned with fighting Roman Catholics as opposed to suppressing African-Americans. In the Klan view Catholic power threatened to overturn American society and values (The Inquisition, seditious secret oaths of the Knights of Columbus, Jesuitical conspiracies etc.) In the 19th century the Church had grown from 50,000 adherents and 35 priests to twenty million faithful with a vast network of clergy, schools and seminarians. Catholic alienism— the "unassimilated hordes of Europe"—threatened American racial purity. Today it's all forgotten so much so that the Klan now recruits Catholics! What a testament to how rapidly and totally immigrants become assimilated into American life.

Surely Digby Baltzell would have heartily approved the election of Barack Obama as the first African-American president of the United States in 2008. President Kennedy's youngest brother, Senator Edward Moore Kennedy, though suffering from terminal brain cancer, made his last public appearance to celebrate Obama's inauguration at the Capitol in early 2009. Baltzell would have cheered.

And he would wonder, given the debates over immigration in the 2016 election, if a decade hence we will shake our heads and wonder what we were so bothered about?

CHAPTER IV

Southward and Westward

THE MIGRATION OF IRISH AND SCOTS IRISH TO THE AMERICAN SOUTH was both earlier and far more numerous than has typically been assumed. The second royal governor of the Georgia colony (1757–60) was the County Monahan–born naval explorer Henry Ellis. In the 1760s Armagh native George Galphin cosponsored a largely Irish settlement called Queensborough. Early place names include Dublin and Burke and Blakely Counties. Georgia's first St. Patrick's Day parade took place in Savannah in 1814. Unlike in the North, many of these immigrants were from Ulster and Presbyterian rather than Catholic, but in the decades that followed, Irish immigration to the American South was not unlike those seen elsewhere in the United States. In the 1820s and 1830s, Irish labor, including for the first time many Catholics, constructed the canals. In the 1840s and 1850s, they built the railroads. By the time the Civil War broke out in 1861, there were enough Irishmen in the South— eighty-five thousand—to raise Irish brigades in eight of the eleven states that made up the Confederacy.

The War of 1812 hero, Indian fighter, and populist Andrew Jackson, soon to be replaced on the twenty-dollar bill by Harriet Tubman, was descended from Ulster Protestants. When he ran for president in 1828 with the enthusiastic support of his co-nationalist frontiersmen, opposition centered on his outsider status, just as it would in 1960 with John F. Kennedy and in 2016 with Donald Trump.

Prominent Georgians of Irish descent include lawyer and former Justice Department federal official Michael Egan, Paul Kinane, and

Terence McGuirk in Atlanta; Michael Toohy in Cartersville; Peter Lyons in Marietta; the late Harry Hagerty in Sea Island; and Bill McKenna in Savannah.

The Irish presence in South Carolina can be traced even earlier, to three ships sailing from Barbados in 1670. On board one of them were several indentured servants from the West of Ireland and Captain Florence O'Sullivan. Soldier, surveyor, and businessman, he would become known as "the Sentry of Charleston Harbor," and Sullivan's Island would be named for him.

From 1670 to 1750 the Irish arrivals were mostly Anglican, from 1750 to 1820 Presbyterian, and from 1820 through the 1900s mostly Catholic. Father Simon Gallagher was the pastor of St. Mary's Catholic Church, the first Catholic parish in Charleston. He was also on the faculty of the College of Charleston in the 1790s and was the first chairman of the Charleston Board of School Commissioners. Of the eight South Carolinians who signed the Declaration of Independence or the Constitution of the United States, four were of Irish descent. By 1883 there were seventeen Irish social, philanthropic, church, or militia groups in the city, including the Charleston Hibernia Society, which still thrives today. In 1920 Eamon de Valera, founder of the Irish Republic, visited Charleston and was welcomed by the second-generation Irish-American mayor John P. Grace and Andrew Riley, grandfather of the current and longest-serving mayor, Joe Riley. Among the many Irish civic leaders in Charleston are Dr. Duke Hagerty, Judge Michael Patrick Duffy, and restaurant owner Tommy Condon. Other well-known South Carolinians include the Snows of Beaufort, Morans of Greer, Harkins of Mount Pleasant, and the popular Lowcountry novelist Pat Conroy, who died in 2016 at the age of seventy.

New Orleans is best known for its French, Spanish, Cajun, Creole, and African associations, but the Irish have long been present there as well. Its first St. Patrick's Day parade was even earlier than Savannah's, in 1806, just two and a half years after the Louisiana Purchase. Among the seventeen toasts drunk that day were "To the Irish shamrock—may it find congenial soil in the plains of Louisiana" and "To the fair ladies of Louisiana—may the sons of St. Patrick ever deserve and be blessed with their families!"

The first Irish Catholic church was seven blocks upriver from Canal Street. Others then sprouted up in today's Warehouse District. Finally the neighborhood known as the Irish Channel was settled, between Felicity Street and Jackson Avenue, between the Mississippi River and the lower Garden District. St. Alphonsus Church is still a centerpiece of this neighborhood.

Among the prominent Irish-American New Orleanians, the various strains of the Brennan restaurant family surely have pride of place, feeding and watering natives and visitors from all over the world at places like Brennan's ("for Breakfast," best taken with a powerful milk punch), Mr. B's, and Commander's Palace. Lauren Brennan Bowers and her far-flung family lovingly look after their long tradition of hospitality and look forward to passing it on to future generations.

THE SOUTHWEST

Texas also boasts a somewhat submerged Irish presence. After the battle of Kinsale in 1602 and the defeat of the Irish armies, harsh penal codes were imposed on Irish Catholics, resulting in their flight to France, Spain, and Austria, and eventually to New Spain and Texas. Hugh O'Connor was born in Dublin in 1734. He later escaped to Spain and, as Hugo Oconor, served as the Spanish governor of Texas from 1767 to 1770. John McMullen and James McGloin established the San Patricio colony south of San Antonio in 1828. In that same year James Power and James Hewetson established the Refugio colony on the Gulf Coast. At least eighty-seven Irish-surnamed settlers settled in the Peters colony, which included much of present-day north central Texas, in the 1840s. Fourteen Irish died defending the Alamo in 1836, and about one hundred participated in the Battle of San Jacinto. "Dick" Dowling was Irish Confederate commander in the Civil War, famous for saving Houston by fending off a five-thousand-man Union Navy flotilla. He became known as the Hero of the Battle of Sabine Pass, and a statue and road in Houston honors him to this day.

The 1850 census in Texas listed 1,403 Irish. By 1860 that number had almost tripled, and it continued to grow going forward. Today there are St. Patrick's Day and Irish cultural celebrations throughout the state, including in Abilene, Clifton, Dallas, Fort Davis, Fort Worth, and, of course, Shamrock.

Among the prominent Irish-American citizens in Texas today are the McNairs in Houston, owners of the Houston Texans; the McMahons in Wichita Falls; the McWhorters, Dunigans, Buckleys, and Conways in Dallas; and the Colberts and O'Higginses in Austin.

WESTWARD

Unlike Boston, New York, or Philadelphia, Chicago was not settled until the 1800s. So the Chicago Irish did not face the worst kind of anti-Catholic, anti-Irish bigotry from established, native-born elites. This also allowed early Irish immigrants to get in on the ground floor of Chicago, and they took advantage of the opportunity.

"For the Irish, Chicago's emergence as the nascent city on the prairie was timely," writes John Gerard McLaughlin in his book *Irish Chicago*. "The construction of the Illinois and Michigan Canal, which would connect the Great Lakes to the Mississippi River, began in 1836, drawing Irish laborers.... The completion of the canal in 1848 coincided with the mass emigration from Ireland caused by the Great Famine."

Kerry native Dr. William Bradford was among the earliest boosters of Chicago and the opportunities presented by the canal's construction. Bradford, a physician, was also one of Chicago's earliest successful real estate speculators.

Canal work brought hordes of additional laborers—as well as class tension and cries for unionization. It also meant that when the Great Hunger struck Ireland, some Chicago laborers were able to send money, food, and other materials back to Ireland.

Although Chicago was spared the anti-Irish violence of other large American cities, there was no lack of rabid anti-Irish sentiment. The *Chicago Tribune*, edited by Joseph Medill (a descendant of Scotch-Irish Presbyterians), regularly dismissed the Irish as lazy and shiftless. "Who does not know that the most depraved, debased, worthless and irredeemable drunkards and sots which curse the community are Irish Catholics?" the *Tribune* sneered. This came even as Irish laborers worked feverishly to complete Chicago's stately St. Patrick's Church at Adams and Desplaines Streets in the mid-1850s.

Besides Dr. Bradford, another example of Chicago's Irish rising class was Cork native James Lane. In this city which would lead the nation in meat production, Lane is said to have opened Chicago's first meat market in 1836. He marched in the city's first St. Patrick's Day parade in 1843—and was still doing so five decades later, in the 1890s.

Meanwhile, decades before Jane Addams and Hull House became synonymous with Chicago charity, Carlow native Agatha O'Brien and nuns from the Mercy Sisters worked in hospitals, schools, and asylums caring for victims of cholera and other diseases.

By the 1870s the Irish-born population of Chicago was approaching seventy thousand—over 25 percent of the people. Then came a calamity that transformed the city forever.

According to legend, the Great Chicago Fire was started by Mrs. O'Leary's cow. The immigrant family was ultimately exonerated, but the O'Learys were subjected to awful harassment. The fire scorched large swaths of Chicago, including a dressmaking business owned by Cork native and future labor leader Mary Harris "Mother" Jones, who entered the labor movement soon after the fire. The newly rebuilt city saw further upward mobility for the Irish. A priest at St. John's parish on the South Side, Father Woldron, watched "in sorrow as hundreds of beloved families surrendered their humble homes and moved."

By the 1880s 30 percent of Chicago's police force and other civil service jobs were held by Irish Americans. Many of Chicago's Irish Americans now earned enough money to move to neighborhoods such as Englewood, where (much to the dismay of local Protestants) they laid foundations for working- or middle-class parishes such as St. Bernard's.

The Irish, as they did in many other cities, proved adept at politics as well as parish life.

Again, Chicago is unique in that while the Irish were the largest immigrant minority group in other large cities, they were just one of many in Chicago. Germans, Poles, Jews, and other Eastern Europeans flocked to Chicago in large numbers. "Second generation Chicago Irishmen assumed the role of buffers between the strange speaking newcomers and the native, older residents," Paul M. Green has written.

Meanwhile, Chicago writer Finley Peter Dunne created one of the great voices in American letters at the turn of the century: Mr. Dooley, the saloonkeeper/philosopher with the exaggerated brogue who was beloved by millions in nationwide newspapers and books. When Teddy Roosevelt published his book *Rough Riders*, Dunne wrote a tongue-in-cheek review with the punch line, "If I was him I'd call th' book 'Alone in Cubia.'" The nation laughed, and the partly Irish president wrote to Dunne, "I regret to say that my family and intimate friends are delighted with your review of my book. Now I think you owe me one; and I expect that when you next come east you will pay me a visit."

Early 1900s labor leaders included Margaret Haley, president of the Chicago Teachers Federation, and John Fitzpatrick, leader of Chicago's Federation of Labor.

There was also a dark side to Chicago Irish life, painted most memorably in the 1930s Studs Lonigan trilogy of novels by James T. Farrell. Farrell also wrote another series of novels about a youth named Danny O'Neill, who escaped Chicago and chased his dreams. Chicago groups such as the Catholic Interracial Council also showed that some Chicago Irish were promoters of racial justice.

Deanie O'Banion was the era's most prominent Irish gangster. He grew up in a notorious neighborhood known as Little Hell. Even when he became a full-time murderer, O'Banion sported a rosary in his pocket and a carnation in his jacket. In fact, O'Banion so loved flowers that he opened a flower shop on North State Street, which was where he was killed in 1924, after he had swindled members of Capone's crew.

All in all, Chicago has had a dozen Irish mayors. Early city leaders include John Comiskey (father of White Sox baseball owner Charles Comiskey), John Coughlin, "Foxy" Ed Cullerton, and Johnny Powers. Later, in 1979, Irish American Jane Byrne was the first woman to serve as Chicago mayor.

The most powerful Irish-American mayor ever was Richard J. Daley, who ran Chicago for more than twenty years, beginning with his 1955 election. Daley was a humble, devout Catholic who raised his family not far from the South Side Irish enclave where he grew up. As a multiethnic town, Chicago required a mayor who knew how to reward all ethnic groups, a task that Daley mastered.

Daley became such a key figure in the Democratic Party that he was known as a "president-maker," whose support was needed to nominate any White House candidate.

Daley's image was tarnished by the violent events of the 1968 Chicago Democratic convention. Afterwards he memorably roared in an attempt at Ciceronian rhetoric: "I have been vilified! I have been crucified! Why, I have even been criticized."

But in the mayoral election of 1971, Daley received nearly 60 percent of the vote. He died while in office in 1976. His son, Richard M. Daley, was later elected Chicago mayor in 1989, and another son, William Daley, was a key advisor and cabinet member to Presidents Clinton and Obama.

By the 1980s many Chicago Irish had been in the city for three or four generations. But a whole new wave of immigrants then arrived, escaping an Ireland that was still struggling economically. These immigrants breathed new life into Chicago's Irish-American life and culture. A daughter of immigrants, Liz Carroll is a Chicago native who is one of today's top Irish fiddlers. Then, of course, there is *Riverdance* star Michael Flatley. A native of the South Side, Flatley reinvented Irish dance and brought it to the international masses. Other prominent Chicago Irish Americans include Donald O'Connor, Bill Murray, the late Chris Farley, Chris O'Donnell, Jenny McCarthy, and the Disney brothers, Walt and Roy.

And other families have come to the fore in more traditional businesses, such as the Fitzgeralds, the Cummings, Fitzsimons, and Garvys.

ELSEWHERE IN THE MIDWEST

Detroit's first St. Patrick's was celebrated in 1808. An early leading citizen was George Alexander O'Keefe, who came from Dublin to Detroit to practice law in 1820 and became a dominant figure as a lawyer and probate judge. He was one of the founders of St. Patrick's Day festivities in Detroit, which included toasts such as "Ladies, may you be temperate in everything except in your affections for your husbands."

By 1858 Detroit had its first Irish-born mayor, carriage maker John Patton. Holy Trinity Church, the epicenter of Irish spiritual life, was expanded into the Gothic Revival edifice that still stands today. The city's Irish population swelled, and prominent families today include the Connollys, Fishers, Fitzsimonses, and Thurbers.

Milwaukee's Third Ward was an Irish neighborhood for much of the nineteenth century until a fire swept through it in 1892. The Irish then moved west to Tory Hill (today part of the Marquette University campus) and to Merrill Park. Actors Pat O'Brien and Spencer Tracy lived there before heading to Hollywood. Tom Cunningham, Matt Flynn, and John Carroll all remain prominent citizens of Wisconsin.

St. Louis is historically a French city, like New Orleans, but its ancient Irish Quarter was called Kerry Patch. As the city has moved to the more spacious suburbs, its churches have been torn down and other landmarks, like the James Clemens Mansion, have been left in disrepair, but some ardent preservationists have begun to organize renewal even as many of the younger generation move back into Warehouse District lofts downtown. The Mullins, Murrays, Gillises, Lynches, Fords, and Burkes remain prominent citizens.

Up the river, Minneapolis was famous for the McNights of Minnesota Mining and Manufacturing (3M). William L. McNight was famous for developing a management theory that stressed delegation and proved quite successful over many decades. His son-in-law, James Binger, headed the Honeywell Corporation and also succeeded in the high-risk industries of theater and horse racing.

The first Irish to come to St. Paul were three soldiers from Fort Snelling in 1838. Their number quickly grew, and nine of the ten men who served as mayors of St. Paul between 1932 and 1972 were Irish. The Irish Fair of Minnesota continues to take place annually on Harriet Island in St. Paul.

Tom Pendergast was the dominant machine politician in Kansas City in the 1920s and 1930s. In his capacity as chairman of the Jackson

County Democratic Party, "T.J." was able to use his large network of friends to help elect politicians (through voter fraud in some cases), hand out government contracts, and arrange patronage jobs.

The Kansas City of those decades was a wide-open town with more than forty dance halls and dozens of nightclubs where legendary jazz heroes like Count Basie and Hot Lips Page entertained hard-drinking customers. There was also widespread gambling and prostitution. To those who questioned Pendergast's laissez-faire approach to morality he answered unapologetically as a Democrat with a small "d."

"The upper classed have their own clubs where they can go to have a good time, and less fortunate people should have the same opportunities."

In such an atmosphere it was inevitable that organized crime would try to establish a foothold, and a North Side mobster named Johnny Lazia did just that by kidnapping Pendergast machine election workers who had regularly produced turnouts in excess of 100 percent of registered voters. In the truce that followed, Lazia was given "home rule" on his turf and became the enforcer and collector across the city, lucrative occupations given the highly profitable operations from which he was extorting cash.

In due course this led to Pendergast's downfall as stories of Kansas City's corruption spread across the country, and a federal investigation followed. His increasingly expensive and well-known gambling habit, especially on the ponies, didn't help. Despite Pendergast's sterling record turning out votes for FDR, secretary of the treasury Robert Morgenthau declined to intervene on his behalf, saying, "Let the chips fall where they may."

They did, and T.J. Pendergast went to jail for eighteen months, living out the remaining few years of his life a broken man. A surprise attendee at his funeral in 1945 was vice president Harry S. Truman, the one-time "Senator from Pendergast," who said simply, "He was always my friend, and I was always his."

The Hegartys and Dooners remain prominent Kansas City Irish names today.

CALIFORNIA AND THE WEST

Early Irish immigrants gained land grants from the Mexican government, especially in Marin County, which became known as Little Ireland. Among these early settlers were John Connors with Rancho Punta de Quentin, Timothy Murphy with Rancho Santa Margarita y Los Galinas San Pedro (Marinwood and San Rafael), John Reed with Rancho Madera del Presidio (Corte Madera and Tiburon), John Berry with Rancho Punta de los Reyes, and John Murphy with Rancho Corte Madera de Novato.

With the gold rush San Francisco's Irish population grew to 4,200 in 1852. By 1880 that number had reached 30,000, 37 percent of the city's population. Many of the early settlers became prominent politicians. General Bennet Riley became military and civilian governor of the Territory of California and drafted the state constitution in 1849. John Geary became San Francisco's first mayor in 1850 and was followed by another Irish-born mayor, Frank McCoppin, in 1867. James Broderick was elected U.S. senator in 1857 and H.H. Haight governor of California in 1878.

In business, John Daly had a large dairy and rock quarry south of San Francisco that he subdivided to create Daly City. Samuel Brannan printed San Francisco's first newspaper in 1846. John Sullivan founded Hibernia Savings and Loan and the Hibernia Housing Society. James Phelan established the First National Bank of San Francisco, and his son, James Jr., went on to become mayor of the city and a U.S. senator.

San Francisco's St. Patrick's Day parade started in the 1850s and quickly grew over the next twenty years to six thousand marchers and fifty thousand spectators. The Irish have played a prominent role in the city's civic and business life ever since. And today women are competing on an equal playing field with men. Meriwether McGettigan and her daughter Fay, for example, are prominent jewelers in Presidio Heights. Katherine Tobin's Avanti imports Italian pottery, and Angela Tirrell is a leading trompe l'oeil artist in the city. The Irish Technology Leadership group led by Palm Inc. senior vice president John Hartnett and executives from Intuit, Apple, Intel, Cisco, and Hewlett-Packard aims to help Ireland take advantage of technological opportunities.

Other leading San Franciscans include Henry McGinness, Owen Reid, and Dale Kirby.

In Los Angeles, in addition to the Dohenys, Belfast-born William Mulholland made the city possible by developing the Los Angeles water aqueduct that delivered water to the rapidly growing city. Hollywood has also had an Irish component, from Hal Roach and John Ford in the early days to Roma Downey, Ed Burns, and George Clooney today. There are many Irish organizations throughout the city and, in addition to the Maguire real estate dynasty, the Dunn and Joyce families are also active. Patrick Conway, Michael Phelan, and Michael McDonnell are all prominent as well.

DENVER

After silver was discovered at Leadville, the Irish swarmed to Colorado and in due course built an enduring community in Denver and elsewhere in Colorado. J.K. Mullen learned the wheat trade when he came from Ireland and operated a number of successful flour mills. With his wife he also founded many philanthropic organizations for the poor and built several churches. He was a frugal and serious man who disliked ostentation and disapproved of the St. Patrick's Day celebrations that began in 1883, but they flourished without him until anti-Catholic sentiment put the parade on hiatus in 1921. Then, in 1962, a few regulars of Duffy's Bar & Grill breathed new life into the tradition by merely walking around the block of the tavern in 1962. Within a decade the Denver parade was the second biggest in the country. Today Jeremy Kinney remains a pillar of the energy community.

Seattle and Phoenix also have proud Irish traditions, and the latter's McClelland Irish Library is a leading Irish cultural center.

CHAPTER V

Faith of Our Fathers (and Mothers)

In *Real Lace*, Stephen Birmingham makes many references to the devout ways of the First Irish Families: the Murrays praying the Rosary on car rides and attending Mass in their private chapel in the great house on St. Mark's Avenue in Brooklyn, now torn down; James Butler endowing Marymount College in Tarrytown for his cousin, Mother Marie Joseph Butler, and later buying her the Burden Mansions on Fifth Avenue for Marymount School; the Catholic Church in Southampton filled with Cuddihys, Murrays, and McDonnells on a summer Sunday morning all dressed to the nines. There are also more irreverent anecdotes, such as the young Lester Cuddihy biting Cardinal Spellman!

Birmingham also records that pew number eleven in St. Patrick's Cathedral remained the Butler pew, "the only one still in family possession." Say what? That is certainly news to my family, who had never heard any such thing, nor is there any nameplate or other sign so to indicate. A harmless piece of blarney, perhaps, but perhaps we should be making weekly visits just to make sure . . . This was part of the warp and woof of Irish-American Catholic life, although as part of the recent renovation of St. Patrick's, the price of a named family pew has been raised to $250,000!

My mother often reminisced about being out on the town at the Stork Club on a Saturday night in the late 1930s. Her father, Schuyler Casey, who was of New York Dutch and Irish extraction, would call up the owner, Sherman Billingsley, and tell him he was sending "the kids" down and to put everything on his tab. But Mother would not drink or eat after midnight and would insist on attending the first mass of Sunday morning at St. Paul's Church on Eighth Avenue at what is today the southern boundary of Lincoln Center. It began at 5:00 a.m., not long after the nightclubs closed, and, having assisted at the mass and received the sacrament, one could look forward to a long lie-in the rest of Sunday morning.

Such stories lasted well into the 1950s and 1960s. Christopher Buckley recounts his New Orleanian grandmother, Aloise Steiner Buckley, and her sister going into St. Patrick's Cathedral to make their confessions late in life. Two elderly ladies in mink coats in the grit and grime of the 1960s. When they emerged from the confessional and were praying their penances, one haltingly turned to the other and asked sweetly, "Darling, do you by any chance find anything unusual about your penance?"

"Why yes, darling, I did."

"What was that?"

"Well, the priest told me to say ten thousand Hail Marys and five thousand Our Fathers."

"Why, he told me the same thing, darling! Do you think we should go ask someone what to do?"

And so, clutching each other, these two genteel natives of New Orleans "without a sin to split between them," in Christopher's phrase, sought out a clergyman, who was properly appalled at what they had to say and, upon inspecting the confessional box, found one of New York's homeless installed in it, making the most of his opportunity.

Former Boston mayor and U.S. ambassador to the Holy See Ray Flynn remembers St. Patrick's Day as a day off from school in South Boston, where the mothers were up early to bake soda bread before bringing the family to hear then Bishop (later Cardinal) Cushing celebrate 11:00 a.m. mass. After mass they would head over to the parochial school hall, where hot tea and scones were served. A fiddle and accordion player would play traditional Irish music.

Even as a young boy I would get up and sing "A Mother's Love is a Blessing" on the stage. Before the party wound down one of the nuns would get up and tell the gathering a little story about the life of Saint Patrick.

Years later the celebration of the day would take me to Mass at Saint Peter's with Pope John Paul II, dinner with the president at the White House, and the honor of being named Grand Marshal for the St. Patrick's Day Parade in New York, Dublin and other great world cities. But attending Mass on Saint Patrick's Day in my hometown of South Boston, with my family and neighbors close by, will always be my fondest memory of "my favorite day of the year."

Ray Flynn tells another story indicative of his generation. He was a star basketball player at Providence College and was named the Most Valuable Player in the National Invitational Tournament in 1963. This led to a tryout with the many-time champion Boston Celtics, every Southie boy's lifelong dream. Flynn did very well. In fact, he was the last person cut from the team before the season began. It was a crushing blow. Years later he remembered:

Coach (the legendary Hall of Famer, Red) Auerbach could not have been kinder. He said, "Ray, we'd love to have you, you did everything right. I just don't have the budget or the room. Go out and find something you can excel at. I'm sure you will. Good luck."

I walked out of his office and onto the street in a daze. I felt like my life had ended, and I had no idea what I could do next. I walked for hours. There was no way I could go home, no way I could sleep. But I promised myself I wouldn't go into a barroom, wouldn't take the easy way out. I had to face my failure and myself. Instead, at some point I found myself in a church, and I stayed there for a very long time. I prayed for God's grace and help to let me find the way forward. In the end I got a job working as a counselor in a youth program in South Boston, and slowly I got involved in politics. It was the right path for me.

Cardinal Dolan, in a similar but slightly different vein, waxes fondly about leading a band of New York pilgrims to Lough Derg, the sacred Irish island sanctuary of St. Patrick. In 2015 he wrote: "I know I am looking forward to returning there this August as it will be a wonderful opportunity for prayer. And maybe, after thanking God for the great gift of His mercy, we will stop at a local pub to offer thanks for another of His great gifts!"

In the 1920s, 1930s, and 1940s, the church remained strong, busily building parishes, cathedrals, schools, and hospitals. Vocations to the priesthood and to religious life for women remained high. There were 42,000 priests in 1970, the high-water mark. Religious sisters grew throughout the twentieth century to 147,310 in 1950, reaching a peak of 181,421 in 1966.

Lay Mass attendance as a percentage of American Catholics was over 70 percent on Sundays. But as the fifties ended, and the decade of the sixties began, shifts began to happen. Was it the culture, with the coming of the Beats, the Summer of Love, civil rights protests, and anti–Vietnam War demonstrations, in short a revolt against all symbols of authority? Or was it the church itself, beginning to rot from within? Or was it a bit of both?

Vatican II was a well-intentioned effort, as Pope John XXIII put it, to "open the windows of the Church" to the changing times, and arguments will persist for a long time as to whether it helped or hurt, or even, given the prevailing gestalt, made little difference in what followed.

There have always, of course, been those seeking to purify and reform the church from within, like latter-day St. Bernards of Clairvaux, who railed against the excessive grandiosity of the medieval abbots of Cluny. The magnificent monastery of Cluny had more than 10,000 monks, 1,450 dependent priories around Europe, and more than 460 monks in its home monastery alone. It figured powerfully in the civil and ecclesiastical life of the age. Among other things it was the starting point for the Camino de Santiago, the ancient pilgrimage route to Santiago de Compostela in Spain to venerate the remains of St. James. But St. Bernard attacked the grandeur of its abbots: "Who cannot go four leagues from their house without a retinue of sixty horses in their wake . . . will the light only shine if it is in a candelabrum of gold or silver?" His Cistercian reforms gained influence and won the day. Today Cluny, once the largest church in Christendom (until the building of St. Peter's in Rome), is but a ruin, albeit an awe-inspiring one. The nearby Burgundian cathedral of Vezelay, a Romanesque masterpiece, meanwhile, has adopted a novel governance structure. Three different orders of Franciscan priests, nuns, and a lay apostolate jointly share in its care—a potential model for others going forward.

Unlike St. Bernard, the *Real Lace* Irish were proud to be rich, but they often supported other Irish Americans who devoted themselves to social reform and service to the poor, none more so than Dorothy Day, who was called by her biographer, Jim Forest, a servant of God, saint, and troublemaker.

Can you think of a word that describes a person who devoted much of her life to being with people many of us cross the street to avoid? Who for half a century did her best to make sure they didn't go hungry or freeze on winter nights? Who went to Mass every day until her legs couldn't take her that far, at which point communion was brought to her? Who prayed every day for friend and enemy alike and whose prayers, some are convinced, had miraculous results? Who went to confession every week? Who was devoted to the rosary? Who lived in community with the down-and-out for nearly half-a-century? Whose main goal in life was to follow Christ and to see him in the people around her?

A saint.

Can you think of a word that describes a person who refused to pay taxes, didn't salute the flag, never voted, went to prison time and again for protests against war and social injustice? Who spoke in a plain and often rude way about our "way of life"? Who complained that the Church wasn't paying enough attention to its own teaching and on occasion compared some of its pastors to blowfish and sharks?

A troublemaker.

And there you have Dorothy Day in two words: saint and troublemaker.

To a journalist who told her it was the first time he had interviewed a saint, she replied, "Don't call me a saint — I don't want to be dismissed that easily. . . ."

For Dorothy, hospitality is simply practicing God's hospitality to us with those around us. Christ is in the stranger, in the person who has nowhere to go and no one to welcome him.

Dorothy was close to many artists and writers, including Eugene O'Neill. She used to hang out at a Greenwich Village saloon locally known as the Hell Hole. It was an adventurous time in her life but without much of an anchor. She had a lover who wanted neither marriage nor children. In a desperate effort to preserve their ill-fated relationship, she had an abortion. Her lover abandoned her anyway. Dark times! Dorothy tried to commit suicide but a neighbor smelled the gas and saved her life.

She survived, brought another child to full term, and doted on her, and with the help of Peter Maurin started the Catholic Worker movement. Its eponymous newspaper, which she edited, grew from a print run of twenty-five hundred to one hundred thousand, and Catholic Worker houses were established across the country.

I stayed at the one in Davenport, Iowa, in the 1970s, where my Portsmouth classmate Michael Garvey was working. The King of the Hobos had recently passed through and then died as he napped beside the banks of the mighty Mississippi a little ways downriver. One of his friends eulogized him at the memorial service: "What better way for a hobo to pass over Jordan than asleep beneath a tall oak tree, God's great sky spreading out above him?"

A social worker asked Dorothy Day one day how long the down-and-out were permitted to stay. "We let them stay forever," Dorothy answered rather testily.

No stranger to prison, Dorothy Day was first locked up as a young woman protesting with suffragettes in front of the White House in 1917, when she was nineteen, and was last jailed in 1975 for picketing with striking farm workers at the edge of a grape field in California.

She was, in short, a remarkable woman, now known as the Servant of God, Dorothy Day. The cause for her canonization continues, however much she might dismiss it.

As the 1960s continued, Catholic culture was changing. I can vividly remember being about ten years old, dressed in khaki trousers and a madras jacket and tie one steamy morning at St. Joachim's in Cedarhurst, Long Island, when Father Flanigan, hoarse from shouting without amplification, asked us all to stand to take the Legion of Decency Pledge. My eldest brother, an undergraduate at Johns Hopkins with what seemed to me to be boundless sophistication, was determined to see Brigitte Bardot in *And God Created Woman*. He refused to budge. "Philip, stand up right this instant!" my mortified mother whispered with increasing urgency. It was an early sign of insurrection.

PROFILE:
Portsmouth Priory: The Early Years

Portsmouth Priory School was founded in 1926 by Father Hugh Diman. "A dyed in the wool Yankee" by his own description, he was born John Byron Diman, in Brookline, Massachusetts, to J. Lewis Diman, pastor of the Harvard Congregational Church, and his Unitarian mother, whom he always credited with being the greatest moral influence on his life. The family had old roots in Bristol and may at one time have held slaves, as many in that well-known slaver port once did.

After Diman's birth, the family soon moved to Providence upon his father's acceptance of the chair of History and Political Economy at Brown. An Episcopalian by his senior year, Diman graduated from Brown in 1885 and from there attended Episcopal Theological Seminary in Cambridge. He was ordained deacon in 1888 and became the first permanent rector of the lovely St. Columba's Chapel, then Berkeley Memorial Chapel, on Indian Avenue in Middletown, Rhode Island. Both Louis Comfort Tiffany and John LaFarge designed stained glass windows for the little church that can still be seen today.

In 1896, after teaching and acquiring an M.A. from Harvard, John Byron Diman opened a small school for four or five students called the Diman School, at 22 Catherine Street in Newport, with the help of his sister Emily and the encouragement of the LaFarge family. The school prospered, growing to over forty boys in the next few years, until in 1901 it was incorporated as St. George's School and moved to its present, magnificent site overlooking the ocean at Second Beach in Middletown. His directness and simplicity of manner made it possible for him to get along with anyone. On occasion he was observed riding his bicycle in white tie and tails. Upon being asked his destination, he answered unaffectedly, "I'm having dinner with Mrs. Vanderbilt."

Diman served as St. George's founding headmaster for twenty-one years and also, during this time, demonstrated his breadth of educational vision by planning and funding a vocational school for public school students in Fall River called the Diman Vocational School, which is still in operation today.

Despite these achievements, by 1914 Diman was seeking to resign his headmastership and did so on October 28, 1916, saying only, "In recent years I have become increasingly interested in many subjects—educational and other—for which I wish to have an opportunity for study."

In the late fall of 1915, an attack of acute appendicitis helped to clarify his plans, and, to the amazement of his sister Louise, he asked to see a Catholic priest. On his recovery he began to take regular instruction from Father Higney, pastor of St. Joseph's Church in Newport, who received him into the Catholic Church on December 16, 1917. He never regretted his decision; indeed, he noted later

> *a sense of interior ease and liberty, to which I had been a complete stranger in the perplexed years of my earlier life . . . I was much pleased once when I was told that a good woman somewhere was heard to say to one of her chums that Father Diman was not half so stiff as he used to be since he'd turned Irish. She mixed up her ideas of race and religion a little bit, but she expressed exactly what I felt myself was true.*

Still a layman, he became a captain with the Red Cross in 1918 and served with the Royal Air Force in England in the final months of the war. After the armistice he studied theology in Rome, at Belmont Abbey, and finally at Portsmouth Priory, then in its struggling infancy as a monastery under the leadership of Dom Leonard Sargent. He was ordained, on his own patrimony (meaning he had his own resources and was not under obligation to a bishop or other superior), in September of 1921 and spent a year as a school chaplain and then another in New York as a parish priest before joining the founders of St. Anselm's Abbey, a fledgling Washington Benedictine community founded from Fort Augustus in Scotland, in 1924. In a surprising turn of events, this small group was asked to establish a preparatory school, and Abbot Leander Ramsay of Downside Abbey in England offered to donate the property at Portsmouth for this purpose.

As the founder of two successful schools already, Father Hugh was the obvious choice to lead this new effort, and he set about contacting parents, drawing up the prospectus, and planning the first year for a school of about fifteen first and second formers (seventh and eighth grades).

Cardinal Newman was a crucial influence on Father Diman as well as many of the other early monks at Portsmouth, several of whom were also converts. John Henry Newman was born in 1801 and died in 1890. He was an Anglican priest for two decades, and was one of the founders of the Oxford Movement, which sought to reinvigorate the Church of England. In 1845 he left the Anglican Church to convert to Roman Catholicism. He was ordained a priest soon after, and was elevated to cardinal in 1879.

The richness of Newman's thought and the felicity of his prose remain powerful and provocative today. "To live is to change, and to be perfect is to change often"; "If falsehood assails Truth, Truth can assail falsehood"; and "The Church moves as a whole . . . it is a communion" are but three examples.

Diman's concept was to found a "national Catholic school" along the lines of the St. Grottlesex Episcopalian church schools like Groton, St. Paul's, Middlesex, St. Mark's, and St. George's, all of which he knew well, and the last of which, of course, he himself had founded. In the 1926 prospectus he noted:

The Portsmouth School would be the first Benedictine school in the United States belonging to the English Congregation . . . Americans who are familiar with its great schools on the other side: Downside, Ampleforth, Fort Augustus and Douai know the great role they play in Catholic and national education. There are certain characteristics that mark them all: a genuine appreciation of scholarship, thoroughness in work, and a belief in a broad and liberal education as opposed to narrow specialization. On the other hand the ancient order is in sympathetic touch with the needs of our own times and recognizes the just demands of a scientific age.

In the inner life of these schools there is in all alike a pleasant family association, a large measure of liberty and self-government, a firm reliance on the appeal to honor, a great belief in outdoor sports and games, and a spirit of cooperation and good comradeship between masters and boys in the classroom and on the athletic field.

Religion enters into the warp and woof of the daily life. The Chapel for the (Religious) Community and the School is the same. Boys may enter it and leave it at will. Thus while religion is not thrust upon them, the daily spectacle of the Mass, the occasional presence at sung Vespers or some other parts of the Office, the sight of the quiet and ordered routine of the Community, often reach the mind and the soul of even the most lighthearted looker-on, where calculated effort would generally fail.

The school opened on September 28, 1926. Eighteen students enrolled, of whom the first to arrive were Peter and James Hoguet. Another of the original students at Portsmouth was Christopher Wyatt, brother of actress Jane, whose mother's name, Euphemia van Rensselaer Waddington Wyatt, was the longest name in the *Social Register*. The school quickly grew, doubling in size in its second year. It adopted the colors and motto of Harvard as its own (Father Hugh had twice been president of the Harvard Teachers' Association), and its shield, designed by Pierre de Chaignon La Rose, two rampant lions holding up a loaf of bread, was that of the old Roman family the Frangipani, which claimed descent from the Anicii, from which the school's patron, Pope St. Gregory I, belonged. Word of the new school for Catholic boys spread quickly, and it became known as "Father Diman's school."

By the early 1930s the school had grown to over six forms and attracted students from across the country, including my father, his elder brother, and several of their cousins. A stellar faculty had been recruited, including W.K. Wimsatt, later Sterling professor of English at Yale, chair of that department for many years, and the author of several important studies in eighteenth-century literature; John Howard Benson, one of a long line of fine Newport artists, taught art; and Albert Belliveau, a brilliant Harvard graduate, taught French and founded the school's branch of the Cum Laude Society. For several years Father Hugh had given up the headmastership to an Englishman named G.C. Bateman, who introduced a level of structure and discipline not hitherto seen. "He saved the School when it was becoming unstuck," remembered Carroll Cavanaugh '32. "His famous cane and his equally stinging sarcasm were blessed astringents. A great fellow. Kindest, most humane, entertaining man you'd ever meet."

And yet Father Hugh was beloved as he aged for precisely his lack of structure. He disliked administration and would word letters so they required no reply. Anton Crimmins, a young Anglo Irishman transplanted during World War II, used to serve Father Hugh's mass in the morning to escape the longer community mass. One day Father Hugh called to him, "Anton, there's a man coming to see me I don't want to meet. Tell him I went *that* way"—and he pointed as he started to walk in the opposite direction. He was a notoriously bad driver, and in old age would drift to sleep during study halls, waking as the boys began to raise Cain and murmuring, "Tut-tut," which became his nickname.

Another early student, Jim Baker, recalled, "My fondest memories are still of Father Hugh. Once when Chris Wyatt and I were sitting with him at the head table, Father Hugh was ladling out soup from a soup tureen; and suddenly he said, 'My glasses, my glasses, where are my glasses?' Well, with the next ladle out came the glasses. And through it all he was completely endearing."

And yet he remained steadfast to the end about the Portsmouth Priory's unique mission: "An education of reason without faith can only take its possessors half-way along the road, even if as far as that."

By 1939 the school could count 118 graduates since its first commencement in 1931. Of these, thirty had gone to Harvard, nineteen to Yale, thirteen to Georgetown, and eight to Princeton, a remarkable pattern that persisted for many years. Though its facilities were still modest, Portsmouth Priory's monastic and lay faculty were first-class, and its rating as an academic institution was at the top of the heap.

The monastery had grown, and by the early 1940s included a brilliant second generation of builders, including MIT architect and city planner Dom Hilary Martin, the polymath and wonderfully eccentric Dom Andrew Jenks, star athlete and coach Dom Bede Gorman, and artist and administrator Dom Peter Sidler. Together with the prior,

Dom Gregory Borgstedt, they began to plan the next stage of development for the school.

Father Hugh died after a second heart attack on March 17, 1948 (an appropriate day indeed for one who had "turned Irish"). On March 22 the new bishop of Providence, Russell J. McVinney, celebrated a pontifical requiem for his soul in the priory chapel. Numerous alumni from the three schools founded by Father Hugh attended, and in addition to Portsmouthians and senior officials of Brown and Harvard Universities, the pallbearers included the headmaster of St. George's and the director of Diman Vocational, a fitting tribute to an extraordinary educator and priest.

My father's classmate in the Portsmouth class of 1936, Eric Ridder, a publishing scion, Olympic gold medalist in yachting in 1952, and successful defender of the America's Cup when he co-skippered the yacht *Constellation* in 1952, could have spoken for many when he recalled Father Hugh:

I consider him one of the great men in my life . . . So much can be said for his leadership and his great and gentle mind. I have a very vivid picture in my mind right now of his tall, handsome figure in his black robes and his white shock of hair striding around our athletic fields during football practice. I have a vivid memory of the enjoyment he used to take in playing bridge with a group of us small boys, and I have a very vivid memory of the joy and pleasure that was in all our hearts whenever we saw him.

All three of Father Diman's schools continue to thrive today, each according to its particular charism, and the legacy he left at Portsmouth Priory helped propel it to new heights in the quarter century following his death.

CHAPTER VI

From Counting Houses to Carryout

In the decades after *Real Lace* was written in 1973, the financial world in which so many of the Irish-American families like the McDonnells, the Ryans, the Bradys, and the Meehans had made their mark began to change. Computerization and globalization led to higher trading volumes, a growth in risk arbitrage, and the advent of the eurodollar. Old-fashioned partnerships like Salomon Brothers were assimilated into huge banks or even, as in the case of Goldman Sachs, became publicly traded entities. Investment banking trended from the genteel world of corporate advisory and underwriting services to more aggressive activities. Friendly mergers were increasingly replaced by hostile takeover attempts. Leveraged buyouts, where the target firm's own assets were used to finance the transaction, minimizing the acquirer's cash outlay, became the preferred method of doing business. Exotic financial instruments such as CDOs (collateralized debt obligations) littered the landscape, often with not even the bankers who devised them understanding their underlying value or lack thereof, as the 2015 movie *The Big Short* illustrated.

While the Irish still participated in Wall Street, their involvement was not as influential as it had been. Was it because the brave new world of finance was too data-driven, technocratic, philo-computer, and truly global, and not the collegial, essentially friendly meeting place where colleagues could work hard but look forward to a martini or Scotch over lunch at the Stock Exchange Luncheon Club (now a shadow of itself in the still impressive upstairs rooms of the Exchange)? And whereas there had always been abuses, the motto "Your word is your bond" was sacrosanct on Wall Street, and those who violated it were ostracized. As Billy Salomon approached his one hundredth birthday, his longtime partner Gedale Horowitz said, "Billy sharply limited what you could take out of the firm, with charity being the only exception, and honesty and integrity were uppermost. If you ever even thought about trying to hide a bad trade, you were gone, and never coming back."

Again and again that world receded into the shadows, and yet those who were guilty never suffered penalties, thus accounting for Bernie Sanders's successful critique in the 2016 Democratic campaign of Hillary Clinton's ill-gotten largesse from major Wall Street houses that had helped cause the 2008 financial collapse but successfully lobbied and rigged the system to avoid paying the price themselves, instead passing it along to the taxpayer.

In an eloquent op-ed in the *Washington Post* in 2010, Nicholas F. Brady, a descendant of the Anthony Brady who helped finance the first Thomas Murray and himself the former managing partner of Dillon Read before becoming secretary of the treasury under George H.W. Bush, described the changing climate of finance like this:

When I came to Wall Street in 1954 investment banking was a profession that financed the building of the country's industrial capacity and infrastructure. But year by year the industry's emphasis moved away from this purpose and towards financial innovation for financial profit's sake. According to the Federal Reserve's Flow of Funds data, from 1980 to 1982, the financial sector accounted for an average of 12.8% of U.S. total corporate profits. By 2005 to 2007 the three years average was 23.8 percent.

The money was addictive. It drove people on Wall Street into activities that had no redeeming social value, and it disoriented executive pay scales. The enormity couldn't be contained, and at its height in 2008 it blew up our financial system.

Is there any way of legislating compensation levels? I think not. There is nothing wrong with seeking profit. But I've always been impressed by the military dictum, which is that officers eat last.

In 1989 Brady initiated a Latin American debt reduction program that came to be known as "Brady bonds." Argentina, Brazil, Colombia, and Mexico were some of the countries that participated and have now successfully retired their bonds. After government service Brady returned to the private sector and continued highly profitable investment banking activities in Latin America.

Other significant Irish-American businessmen have included Howard Hughes, James Farrell of U.S. Steel, cable television pioneer John Malone, Heinz CEO Tony O'Reilly, Bank of America CEO Brian Moynihan, Hibernia Bank of San Francisco president Michael Henry deYoung Tobin, and Donald Keough, the longtime head of Coca Cola. Bill Ford is the leader of the latest generation of his family at Ford Motor, and the Maguires are a multigenerational real estate holding family in Los Angeles. Robert McNair built an energy empire in Houston and now owns the Houston Texans, and Francis Rooney is a construction magnate in Tulsa, Oklahoma, who has served as the United States ambassador to the Vatican.

Two other highly successful Irish-American businessmen are Thomas S. Murphy and the late Daniel Burke, who built up the Capital Cities Broadcasting Group so successfully that it was later able to acquire ABC.

Murphy was born in Brooklyn, graduated from Cornell University in 1945, and got his M.B.A. at Harvard in 1949.

He was working at Lever Brothers when broadcaster and author Lowell Thomas hired Murphy to run the WROW station as its first general manager. Murphy's leadership brought WROW-TV to profitability three years later. In December 1957 Hudson Valley merged with WTVD in Durham, North Carolina, to form Capital Cities Communications.

Murphy moved quickly up the ranks in the company thanks to hands-on management and a conservative approach to cost control. In 1964 he became president, and in 1966 Murphy became chairman and CEO. He held this position for the next thirty years. Under his leadership Murphy and his chief business partner, Daniel Burke, built Capital Cities into a multibillion-dollar media company, with holdings such as Fairchild Communications and several daily newspapers.

Through it all, Tom Murphy remained modest and unflappable. He neither smoked nor drank, and, a devout Catholic, attended Mass frequently. I often saw him lunching at the Racquet & Tennis Club, where he was friendly, but direct, and always hurrying to get back to work.

Murphy and Burke's biggest acquisition came in 1985 when they took advantage of their swelling cash flows to buy the ABC television network for $3.5 billion. The difference in cultures between a financially conservative broadcast station group like Cap Cities and the more flamboyant and creative programming executives at the ABC Network was a source of concern to the latter, and they initially expressed fears about being taken over by "the suits" from the East Coast. Murphy and Burke flew out to Hollywood to allay these anxieties and, after a constructive series of meetings, cemented the new alliance after they returned to New York by having a huge bouquet of flowers delivered to the ABC top brass "with love from the Suits."

In 1995 Capital Cities/ABC was bought by Disney, making Chairman Murphy and President Burke very wealthy men.

Daniel Burke died from complications of diabetes in 2001, but Tom Murphy, now in his early nineties, has remained active on several boards such as Berkshire Hathaway, Texaco, Johnson & Johnson, and IBM, and is a major donor to Catholic and other causes.

Among a younger generation of Irish-American executives are Disney's Anne Sweeney and Christine McCarthy, co-chair of Disney Networks and CFO of Walt Disney, respectively; Terry McGuirk, longtime Turner Broadcasting senior executive and now chairman of the Atlanta Braves; and Nion McEvoy, CEO of Chronicle Books. Steve Burke, son of Dan, is executive vice president of Comcast as well as CEO of NBCUniversal. Craig Barrett was the longtime head of Intel who introduced the company to Ireland, where it is now the largest employer. Jack Dorsey is the CEO of two technology companies, Twitter and Square, and Tom Moran is the CEO of Mutual of America. Finally, Richard Cashin has been a highly successful investment banker in New York.

Irish Americans in business are widely dispersed geographically, not simply restricted to Boston and New York.

PHILADELPHIA

The Irish American Business Chamber and Network is based in Philadelphia, and among the prominent businesses there are McCloskey & Co., a multi-generation construction concern. Its longtime head, Matthew H. McCloskey, was the former Democratic Party national treasurer, whom President Kennedy appointed as United States ambassador to Ireland in 1961. Thereafter his son, Thomas D. McCloskey, led the company. After serving in the United States Marine Corps in World War II, he supervised the building of the Philadelphia Mint, Centre Square, Mann Music Center, Veterans Stadium, the Spectrum, and RFK Stadium. By the 1970s development had replaced construction as the company's primary activity. Tom McCloskey died in Palm Beach in 2004, and many of his family continue to reside there at least part of the year.

Among other Philadelphia business leaders are Ed Hanway, chairman emeritus of Cigna Corporation and an active educational philanthropist via the Faith in the Future Foundation, which seeks to rejuvenate Philadelphia's Catholic school system. J. Brian O'Neill of the O'Neill Properties Group, Jerry Sheridan of AmeriGas Partners, Tom Gallagher of Pepper Hamilton LLP, Michael Mahoney of Commonwealth Telephone, and Michael Hagen of Lifeshield Inc. also serve on the Faith in the Future board, as does former NBA coach James F.X. O'Brien.

But the first family of Irish Philadelphia remains the Kellys. John B. Kelly Sr., born in 1889, was one of ten children born to an Irish immigrant. He apprenticed as a mason and later built a prosperous bricklaying business in the city. A great amateur athlete, he played football professionally and won all twelve of his boxing matches while in the army in World War I, but it was in rowing that he made his greatest mark. He became the first oarsman to win three Olympic gold medals and set a record with 126 consecutive single scull wins in competition, but he is best remembered for being denied the opportunity to row for the 1920 Diamond Sculls title in Henley's Royal Regatta because the rules forbade entrants who had done manual labor. Kelly had not planned to row in the Olympics that year, but after his snub he determined to go to Antwerp to meet and defeat the Diamond Sculls winner, the Englishman Jack Beresford. After a thrilling duel to the finish, Kelly beat the English champion by one second. Afterwards they became good friends, and Kelly sent his rowing cap to King George V with a note that read, "Greetings from a bricklayer."

John B. Kelly Sr. is also well known, of course, for fathering actress Grace Kelly, widely considered the world's most beautiful woman, and supplying a two-million-dollar dowry when she married Prince Rainier of Monaco. Princess Grace retired from the screen and devoted herself to family and philanthropy. She died at age fifty-two after a stroke while driving back to Monaco from her country home. At a memorial service in Beverly Hills after the requiem mass in Monaco, James Stewart delivered the following moving eulogy:

> *You know, I just love Grace Kelly. Not because she was a princess, not because she was an actress, not because she was my friend, but because she was just about the nicest lady I ever met. Grace brought into my life as she brought into yours, a soft, warm light every time I saw her, and every time I saw her was a holiday of its own. No question, I'll miss her, we'll all miss her, God bless you, Princess Grace.*

John B. Kelly Jr. continued the family rowing tradition, winning at Henley and capturing a bronze medal at the 1956 Olympics. He was later elected president of the American Amateur Athletic Union.

Another family tradition that endures to this day is the Kelly family's annual pilgrimage to the Kentucky Derby, still going strong with the latest generation after seventy years. John B. Kelly Sr. was a great racing fan and had just been installed as president of Atlantic City Racetrack in 1946 when he received a call from Churchill Downs' chairman asking him to come down for the Derby. He immediately said yes, rented a private railroad car, and brought along twenty of his best friends for a raucous sporting weekend. Last year Prince Albert of Monaco joined his cousins and newspaper publisher Brian Tierney for the seventieth renewal of the Derby excursion, although, unlike in 1946, the Kelly gang now travels to Louisville by plane, not train.

Other prominent Philadelphian Irish include baseball's Connie Mack, MSNBC's *Hardball* host Chris Matthews, Ethel Barrymore, Philadelphia Museum chairman Henry McIlhenny, rapper Jamie Kennedy, Jeanette McDonals, sportscaster Jim McKay, Kevin Bacon, Kim Delaney, author Michael Connelly, Mike Douglas, composer Samuel Barber, pitcher Tug McGraw, cartoonist Walt Kelly of Pogo fame, and, of course, "I'd rather be in Philadelphia" comedian W.C. Fields.

PITTSBURGH
The Donahues
In addition to the Rooneys of racetrack and Pittsburgh Steelers fame, the Donahue family of Federated Investors are longtime business leaders. John Donahue started Federated in 1955 to sell mutual funds after previously selling other funds door to door. His son Christopher Donahue joined the firm in 1972 after graduating from Princeton and concentrated on the then novel concept of money funds that gave investors access to a liquid account that also earned a market rate of interest. Federated's money fund assets rose with the industry, and it grew to be an industry leader behind only Fidelity Investments and JP Morgan Chase & Co., making up 75 percent of Federated's total assets of $356 billion in 2012. In recent years he has had to defend Federated's primary business from regulatory restrictions in the wake of the 2008 global banking crisis. The far-flung Donahue family are active Catholic philanthropists in education, practicing their "Three F's," "Faith, Family, and Federated."

The McGuinns
Longtime Mellon Financial Corp. chairman and CEO Marty McGuinn is another prominent Pittsburgh Irish American. McGuinn steered Mellon through some turbulent competitive seas and restructured the company to meet the changing business and regulatory environment until retiring in 2006 after twenty-five years. In recent years he and his wife Ann have become more focused on philanthropy. In 2013 they became the largest donors to Pittsburgh Promise, the city's scholarship program for public and charter school graduates who are going on to postsecondary education in Pennsylvania. McGuinn also sits on the board of the Carnegie Museum of Art and the University of Pittsburgh Medical Center.

CHICAGO
The MacArthurs

John D. MacArthur was among Chicago's business titans. He started selling insurance door to door, often in poor neighborhoods, and wound up leading the immensely successful Bankers Life and Casualty Insurance Company. He also amassed real estate holdings in Chicago, New York, and Florida that proved to be very valuable. During their lifetime the MacArthurs quietly supported causes in Chicago and Palm Beach, where they lived, but upon their death they created the highly innovative John D. and Catherine T. MacArthur Foundation, which will be discussed in detail in a later chapter on philanthropy.

MacArthur's brother, Charles MacArthur, was a writer best known for his plays with Ben Hecht, *Twentieth Century* and *The Front Page*. He had a long and happy second marriage to actress Helen Hayes. Their son, James MacArthur, became a successful actor, appearing in the Disney movies *Kidnapped* and *Swiss Family Robinson* and for eleven years as Danno on the popular TV series *Hawaii Five-0*.

The Galvins and Motorola

Paul Galvin founded the Galvin Manufacturing Company in 1928, which became Motorola, so named because it was a hybrid of "motor" and "victrola."

Under his son Bob the company was transformed from a car radio and wartime walkie-talkie manufacturer into a global maker of color television sets, pagers, hearing aids, cell phones, semiconductors, satellite communications, and other high-tech electronics. In the three decades after he took control in 1956, the company grew from $290 million in sales to $10.8 billion. Galvin exploited new markets, diversified profitable product lines, and introduced the Six Sigma quality system, later adopted by General Electric under CEO Jack Welch.

Bob Galvin was a longtime supporter of Illinois Institute of Technology and other causes. In 2005 he created the Galvin Electricity Initiative, a nonprofit organization dedicated to transforming the electric grid.

Bob Galvin was succeeded by his son Christopher Galvin as CEO in 1986. After some initial missteps Chris Galvin had positioned the company for a new period of growth when, in 2004, the board, led by Procter & Gamble chair John Pepper, suddenly ousted him.

In a 2014 review of the book *Boards That Lead*, *Wall Street Journal* deputy managing editor Alan Murray wrote of this incident:

> *The authors tell the story of the board of Motorola Inc., which the authors blame for destroying the company. In 2004, it pushed out CEO Christopher Galvin (a grandson of the founder) just as his strategy was starting to deliver success, then replaced him with CEOs who enjoyed some early successes based on Mr. Galvin's efforts, and then presided over the company's decline and breakup.*
>
> *The authors attribute this blunder to not backing a bet on solid technology or strategy, of which investment in technology had been the heart and soul of the Motorola culture, and having a reflexive response to the demands of investors, some of whom where short-term traders.*

After being ousted from his family company, Chris Galvin served as chairman of Navteq Inc. and brought it public in 2004. In 2008 Nokia bought Navteq for $8.1 billion in cash, generating a 255 percent ROI to shareholders in at the time of Navteq's IPO.

Chris Galvin has gone on to found Harrison Street Real Estate Capital, which invests in education, health care, and storage sectors of the real estate market. He has served on the board of several companies, including Bechtel. He also serves on the board of his alma mater, Northwestern University, the Tsinghua University School of Management and Economics in Beijing, the American Enterprise Institute, and the Rand Corporation.

PROFILE:
Tom Monaghan and Domino's Pizza

Another striking example of Irish-American business entrepreneurship since the original *Real Lace* is Tom Monaghan and Domino's Pizza.

Monaghan's father died when he was four years old. When he was six, his mother placed his younger brother and him in St. Joseph Home for Children in Jackson, Michigan. It was run by the Felician Sisters, one of whom inspired Monaghan's deepening Catholic faith. He later entered St. Joseph's Seminary in Grand Rapids, but, after being expelled for misbehavior, realized he did not possess a vocation for the priesthood. Instead, after a stint in the Marine Corps and at the University of Michigan, he set out to be an entrepreneur.

Tom Monaghan borrowed several hundred dollars to purchase a small pizza store called DomiNick's in Ypsilanti, Michigan. After settling a trademark lawsuit from Domino Sugar, Tom opened three additional stores and bought out his brother's share by giving him a Volkswagen Beetle.

Monaghan focused on delivery to college campuses and expanded his network of stores through a franchising system, which focused on college town markets. Monaghan sold his shares in Domino's Pizza in 1998 to Bain Capital, a Boston firm headed by future Republican presidential candidate Mitt Romney, for what contemporary newspaper accounts estimated was one billion dollars.

Original Real Lace *Families in Business*

Michael Meehan of the well-known Wall Street trading family made his mark on Wall Street in his own generation as a partner at Salomon and has gone on to other successful investing ventures.

The heirs of Thomas Fortune Ryan went on various paths. Ryan's eldest son, John Barry Ryan (1874–1942), became a financier and writer. He married Margaret Kahn Ryan.

Mrs. Ryan, known as Nin, was a daughter of the financier Otto Kahn, a turn-of-the-century multimillionaire who became a benefactor of the Metropolitan Opera even though the Met at first would not assign him a box in its "diamond horseshoe," where rich New Yorkers hobnobbed at intermission.

She joined the Met's board in 1956, and after the company moved to Lincoln Center in the 1960s and announced that it was facing a financial crisis, she worked on an emergency fund drive to raise three million dollars. She became an honorary director in 1981.

Mrs. Ryan was also an art collector whose French Impressionist paintings hung on the walls of her triplex apartment on the East Side of Manhattan and, in summers when she went to London, in the Metropolitan Museum of Art.

Otto Kahn was a power at the Met until a few years before his death in 1934. When Kahn first became involved with the company, the Met had an unwritten rule that no Jew could own a box. He was finally permitted to buy one, in the diamond horseshoe, seventeen years after he had joined the board.

In 1951, two years after Mrs. Ryan's mother, Addie, died, Mrs. Ryan and the other Kahn heirs sold Rembrandt's *Portrait of a Young Student* for ninety thousand dollars. They gave the money to the Metropolitan Opera. The Met put up a plaque, first at the old house on Broadway and later at Lincoln Center, that said the money had made possible new productions of Verdi's *Don Carlo* and Mozart's *Cosi Fan Tutte*. The *Don Carlo* was Rudolf Bing's first production at the Met.

Thomas Fortune Ryan's grandson, Allan A. Ryan Jr., born in 1903, was a New York state senator from 1939 to 1942. His father had been disinherited by T.F. Ryan after heavy speculation, and the fortune passed to young Allan, who worked his way from the bottom up on Wall Street and opened an investment banking firm with Charles H. Sabin Jr. He also bred Aberdeen Angus cattle in Dutchess County near his country home in Rhinebeck, New York. He went to Canterbury and Princeton, married four times, and lived until 1981.

Another Thomas Fortune Ryan granddaughter, Sally Ryan, was a noted art collector.

A great-granddaughter is Virginia Fortune Ryan Ogilvy, Countess of Airlie, wife of David Ogilvy, thirteenth Earl of Airlie. Grandson Joseph Bondurant Ryan (1906–1950) was the visionary developer of the Mont Tremblant ski resort in Quebec. Joseph's son Peter (1940–1962) was the first Canadian to compete in Formula 1 auto racing and the winner of the first Canadian Grand Prix in 1961.

Real Lace described how Clendenin Ryan (1905–1957), publisher and owner of *The American Mercury* and a one-time aide to Mayor Fiorello La Guardia of New York, having run through a fortune estimated at fifty million dollars, committed suicide in the same Ryan mansion on 79th Street as had his father, Allan J. Ryan Sr. His son Clen died in the late 1970s, but two other sons survive. Cyr Ryan owns a fiber optics company and lives quietly with his family in rural Allamuchy, New Jersey, the Ryan county seat. Robert J. Ryan inherited the political gene in the family and has been active as an advisor and election campaign strategist to several politicians, including Governor George Pataki, who named him head of the Roosevelt Island Authority.

The Butler grandchildren and great-grandchildren also have generally followed quiet working lives in banking, the law, and on Wall Street, although two, Ewing Butler and Father Luke Travers, became educators. Pierce Butler MacGuire enjoyed a highly successful forty-year career at Tiffany & Company, as did his cousins Judy MacGuire Renicke and Eileen McCarty McGill. James J. MacGuire, a son of James Butler Mac-Guire and Mary Jane Cuddihy MacGuire, is a noted chef, baker, and food writer in Montreal. Finally, his brother, Sean MacGuire, inherited some of his great-grandfather Murray's genius and has patented several software innovations. He now lives in Key West, Florida.

CHAPTER VII

High (and Low) Society

In the years after *Real Lace* was published, Catholics of at least partly Irish extraction played an important part in business, politics, society, and the arts. One of these was Carter Burden, a Vanderbilt descendant and graduate of Portsmouth Priory.

Burden's father, Shirley, was a photographer who married Flobelle Fairbanks, a niece of Douglas Fairbanks, in Beverly Hills in 1934. According to Lucius Beebe in *The Big Spenders*, Burden's grandmother, Mrs. Hamilton McKown Twombly, last living grandchild of "the Commodore," Cornelius Vanderbilt, was past eighty but determined to attend the wedding.

Mrs. Twombly was forbidden to fly. The family private Pullman car had long been discarded, and Mrs. Twombly wouldn't even toy with the idea of renting one from the New York Central, let alone ride in a public train. Driving the entire 3000 miles from Newport to the church was the only solution, but it, too, was fraught with grave perils and the ever present dangers of the Great Plains and other accidents of violence in the howling wilderness west of St. Louis. The James boys, she understood, were no longer in operating condition but who knew about others, the Daltons, for instance? And there was always the chance of hostile Indians. If they recognized her she would be held for ransom, a most inconvenient possibility.

Finally a solution presented itself. For 3000 miles going west and an equal distance coming back, the last grandchild of Cornelius

Vanderbilt dressed as her personal maid, rode in the front seat next to the chauffeur in one of the Twombly Rolls Royces while for an equal time and distance Mrs. Twombly's maid dressed as Mrs. Twombly, rode in lonely state, in the back seat.

Carter Burden: A 1960s Legend's Legacy

In 2014, nearly two decades after his death, the Morgan Library mounted a splendid exhibition of masterpieces from Carter Burden's magnificent collection of modern American literature. *From Gatsby to Garp* brought together nearly one hundred works including first editions, manuscripts, letters, and revised galley proofs. Among the authors featured were such twentieth-century titans as William Faulkner, F. Scott Fitzgerald, Allen Ginsberg, Ernest Hemingway, Langston Hughes, John Irving, Henry James, Jack Kerouac, Norman Mailer, Toni Morrison, Sylvia Plath, Ezra Pound, Philip Roth, J.D. Salinger, John Steinbeck, John Updike, Tennessee Williams, and Richard Wright, among many others, along with their nineteenth-century predecessor Henry James.

Burden's commitment to Harlem (part of which he had represented on the city council) was signified by an especially strong selection of Harlem Renaissance writers such as Wallace Thurman, Jean Toomer, and Zora Neale Hurston. Other areas of emphasis included the Lost Generation in Paris and the Beats. But what was on the walls and in the display cases of the Morgan (of which Burden in his lifetime was a trustee) was but a small fraction of the immense holdings he built up, at one time including eighty thousand volumes representing seven thousand authors. At the height of his collecting, indeed, now nostalgically recollected by rare book dealers as "the Burden Decade," Burden *was* the market, outbidding anyone who tried to compete with him. In later years he winnowed his list of collectible authors from seven thousand down to six hundred and deaccessioned many of his holdings, but when he and Susan moved into their baronial Mark Hampton–designed digs on Fifth Avenue, he had bookcases designed and installed there that held fifteen thousand of those volumes, with another twenty thousand or so still in storage.

My wife and I were lucky enough to be invited there one evening in the early 1990s in large part because, in addition to the fact that our parents had been friends, Carter and I had shared the same housemaster, the charismatic connoisseur and Benedictine monk Father Hilary Martin, and in fact the same room—eleven years apart—at Portsmouth Priory. The apartment had spectacular views of Central Park and the Metropolitan Museum, but the most overwhelming effect was of the bookcase-lined, seventeen-foot-high, mahogany-paneled living room complete with columns and pediments by its entrance. I also seem to remember an over-the-top gentleman's dressing room that Hampton had decorated so lavishly that, after a couple of glasses of very good champagne, I had difficulty divining the location of the loo I had been directed to within it.

Carter Burden's book-collecting mania began when he ran across a first edition of Henry Miller's (on whom he had written his Harvard undergrad history and literature thesis) *Tropic of Cancer* in a Sotheby's catalogue. "Suffice it to say that what began with one lousy book by one lousy author turned into an eighty thousand volume monster a mere twelve years later. . . . when I started, I'd given myself an all-in budget of $25,000, a figure I immediately surpassed with my first telephone order."

What made the book collecting possible, however, was that in an earlier decade Burden had collected contemporary artists such as Frank Stella, Jasper Johns, Any Warhol, and Roy Lichtenstein, when fine works by these rising artists could be had for a song, say $2,500.

"The $2,500 figure comes to mind because it's the precise amount I paid in 1970 for Stella's *Quathlamba*, which I sold at auction seventeen years later for $1.3 million. . . . The point is, one *Quathlamba*, if deaccessioned at the right moment, buys a lot of books, and it did."

Collecting, however, was only one of Carter Burden's multifaceted pursuits. For a period of time he was one of the most prominent of the City's Beautiful People, so much so that a *New York* magazine cover story by Judy Baumgold in 1970 speculated he could become the president of the United States.

He was a great-great-great-grandson of shipping and railroad magnate Cornelius Vanderbilt, "the first tycoon." His father, Shirley, though a partner in the family banking firm, William A.M. Burden & Co., was something of a dreamer, warmhearted, kind, and a gifted photographer.

His mother, Flobelle Fairbanks, was a niece of the actor Douglas Fairbanks, herself an ever elegant beauty, and both father and mother were prominent in Los Angeles and New York social circles.

His first girlfriend was Geraldine Chaplin, to whom he remained grateful for the tutelage that decisively overcame the deficiencies of a Catholic education. The year after graduating from Harvard, in 1964, following a bachelor party at an elegant Upper East Side brothel called Daphne's organized by Bartle Bull, which Carter once told me (no ladies were within hearing range) was "the greatest night of my life," he married Amanda Jay Mortimer, daughter of Standard Oil heir Stanley Mortimer and Babe Paley. A law student at Columbia at the time, he and "Ba" moved into the Dakota and gave parties there for guests including, according to his *New York Times* obituary, Truman Capote, Andy Warhol, Norman Mailer, George Plimpton, Larry Rivers, Robert and Ethel Kennedy, Joan and Teddy Kennedy, and, once, Prince Philip of Britain.

After graduating from law school, he went to work for Bobby Kennedy, as one of many idealistic young reformers whose dreams were dashed when Kennedy was assassinated. But Burden ran for office himself and, with the help of campaign managers Tim Hogen and Bartle Bull and a fiercely dedicated staff, was elected to the city council in 1969, serving until 1978 and launching early initiatives in gay and tenants' rights. Tim Hogen recalls: "For a person of such total privilege he was incredibly zealous, driven and completely enmeshed in all of the relevant issues. He could have been lying on a beach somewhere, but he wasn't. In that sense, and also because one felt he didn't want to let people get too close to him, he was something of an enigma."

In 1969 Carter Burden also became the majority owner of the *Village Voice* (Bartle Bull and Alan Patricoff were among those who had minority stakes), which he merged with *New York* magazine in 1975 before selling his interest to Rupert Murdoch. In addition to books and contemporary art, he also collected masterly drawings, including works by Sargent, Picasso, and Matisse. His many philanthropic activities included the Bedford-Stuyvesant Development Project, the New York City Ballet, the New York Public and Morgan Libraries, and the Burden Center for the Aging. In later years he also founded a radio station holding company,

Commodore Media. He and Amanda were divorced in 1972. "They married very young," explained Bartle Bull, who introduced them. "You have to understand."

Amanda went on to lead the New York City Planning Commission and is now a principal at Bloomberg. In 1977 Carter Burden married Susan Lombaer, a psychotherapist. Their life was a happy one in New York. In town one occasionally spied Carter lunching near his Rockefeller Center office at the Sea Grill or dining with Susan and friends at Girasole, a friendly neighborhood joint just a couple of blocks east of their splendid pad. On such occasions he was always friendly, witty, and very bright. They also enjoyed Southampton and frequent travels. Once, outside the Uffizi Museum in Florence, he gazed at her walking ahead of him and said admiringly to his old teacher, Bill Crimmins, who had happened upon them, "Can you believe how beautiful my wife is?"

Carter Burden was only fifty-four when he died, the same age, remarkably, as his mother, and of the same heart ailment. His funeral took place at the Church of St. Ignatius Loyola and featured selections from Faure's *Requiem*, chosen by his close friend and collaborator, interior decorator Mark Hampton, whose own life was to end too early a few years later. Carter's son, Carter III, spoke affectionately of his father that day, and he and his sister Belle remain active in New York. One is left to wonder what this protean player on the landscape of New York's Fun City era in the 1960s and 1970s would be doing were he still here today, but his legacy lives on in multiple dimensions, prominent among which is the finest collection of twentieth-century American literature yet assembled.

HOLIDAYS OF YORE

Remembering the 1960s and 1970s in New York City brings back many memories. Recently I ran into my old friend and fellow chamber music aficionado Peter Duchin at the Sutton Place stop of the M31 now that he has relocated uptown. The experience reminded me of the great bands that used to play various New Year's venues—Guy Lombardo and the Canadians at the Waldorf, to name just one, but others my parents particularly enjoyed like Peter's father, Joe Carroll, and Ted Straeter. And I remembered a bit sadly wandering into a deli one New Year's Eve fifteen years ago or so and finding Lester Lanin ahead of me on the line. He had gotten started in his amazingly long and successful career at the beach club on Long Island where my brothers and I grew up and still came to play the Labor Day dance there every summer as a gesture of appreciation, but this night he just shook his head and said, "It's the first New Year's Eve in over forty years I haven't had a date. Can you believe it?"

The holidays around New York hold some of the greatest memories of being young. Hundreds of prep school kids converged on Penn Station by train the night before Thanksgiving, going to the Rangers game at the Garden and afterwards carousing out on the town until the Long Island Rail Road milk train (my old man called it "the vomit comet") got one home in time for breakfast; touch football (a brother christened that game "the Toilet Bowl") on the third fairway of the Hunt Club; and the gathering of the clan, where my mother was more than up to the task of keeping the seventeen or so cousins around the table in line, which was not always true of the assembled uncles and aunts!

In any case, by the time that weekend was ended, it would be back to school or college for exams and then a return to New York for dances that could be dreadful or delightful but were always improved by a cozy pre-event dinner at the Regency Whist Club and the gigantic mai tais at Trader Vic's in the Plaza *après*. And of course the night could not be considered properly concluded unless one headed out—not downtown as today—to the various gin mills that catered to the young on the Upper East Side: Doug Fry's, Dick Edwards's, and a few blocks apart on 79th Street, Don Denton's and Mike Malkin's, where no one was ever carded. The drinking age was eighteen back then, remember, and I was served my first Bloody Mary at P.J. Clarke's when I was four years younger than that, under the baleful eye of P.J.'s owner, Danny Lavezzo Sr., and his longtime maître d', Frankie Ribando.

It was at Denton's one night that its then sometime bartender, Michael R. McCarty, now the impeccably reformed impresario of the eponymous Restaurant and Saloon in Palm Beach, decided to liven up the evening. Rising from one of the backgammon tables then much in use, he retreated to the men's room, emerged in his raincoat, and crossed the street to the Laundromat across 79th Street. There he took off the raincoat and in his well-endowed starkness flashed back across the street, burst into Denton's, and ran down the bar back to the bathroom. All had gone according to plan thus far, but now things went seriously awry. As Michael pulled at the door to get in, it wouldn't budge, and soon he began to suspect he could hear the uncontrolled giggling of two of his best friends, Nicky Emmanuel and the late, lamented Artie Schoen, holding the door fast against him. So in due course, as the owner/auteur Don Denton ("of Denton Avenue in Hempstead," as he was prone to point out late at night) ambled down the bar to interview Michael on what he thought he was doing, there was nothing for the noble McCarty to do but run back up the bar and out the front door, cross 79th Street, and retreat to the Laundromat. If only someone had thought to grab his raincoat in the interim!

At any rate, Malkin's, between First and Second Avenues, was often the last stop of the night, with the owner and his friend Diego del Vayo attentively surveying the preppie population therein. One night my great childhood chum Lars Potter had arrived from the toga party his St. George's upperclassman, Howard Dean, was throwing in Big Howard and Andree's Park Avenue pad (the older Deans were safely in East Hampton, where all parents should be when the younger set parties). Lars's date was Margie Lindsay, the mayor's tall, beautiful, brown-tressed daughter, just down from her junior year fall term at Dana Hall.

(Speaking of Dana Hall and girls' boarding schools, twenty years later my friend and publishing colleague Charlie Scribner called me one morning at Macmillan and said, "I'm having the most *awful* problem." "What's that, Charlie?" "Well, I'm filling out this questionnaire for my twenty-fifth reunion at St. Paul's and it asks, 'What was your most memorable moment?' I want to write, 'During the first St. Paul's/Concord Academy exchange program, when the future Queen of Jordan lost her virginity,' but I'm not sure I should." Maybe not, I advised.)

At any rate, back to Margie Lindsay. Margie had imbibed a bit too much of the future Dr. and Governor Dean's powerful grain alcohol punch and had taken a recovery nap in Mr. and Mrs. Dean's bedroom before coming to Malkin's. We intelligently decided once there that a restorative Black Russian or two would make her and all of the rest of us feel better. If you've never tasted one, please don't start now. Black Russians are a disgusting mixture of crème de cacao and vodka and go down the throat like old sludge. Anyway, once we were thus infused, the night went on riotously until it was four o'clock and the lights came on. At that point Potter realized he couldn't find Margie, and it was not until several minutes later that we discovered her receiving the ministrations of the Chinese attendant who tried to keep the two loos at the bottom of a steep staircase in working order through the long nights at Malkin's—a Sisyphean task if there ever was one, and occasionally an Augean one as well.

Thereupon, supporting her on either side, we walked her the ten blocks or so home to Gracie Mansion. As the police guardhouse at the front of the mansion hove to, I courageously said, "I'll let you take it from here." Lars looked *extremely* disappointed in me but resigned to the drubbing he knew he was about to take. When I asked him what happened the next day, he said,

Well, we were shown into this little anteroom, and Mrs. Lindsay came downstairs. She gave me the dirtiest look I've ever gotten in my life, and took Margie away. I stood up to go, and the cop said, "You ain't goin' nowhere." So I sat down, and pretty soon the mayor came down wearing a paisley bathrobe. "I'm not very happy about this, you know," he said in a loud voice so Mrs. Lindsay could hear upstairs. As I stammered out my apologies, his face slowly broke out into a wide grin, and he told me to sit down. We talked for about ten minutes; he asked about school and my plans for the vacation; and then he shook my hand and wished me good night. I can't imagine anyone being kinder or more understanding.

And so it was on a typical night in the holidays of yore.

RESTAURATEUR MICHAEL MCCARTY

After bartending in New York at Don Denton's and Newport at the Clarke Cookhouse as his alternative education, Michael opened his first joint in 1972 on Second Avenue just north of 72nd Street. It had a Park

Avenue–like canopy; palm trees framed the entrance (transported by Jake Burton Carpenter from Dede Littlefield's recent benefit). Jake had not yet become the king of snowboarding, and for the next year tried unsuccessfully to renegotiate his fifty-dollar fee. It had a red taxi light hung outside the door. The glassware, china, and silver were hotel quality, and coats and ties were required, but the drinks were plentiful and cheap. In short, it was an Upper East Side "21" for youngsters on starting salaries.

The bar had the best-educated bartender in New York—Jimmy Ferrer, moonlighting from his day job as the assistant headmaster at Buckley School. McCarty dressed in bespoke suits and presided over the scene, from after-work drinks through dinner and onto the 4:00 a.m. closing, when he closed up with a leisurely nightcap or two and walked home in the soft light of a Manhattan sunrise.

Occasionally Michael would take a busman's holiday, rent a limo, and pick up a date at her building. "Would you like some wine?" he would ask the young lady once she was seated, and point to the chilled bottle of Dom Perignon cooling in an ice bucket in the backseat. Then it was on to some chic restaurant. One night, in a rare show of nerves, he had made a reservation in another name, and Bruce, the maître d' at "21," furrowed his skeptical brow and said, "Auchincloss, Auchincloss . . . would you mind spelling it, sir?" Spelling was not Michael's strong point! So he headed for the exit . . .

Swells was often bursting at the seams, and through it passed a panorama of young New Yorkers—Don and Susan Ross; Macy Jones and Lisa Fisher; Tom Quinn, not yet the inspiration for the tobacco lobbyist in Christopher Buckley's *Thank You for Smoking*; Pandy and Mike McDonough; *People* publisher Chris Meigher and his glamorous wife, "Grace the Face"; and Bill Doyle gallerists Barry and Linda Donahue.

Ultimately too many late nights and poor lifestyle choices closed Swells, its successor, and two other east side joints Michael McCarty opened, but, after a near-death experience or two, he reformed, went to work for the Smith & Wollensky chain in New Orleans and Chicago, and in 2004 realized his dream of opening Michael R. McCarty's Restaurant and Saloon in Palm Beach, taking over the location long occupied by another popular hangout, Dempsey's. He made an instant splash as the only restaurant to be open five days after the 2005 hurricanes, and one that sent out free sandwiches to shelters and rescue workers during the messy aftermath of the storm.

The place did a good lunch business but really sizzled with the young late at night. Nearly nine lives after his first success on Second Avenue, McCarty often found himself welcoming the children of his former customers: Elizabeth Meigher, Mike and Lucas McDonough, Whitney Tower III, Piper Quinn, and Nevin and Clay Donahue. "I get a tremendous kick seeing these kids, and I love it when they ask me about the old days," McCarty says. "But sometimes I have to bite my tongue remembering their parents."

The parents appreciate McCarty's discretion in not revealing too many details of New York's Studio 54 years. Moreover, they trust him to look after their kids and run his place the right way. They know he has not had a drink in thirty years ("Giving up drinking was the best thing that ever happened to me, and the general public as well."), that he will not ever serve the underage, and will quickly cut off anyone who looks the worse for wear. They know he is not shy about relieving the occasional young patron of his car keys, keys and car to be returned the next morning, after McCarty emerges from the early mass. He spends most Sundays visiting with patients at a local substance abuse center.

The restaurant closed in the summer of 2016, but Michael McCarty remained grateful and philosophical. Suntanned, youthful, and still elegantly, if somewhat more casually, dressed, McCarty said "Sometimes I had to pinch myself to make sure it was really true. I couldn't have asked for more."

EDWARD RILEY BRADLEY

A *Real Lace* Irish American who played a prominent role in establishing Palm Beach as the leading winter resort was Col. Edward Bradley. His amazing career was not mentioned by Stephen Birmingham and deserves to be recounted here.

When asked his occupation by a U.S. Senate committee in 1934, Bradley famously testified that he was a "speculator, raiser of race horses and gambler."

He was born in Johnstown, Pennsylvania. At age fourteen, Bradley labored in a steel mill before decamping to Texas in 1874 to work as a cowboy. He later worked as a scout for Gen. Nelson A. Miles during the Indian War campaigns; was a friend of Wyatt Earp; and considered Billy the Kid to be "bad news."

Bradley became a gambler and bookmaker with a network across the Midwest. He married a St. Louisan girl, Agnes Cecilia Curry, and also acquired a hotel and other business interests in Chicago.

Recognizing the potential of Florida real estate, Bradley next went there. The exclusive restaurant and private gambling casino he opened in Palm Beach in 1898, "Bradley's Casino," made him enormously wealthy.

In 1906 he bought Idle Hour Stock Farm, a four-hundred-acre property near Lexington, Kentucky. In time it became the leading Thoroughbred breeding operation in the American South.

Bradley was close friends with grocery chain owner James Butler and often stayed with him at Butler's Eastview Farm in Westchester, where the Butler grandchildren remember him giving them each one hundred dollars on Christmas mornings—a princely sum in the 1920s. Later Bradley gave young Bea MacGuire, called "beauteous Beatrice MacGuire" in the society columns around the time of her debut, a racing interest in a champion filly he had named for her. All of Bradley's horses were given names that began with "the Bradley 'B,'" and this one was called Bee Mac. She went on to become a stakes winning filly and successful broodmare.

One day, James Butler and Bradley were hurrying down the Garden State Parkway when a New Jersey policeman pulled their chauffeur over for speeding. "I'll take care of this, Jim," said Bradley, and got out of the car to discuss the matter with the cop. He came back a while later and said, "No luck." Then Butler got out of the car and tried. When he came back, he was poker-faced and merely said to the driver, "Drive on."

Finally, Bradley couldn't control himself and said, "What the hell did you say to him? I couldn't get anywhere."

"Why, I told him I was riding with the great Edward Riley Bradley, and he let us off the hook straightaway."

Bradley won an unprecedented four Kentucky Derbys with Behave Yourself (1921), Bubbling Over (1926), Burgoo King (1932), and Brokers Tip (1933).

He also owned the Fair Grounds Race Course in New Orleans from 1926 to 1934 and invested in Joseph Widener's Hialeah Race Track in Miami in 1932. Edward Bradley served as president of the Thoroughbred Horse Association and was honored with a "Kentucky colonel" title by the governor of that commonwealth.

Edward Bradley and his wife Agnes had no children but were generous to others' and took a special interest in the welfare of orphans. When Mrs. Bradley died in 1926, Col. Bradley left a part of their Palm Beach property to the city and another lakefront parcel to St. Ann's School for Girls.

Edward R. Bradley died at Idle Hour Farm in 1946 at age eighty-six, having had one of the most successful Thoroughbred racing and breeding careers in the history of the American turf. Parts of Idle Hour remained in the hands of august old-line family racing stables for decades thereafter, the Kleberg's King Ranch acquiring one section and John W. Galbreath's Darby Dan Farm another.

A "21" CHRISTMAS

Another favorite tradition of the Irish in New York, but also of Protestant and Jewish New Yorkers, is Christmas at "21." Of all of New York's landmarks, the "21" club stands out as a symbol of another age, adapting itself to the demands of a new century. Founded as a speakeasy by cousins Jack Kreindler and Charlie Berns, it moved to its present location at 21 West 52nd Street in 1929. Although it was raided frequently during Prohibition, an ingenious system of levers tipped the shelves of the bar, sweeping the liquor bottles through a chute and into the city's sewers, and the joint was never closed.

My mentors Murray McDonnell and Charles Wohlstetter used to take me to memorable lunches at "21," receiving the royal treatment as members of the family. Wohlstetter recounted how he built a network of previously unconsolidated phone companies into Contel and then merged it into GTE (now Verizon) for a pretty penny; but my favorite story of Charlie's was how the color bar was broken at "21": "One night in the '40s when Lena Horne was the toast of Broadway, George Jessel brought her in on his arm and asked to be shown to his regular table. The maître d' gulped and tried to stall for time. 'In what name is your reservation, sir?' 'ABRAHAM LINCOLN!' answered Georgie and walked right on by him with Lena. There was never a problem after that."

I can count four generations of my own family at "21." My mother used to laugh that Kreindler would always produce a waiter who had known her father, Schuyler Casey, when she and Dad would come in from Long Island for a night at the theater and on the town after the war, until finally there was not a one left. The most loyal of my family's "21" supporters was my cousin, Mary Ann Travers, an Auntie Mame if there ever was one. She was long past her drinking days (her husband, a minor Danish aristocrat, had been paid off to go back to Copenhagen, and she had reformed), but whenever she brought us in, the staff pampered her and plied her underage cousins with drink. One day Kreindler introduced her to Nelson Rockefeller, and Mary Ann reminded Rocky that their grandfathers had been friends in adjacent places, Pocantico Hills and Eastview, near Tarrytown. "You were a much better neighbor than Union Carbide," the governor replied, that company having turned Eastview, her family farm, into a corporate headquarters. Mary Ann once threw her mink coat onto a roulette table at the Piping Rock Casino in Saratoga and cried out, "Put that on black." When she died, her priest nephew began his homily, "Mary Ann always said she wanted to die overdrawn at the Chase Bank. Mary, you got your wish." When she gave another nephew his twenty-first birthday dinner dance at "21," she had her doctor sit beside her and had been preadmitted to his hospital, "just in case."

The contents of the wine cellar at "21" is still the stuff of legends, the jockeys outside on West 52nd Street still bear some of the most august racing colors in the history of the American turf, and inside the restaurant there still hang a unique collection of sports and business memorabilia and important American paintings. The days of calling for a phone to be plugged in by your table have now gone by the boards, and the age of publishing lunches gone by when one Time Inc. exec stayed through from lunch to dinner on such a regular basis that his nickname became "42" are but a distant memory.

But of all "21"s traditions, by far the most beloved is that of the Salvation Army Band playing and caroling during the Christmas season. It started more than seventy years ago on a frigid, snowy night when Jack Kreindler took pity on a shivering, small band of missionaries and invited them in out of the cold and wet for tureens of hot soup. They accepted but, once warmed and restored, insisted on offering something of themselves in return, and began to regale the diners with songs of the season. The spontaneous outpouring from the patrons of all religions or none was overwhelming, and Kreindler had the presence of mind, and the generosity of heart, to pass a hat around the room, which was overflowing in no time.

And so it has gone ever since, putting the lie to the myth of New Yorkers being a hard-hearted, Scrooge-like lot. So if you want to experience the true spirit of the season in New York City, there can be no better way than a "21" Christmas.

THE LAST SALOON

Speaking of saloons, for many years I have lived on East 55th Street between First Avenue and Sutton Place. It was a convenient commute by foot to the two publishing companies where I spent most of the 1980s forgetting to get rich, and although I found it rather faceless at first, in time I saw a neighborhood there.

I got to know some of the shopkeepers, janitors, and doormen as I made my morning and evening rounds. Thanks to a rent strike, I even achieved that relative rarity in Manhattan—an acquaintance with other people in my building. And during those years I saw the neighborhood change. Big buildings began to arise all around the neighborhood, and many of the mob-operated porno shops and the rougher gay bars on the 53rd Street strip closed down.

There is one place in the neighborhood, however, which has not changed much. I'm talking about my local bar during my bachelor years in the 1980s—P.J. Clarke's.

There are other watering holes in the community, but I like Clarke's best. It is older, dirtier, cheaper, and serves a more limited menu. But the real reason I like it is that, while over the last fifty years the neighborhood around it has shifted and changed beyond recognition, Clarke's remains what it always was: a New York ethnic bar with a patina of criminals and celebrities, successes and failures, young and old. Most importantly, it is a place where people talk, a rare commodity nowadays.

On a recent visit around three o'clock on New Year's Eve afternoon, I pushed the swinging wooden door open to see two dozen people standing and sitting around the bar, a slab of unfinished oak soaked in the spilled spirits of a century. Behind the bar white-aproned bartenders ignored the customers and discussed point spreads in the upcoming weekend's football games. Irish and American flags waved proudly from a dirty mirror, and there were no fewer than three portraits of Lincoln, while FDR and JFK merited one apiece. There was a Union Pacific calendar, an ancient ad for Glenlivet, bad check lists, a jukebox, two clocks, three antediluvian cash registers, and a Tiffany glass window on top of the door to the men's bog. Near the door a faded blue sign said "UN: We believe." And further down there were photos of the dismantling of the Third Avenue El, and a poignant portrait of Michael Collins, the doomed hero of Irish independence, dressed in a military uniform outside the Dublin Post Office, his face creased in a confident smile.

After fighting for a beer in the bar, I meandered into the middle room, its ten tables covered in red-and-white-checked tablecloths, and on into the back. The back room is darker and larger. There are old gas lamps, now fitted out with electric lights, and the walls are covered with pictures: of Terence MacSwiney, the martyred mayor of Cork; of Daniel O'Connell, the Great Liberator; of Charlie Conerly; of McSorley's; of the pedestrian bridge at Broadway and Fulton Street in 1866; and of Skippy, the late house-dog. These are not the ersatz tchotchkes of a fern bar reaching futilely for some archetype of the authentic, but the archeological detritus of one of the proudest and most turbulent eras of this city's history.

Throughout the first half of the nineteenth century, mid-Manhattan remained undeveloped. Fifth Avenue was called the Middle Road, and there was a sheep meadow at the site of today's Tiffany & Co. Irish and German immigration poured into New York in the 1840s, however, and the city swelled northward.

At that time, as is true again today, many of the immigrant Irish were employed in construction. Others worked in the slaughterhouses situated where the U.N. now sits nervously. Still more were employed at Peter Doelger's brewery on Sutton Place, then called Avenue A. (Breweries were abundant in midtown—Cook's, Rheingold, Schaeffer—thanks to the confluence of four natural streams, which have now been plugged.) Sutton Place soon became a street of typical four- and five-story tenements, and one of the most venerable of P.J. Clarke's waiters, Tommy Joyce, white-haired, handsome, and still working at seventy-six years of age in the 1980s, grew up in one of them on 59th Street.

My uncles both had full-time jobs, but they also worked for the city as lamplighters. They would get up at five in the morning and go outside to light the lamps, and before they went to bed they'd snuff them out.

We were poor, but in those days it was safe to play in the street. And in the summertime the city brought portable bath lockers down to the edge of the East River. Before the FDR Drive was built, there were just rocks on the bank, no big embankment like today. We called 54th and the river Allen's Point, and if the tide was running right, we'd swim. I used to swim all the way to Long Island City. But if the tide was running north and bringing all the crap up from the slaughterhouses, why then, of course, we wouldn't swim.

In the last years of the nineteenth century, the neighborhood was linked to distant sections of the city by the newly constructed Second and Third Avenue Els. The forerunner of P.J. Clarke, a publican named Jennings, located his saloon close by the Third Avenue El to cater to the Irish laborers who rode it to work. Although city records date the building from 1868 (it replaced squatters' shacks), nobody knows for sure how long ago "Jennings" opened. "Forever" is the closest estimate I have heard. But it was there in another incarnation, owned by a Mr. Duneen, when an Irishman named Paddy Clarke came off the boat in 1902. After ten years of hard work behind the bar, the original P.J. bought the place and renamed it.

The Clarke family owned the bar for thirty-six years, from 1912 to 1948. The neighborhood changed steadily through those years. Migration to the suburbs grew. Doelger's brewery and the tenements were sold to developers, who built luxury apartment houses along Sutton Place. The el was torn down and high-rise office buildings were thrown up on Third Avenue. St. John's Church, designed by Renwick and built in 1881, long the center of neighborhood life, was demolished by Cardinal Spellman in 1969 to make way for an undistinguished high-rise office building that houses the archdiocesan offices. Through all these changes Clarke's survived.

The original Mr. Lavezzo, who had immigrated from Italy and built up a successful antique and furniture restoration business, bought the building from Paddy Clarke for nineteen thousand dollars in 1942. Six years later, after P.J.'s death, Mr. Lavezzo's sons bought the bar from twenty-six beneficiaries of the Clarke estate. Longtime employees got along with the new regime, and one member of the Clarke family, Charles Clarke, who was born in a room upstairs, continued working there until he retired in 1989.

By the fifties, more businesses were moving uptown, and Clarke's had become a popular spot for the advertising crowd. Always a favorite with sports personalities, its late hours (P.J.'s closes at four in the morning, though anyone who knocks and is known can get in until dawn; the problem is that people seldom do anymore) made it a favorite with show business folks as well. When the Tishmans assembled the block for the Marine Midland Bank building, they held long negotiations with the Lavezzos and in the end agreed to buy the building and its air rights, contingent upon leasing it back to them for ninety-nine years.

So P.J.'s survived. But what made Clarke's so special?

Was it Frankie Ribando, the dapperly dressed maître d', whom a disgruntled patron once likened to a Lionel conductor? It could be, if you can get him to talk to you about New York architecture. He has been studying it all his life. He also knows furniture, having started with the Lavezzos at age fourteen in their antiques store upstairs. But what he knows best of all is Clarke's.

"This is a place of history, you know," said Frankie to me one night in his prime in the 1980s.

Everybody passed through here. Hedy Lamarr, Eugene O'Neill. Alice Faye still comes to Clarke's. Teddy Kennedy came to P.J.'s for lunch the day after he lost the nomination to Carter in 1980. He stiffed the waiter out of his tip. Frank Sinatra loves to hold forth at Clarke's. He doesn't stiff. The old-time editor, Dennis McEvoy, used to come in at 3:00 a.m., stand on his head in a chair, and sing an aria from Pagliacci in Japanese. They don't make them like that anymore!

I wandered into Clarke's by happenstance one night in the early eighties and ran into a friend of mine from the racetrack. "Come over to the house table," he said, "and meet a couple of friends of mine."

There were two older guys sitting there, both in beat-up-looking clothes, one of whom proved to be the owner, Danny Lavezzo Sr. He had the face of a hound dog and thick black eyebrows. His friend, Bill Healy, a stockbroker born and raised in Providence, wore a once-stylish tweed jacket and spoke in a voice with all the delicacy of a foghorn.

"I don't care what you say," he bellowed, "Mayor Crotch is nothing but an uptown Manny Skolnick." The reference, as I later learned, was to a star of the Yiddish theater.

"That may be," Danny answered, chewing his cigar. "But the fact is that he knows how to run the city without putting it up to its ass in debt. I remember Toots Shor talking about his first job in Jersey waiting tables at the Shore. 'Those were great days,' Toots said. 'I was making twenty dollars a week at the restaurant and betting two hundred a night on the fights.' And it was the God's honest truth. The problem is that's how every cretin since La Guardia has tried to run this town, including Lindsay, the glamour-puss. He was the biggest 'fubar' of them all. His administration was a living illustration of what Franco said in the last speech he gave before he died: 'Four years ago we were on the edge of the precipice. Today we have taken a step forward.'"

Danny Sr. and Frankie were not the only characters at Clarke's. Another was the house manager, Jack Sterling. He sat silently at a table in the middle room nursing a Campari and soda, his face a scowl of Buddha-like impassivity. Jack was not born into the business. He started out as a gentleman horse trainer. "Had a big place on the Eastern Shore. Three hundred acres. Fourteen in help. Didn't have to pay much in those days. Came up north with a string of race horses and ran pretty well until the Crash. I struggled as long as I could, but I finally had to sell the farm in 1938."

A Maryland beau of the twenties, lame, squinty-eyed, but still going forward, fifty years later or more.

"How did you get into the saloon business?" I asked him one night.

When I went under I had a lot of debts around town, and the Copa offered to let me work off my bill there. I'd been married to Liz Altemus (who briefly married John Hay Whitney instead) and spent a lot of money courting her I didn't have. They fired me within two weeks. They said that I'd given away more free booze in two weeks than anyone else had in a year. So I worked the nightclubs and casinos in Saratoga for a few summers, but eventually Senator Kefauver had to screw that up. I was getting tired anyway. Glad-handing mafiosi like Three-Eyes Paserolla and Irish Moshie Blumberg all night long and then going down to the whorehouses on Caroline Street to unwind. But damn if those girls would leave me alone. It was exhausting.

Eventually Danny's father gave me this job. It suits me fine so long as the unions keep their noses in joint. I'm management.

Clarke's is a union shop, although what difference that makes is hard to figure. No one ever tells anyone else what to do, and when they do, they are ignored. Yet the place runs night after night, day after day, 365 days a year, like a finely oiled machine.

There are the good nights, like those in the eighties when Geraldine Page or Liza Minnelli lit up the place. There are funny nights, such as the one when Lord Carrington and Giscard d'Estaing found themselves cramped at adjacent tiny tables, while Frankie saved a big empty one for a really important politician, ex–city commissioner Neil Walsh, whose claim to fame is that since the Equal Opportunity people forbade the city from doing it, he now pays for the green stripe that's painted down Fifth Avenue each St. Patrick's Day. There are interesting nights like the ones when veteran Broadway columnist Jack O'Brien, who hated Neil Walsh, told stories about Walter Winchell and Damon Runyon as he sipped his Jack Daniel's.

Moses Hurwitz, aka Moseley, who owned two dirty bookstores in Times Square, was a frequent visitor to the bar until his death. Another haggard, unshaven character with haunted eyes is known simply as "the General," or more colloquially as "the Lifter." He has an unusually large overcoat, and his vocation in life is to remove from the shelves of department stores, groceries, liquor shops, or wherever articles of interest to his customers, which he sells to them for half their retail price. He is almost like a private shopper, you might say, although he costs less.

Most days Clarke's has its own resident bookmaker, George Miller, a distinguished-looking gentleman in Savile Row threads, who reads *Debrett's Peerage* in bed at night, knows who lives in every Park Avenue apartment from 60th to 94th Street, and keeps the back-room phone booth as his exclusive preserve from four thirty in the afternoon until well past midnight, specializing in college football action. He used to patronize Mortimer's, the society boite on Lexington Avenue, but he was barred for his honesty. He was sitting at the bar with the owner one night when Claus von Bulow walked in, in mid-trial for having murdered his wife and having resigned from his New York clubs. "I see that Claus is with us again tonight," said the proud proprietor. "That makes the third time this week."

"Yes, Glen," responded our hero. "He's going to prison next month, you know, and he wants to get used to the food."

Danny Lavezzo Sr. himself became a casualty of the eighties as the decade wore on. A recognized authority on Thoroughbred breeding lineages, Dan bred a Triple Crown candidate and named it for one of his best friends, the greatest of Giant quarterbacks (with no disrespect meant to Tittle, Simms, or Eli), Charles Conerly. The colt won two Derby Preps, the Bay Shore and the Gotham, but could not at that point in his career stretch out beyond seven furlongs. Chas. Conerly was sold some months later. Nonetheless, his success brought great cheer to 55th Street.

Unbeknownst to anyone then, however, Dan's fascination for another aspect of the racing game—high-stakes betting—was about to change his life radically. Big Dan had a taste for long shots and doubled up heavily when he lost. As his losses mounted, he borrowed money from some, uh, high-interest sources. Eventually his lenders invited him to pay his debt, then around two million dollars. He has reportedly been living in a series of motels ever since. Dan Sr. has been sighted occasionally—in the grandstand at Atlantic City; at Charles Clarke's retirement party in the back room of Kennedy's on Second Avenue; and even, by some accounts, in the wee hours of Friday mornings, when a solitary figure emerges from a car and enters the side door at Clarke's to collect enough cash to live on from the old bar's safe before the weekly deposit gets made.

Later the place was managed by Danny Jr. But I missed Dan Sr., and so did all of Clarke's. He was funny, cranky, and eccentric—all admirable qualities in a saloonkeeper. He set a certain tone of reasoned iconoclasm (reasoned in his conversation, if not always in his conduct), and he could tell a story wonderfully well. Once he was recounting how in the sixties he had first broken the rule against unaccompanied women at the bar (a rule originally imposed to discourage prostitutes and their accompaniment, the bribe-seeking worthies of the N.Y.P.D. vice squad, who, before the Knapp Commission, used to come around threatening to close the place down):

> Tommy woke me up at eleven one morning and said, "You'd better get over here. We got thirty broads with their arms linked surrounding the bar."
>
> When I got over there, I looked at the first broad I saw and said, "Take me to your leader." She did. I introduced myself and asked, "What is it you ladies want?" She said, "We want a drink." I looked at the bartenders. They were standing with their hands clasped behind their backs. So I said, "Give them a damn drink."

Behind a gruff exterior, Danny was a soft touch. He never pressed anyone to pay his bill and even sent occasional presents to his house accounts. At lunchtime to this day, Clarke's patrons write out their orders with a pencil on a yellow pad. The origin of this quaint custom is that Dan wanted to promote a hard-working Chinese busboy to waiter, but the busboy couldn't speak English. So Danny installed writing pads at every table, and the new waiter only had to hand the order slip to the cook.

I walked in for a late supper one night in the mid-eighties. Just as I entered the back room, a shouting match broke out between Frankie, the maître d', and a young man with a date who objected to being seated at the table nearest the kitchen. The kid was screaming.

"Oh no, I ain't waited twenty minutes to sit at no crummy table like that."

"Yeah you have. You'll sit right there."

"Aw, no I won't. I won't sit anywhere like that."

"Yeah you will. You'll sit there or you'll get out of the restaurant."

At this point two things happened. The young guy's girlfriend said, "Larry, let's sit down. I think we ought to sit down."

Then Danny Sr. limped into view, nursing a bad leg, wearing loose sneakers beneath his baggy trousers, a cigar in one hand, and a glass of beer in the other. He raised his voice in rage. "Don't tell him he has to sit at that table. Never tell a customer he has to sit somewhere he doesn't want to. How many times do I have to tell you that? Isn't thirty years long enough?"

Frankie might reasonably have been expected to do his boss's bidding. Instead he looked at the owner contemptuously and spat hard on the floor. Then he turned and said, "You take that first table, kid, or I'm running you right out of here. Jamie, you take the big one on the right."

The big one on the right was Danny's table. He was giving me the owner's table! I didn't move to it right away. Danny swore and walked out in disgust. A minute later Frankie came over and, with an air of saintly resignation, said, "He was lookin' for an excuse to blow up all !@?! night."

Later Danny came back in with some friends and joined me. The group included Billy Mack, a wisp of a man with four generations of family in Greenwich Village who used to manage Jimmy Weston's, a nightclub that closed last year. Billy was fresh out of a rehab home in New Jersey and was making a good start toward unconsciousness in his first three hours back on the town. Then there was John Nostrangelo,

"Johnny Angel"; he had been a partner in one of New York's greatest dives—the Chez Madison, by the Westbury Hotel—years before. Phil Kennedy, the old Cardinal infielder who used to save me a stool at the bar while I was at mass on Sundays so we could watch the Giants game on TV together, was there as well, and Jake LaMotta was sitting by himself at a table along the wall. (LaMotta likes to sit in the back room. When he was still alive, Rocky Graziano preferred to sit beneath his photo in the middle room of P.J.'s, dressed, appropriately enough, in his pj's.)

Danny told stories about the actor Larry Tierney coming in to memorize his scripts in the men's room. "He hid them in the nook right above his stall. I think one's still there."

Then Charles Clarke, who was running the service bar behind our table, began to reminisce. He had been born upstairs, and during Prohibition the liquor had been kept there. "Downstairs the green shades were drawn, the cops were paid off, near beer was served, and stronger stuff was available if you knew how to ask for it. The original P.J. always said that the Volstead Act was 'like a bad cold—someday it will go away.'"

"Yeah," said Phil Kennedy. "I agree with Ring Lardner, though. 'Prohibition was better than no drinking at all.'" Then employed as a "career consultant" to the Penthouse Pet of the Month, Kennedy continued: "Remember the night we were all here, and a guy came in on crutches around midnight, and we helped him to his table and then came back to this table. Six thirty in the morning we're still going good. I'm getting ready to go down to the Waldorf for my seven o'clock shave, Billy Mack here and Jack Price are asleep on the table, so I look up and see that the whole joint is deserted, and on the back wall is hanging a pair of crutches. 'Danny,' I says, 'you got the only miraculous saloon on Third Avenue.'"

We laughed.

"You're young," Johnny Angel said to me then. "Why don't you have a goil?"

"Yeah," said Eddie Tru. "You should get married. You're the right age."

"Yeah," said Billy Mack. "Why should you be happy?"

Everyone else grunted their assent.

Thrice-married Phil Kennedy simply shrugged. "As George Bernard Shaw put it so well, 'Women, if we knew what they wanted, we'd give it to them.'"

When he died the next spring, it was only fitting that his ashes were placed on top of the ladies' restroom.

I married happily in 1990, and however natural it felt to move on to a new phase in my life, I still missed Clarke's. I missed the likes of Don Nexer, who used to operate the burger grill by the front door and as a sideline sold two products—rosaries and porno postcards—from a shelf underneath. I missed Jimmy Ennis, an Andover alumnus who went to work at Clarke's thirty years ago to pay off his bill and is still at it. I missed Pat, my favorite waitress. I missed Louie and Lefty and Joannie, who are all gone now. I missed Alice Gold, a schoolteacher who came in on Saturday nights and had a heart just like her name.

I missed all the patrons and all the staff and all the talk going on night and day, and all the ghosts of all the people who have passed through, and all the echoes of all the talk that has taken place there in the last hundred years.

A priest I know who works at Cardinal Hayes High School in the South Bronx, Father Joseph O'Keefe, grew up in a tenement on 56th Street by the old St. John's, and one day he said to me,

> When I was a kid, my parents knew everybody in our building, and everybody in our neighborhood, and everybody at church, and everybody in the local bars. And they knew all their families and where they all came from, and what they all did, and how they had all gotten into trouble. That's something these kids up here don't have at all, and I feel sorry for them because it's a great thing.

Clarke's is still a great thing. Today it is owned by Phil Scotti and an investor group that includes George Steinbrenner's family and Timothy Hutton. They have realized Big Danny's dream of branching out to the West Side, downtown, even to Washington, D.C. But within its walls much of what has been still survives, not only in the daily routine but, more importantly, in the human memories of those who pass through its doors.

It was my dumb luck to have heard those voices over a decade. After chatting with him on and off for five years, I learned that Jack Sterling, the house manager, knew my grandfather. After seeing him on a weekly basis for over ten years, I learned that, as a boy, Tommy Joyce had once worked for my great-grandfather. Frequently over the years I ran into people whom I had not met before who knew my aunts and uncles, cousins and brothers. And I enjoyed listening to them spin their yarns, adding unfamiliar threads to the tapestry of my relations' lives which, once added, seemed instantly to become a part of the whole.

In good times New Yorkers come to take the cosmopolitan side of the city for granted, to grow nonchalant about luxury and glitz. But there is another New York, too, and a place like Clarke's is the crossroads where the two sometimes meet.

Cosmopolitan New York is fickle. When the bad times come, it can even disappear—hightailing it to Connecticut, or staying at home in Corpus Christi. But the other New York, the real New York, is here all the time, quietly flourishing in the shadows far from the limelight. When cosmopolitan New York—which might almost be defined as that part of New York which writes about itself, reports its assets, celebrates itself—comes to town, it often misses the jobs, the adventures, the lives that go on ticking, recession or no, in the real New York, in the city's heart. Look for that other New York and you will find it, like Clarke's, tucked away in crannies and nooks, surrounded by the monuments of a cosmopolitan city. Just like Clarke's, it will always be there.

ALTERNATIVE EDUCATIONS: SUMMER IN SPAIN

Several seasons ago in Palm Beach, my old friend Barry Donahue turned me onto a wonderful memoir, *The Empress of Ireland: A Chronicle of an Unusual Friendship* by Christopher Robbins. It tells the story of film director (*A Christmas Carol*, among others) Brian Desmond Hurst, the Belgravian Irish bugger and bon vivant and his ultimately quixotic quest late in life to make a film on the events leading up to the birth of Jesus. The book moves from the bawdy ("I'm trisexual—the Army, the Navy and the Horse Guards") to the mystical (the story of how a Turkish soldier with a face Brian could not at first place led him back to his own lines after he got disoriented and wandered into a Turkish camp one dark night at Gallipoli; only later did Brian realize the face was his mother's), and moves from London to Morocco, Ireland, and Hollywood. The dramatis personae include Noel Coward, Siobhan McKenna, John Ford, Michael Redgrave, and Noel Coward, and the sum effect on the author was an alternative education in the many ways of leading a life.

Reading it called to mind the closest such relationship in my own life, the friendship offered me by Dennis McEvoy, father of my boarding school roommate Nion, today the owner of Chronicle Books in San Francisco. Dennis was a Falstaffian figure, a hard drinking ex-Marine whose father, J.P. McEvoy, had been a journalist and playwright, and a member of the Algonquin Round Table. Dennis himself at the time when we met in the summer of 1973 was the senior editor for Europe of the *Reader's Digest*, having successfully launched the Asian edition of the *Digest* in Tokyo after World War II.

I arrived at his beautiful penthouse pad in Madrid after an all-nighter at the Crazy Horse and the Café de Flore in Paris, and Dennis apologized that his vacation had to be delayed for a couple of days due to an impending deadline. He handed me the keys of his baby blue Mercedes 425 SL convertible so I could drive his apparent girlfriend, a beautiful English nurse named Vivica who had cared for him during a recent hospital stay, down to the Costa del Sol. We got as far as Granada the first night, and after dinner I rather boorishly passed out. The next morning Vivica made it absolutely clear that Dennis was not her boyfriend, and things got better and better.

Eventually we made our way to the Alhambra, and later that day drove south. At some point we stopped for a siesta in an olive grove that I thought was shielded from the road, but a passing truck driver stopped and somewhat shattered the mood as far as Vivica was concerned by calling out, "Hey hombre, how about some for me?"

Once we got to Torremelinos, Dennis joined us from Madrid and Nion flew in from the States. Vivica explained the new situation on the ground, and Dennis was philosophical and forgiving. Soon he was calling me, in Charlie Chan fashion, his "Honorable Number Two Son." Dennis had led a picaresque childhood. His father had foreseen that the world would become smaller and was determined that Dennis be prepared. He had lived and studied in Germany, China, and Japan, and in addition to those languages spoke perfect French and Spanish and a good deal of Arabic to boot. He knew every broke aristocrat and wealthy gangster on the Costa del Sol, and our first stop was at the Marbella Club, presided over by Count Alphonsus Hohenlohe, where I was able to lie under the Steinway grand on which Artur Rubinstein was rehearsing.

Next there was golf at Soto Grande, and from there we made our way south toward Algeceris, staying at the finest hotels and resorts, Dennis never forgetting to negotiate the lowest possible rate on the premise he would be writing a story on the venue. Dennis's favorite expression was "It's BUTTB time, boys," which translated into "Belly up to the bar." This happened a little after noon on most days until a long lunch ended in an extended nap. Then we would belly up again around nine at night, sup at midnight, and party on. Drawing on his endless fund of stories and good cheer, Dennis drew people to him, and most nights we closed whatever nightclub we found ourselves in at 4:00 a.m., usually with a performance of Dennis's pièce de résistance, in which he, then a sixty-year-old man, stood on his head in a chair and sang an aria from *Pagliacci* in Japanese to the cheers of the remaining customers gathered 'round.

After too short a sweet sojourn together, Vivica had to get back to work in Madrid, and when Nion and I expressed a desire to go to Tangier by ourselves for a couple of days, Dennis instructed us to look up Mohammed, the porter at the Palace Hotel. When Nion asked why, Dennis answered, "Because I know damn well why you're going, and he's got the best kef in all of Morocco." And so he did.

Dennis was friends with James Michener and drank with Hemingway during the running of the bulls at Pamplona. He also knew Sophia Loren, but perhaps his best American friend in Madrid was Ava Gardner, and therein lies a story. One night Dennis was smoking in bed and fell asleep, and his house caught fire. The next morning Ava called up and said, "Dennis, honey, I heard what happened; you just come on over here and move in with Ava until your place is ready." Like any sensible man, he did as he was told. Then the American ambassador at the time, Angier Biddle Duke, called him at the office and said, "Dennis, we're having a state dinner for Generalissimo and Madame Franco next month. As one of the leading American businessmen in the country, you have to be there, and I hear you're staying at Ava's, so bring her too."

"I don't know, Angie, Ava's been on a bit of a tear lately, you know how wound up she can get. I don't think that's such a good idea . . ."

"Nonsense, the Spaniards love to see Hollywood stars. Bring her with you and see that she behaves."

The appointed evening came, and Ava looked radiant and dressed to the nines. But at dinner things began to go south when an American lady on the other side of the table unwittingly commented that she thought Ava's most recent film, *The Night of the Iguana*, had been "indecent." Ava tensed, poked Dennis in the ribs, and said, "You hear what that fat cow just said about my movie?"

"Now Ava, don't cause a scene."

"Oh, I won't cause a scene . . . *Excuse me!*" The whole room went silent, and Ava leaned over to the lady and sweetly asked, "Do you mind if I ask you a question? Would you tell me your definition of 'indecent'?"

The lady was flustered by now and could only say, "Well, I don't know, just indecent."

"Well, would you like to hear what my definition of indecent is?"

"Oh yes," quoth the lady, feeling let off the hook.

"Well, my definition of indecent is if it's in long enough, wide enough, and hard enough, then it's *in decent*."

At that point the room collapsed into chaos and up on the dais a puzzled Madame Franco asked Ambassador Duke for a translation that was not forthcoming.

That summer was *my* alternative education, and Vivica and Dennis were generous teachers. Vivica got married to an English guy the following year. Dennis retired a couple of years after that, briefly moved to San Francisco to be closer to Nion, and then, expat at heart that he was, returned to Spain, where he died too young on Mallorca in 1982. Nion and I remain the best of friends, and just the other day over lunch promised each other we would mark our upcoming birthdays next year with a special trip, and what better destination than those haunts his father introduced us to nearly fifty years ago? I hope Mohammed will be waiting!

ST. PADDY'S DAY AND THE FIGHTING SIXTY-NINTH

As for Ray Flynn and other Bostonians, St. Patrick's Day remained a big event in New York for *Real Lace* families.

In the 1950s Mother bundled us into the station wagon and drove us into town, dressed in gray flannel shorts that left one's legs stinging with the cold and rain as one tried to peer through much larger people lining Fifth Avenue as the parade went by. Mother always had a plan B, of course, which was to importune her favorite salesman at Saks Fifth Avenue to let us gaze down on the parade from an upstairs window, a far warmer and drier vantage point. Our beloved nanny, Theresa Gateley, was a diminutive but domineering presence inside our house and out. She headed every Hibernian organization on Long Island and each year proudly carried the flag for County Roscommon's marching contingent. We would look for Nanny and cheer. Whereas Theresa would be out all night at the ceilidh at the Jaeger House in Yorktown before catching the early-morning train to be home to get us dressed for school, we would decamp to Schrafft's for lunch, the Irish waitresses in their black uniforms serving Mother a well-earned Scotch and the rest of us ice cream sodas. If we were good, Mom would treat us to a box of fudge to nibble on en route back to Long Island.

I went to the parade several years ago and saw Al Smith V, great-grandson of the New York governor who was the first Catholic to run for president (he lost to Herbert Hoover in 1928), leading the march as grand marshal. The line of march is actually led by the honor guard of the Sixty-ninth Regiment of the New York State National Guard, the storied "Fighting Sixty-ninth." And therein lies a tale.

The 1850s was a turbulent time in New York as the city grew and immigrant groups like the Irish faced opposition and bigotry ("No Irish Need Apply") from Nativists and Know Nothings, as viewers of Martin Scorcese's *Gangs of New York* will remember.

Irish Americans decided it was time to form an Irish brigade to defend their interests and, possibly, to fight the English for Ireland's independence back on the Auld Sod. That never happened, but when the Civil War arrived, the Irish Brigade, now reorganized as the Sixty-ninth Regiment, volunteered to fight for the Union cause and were soon noted for their willingness to tackle tough missions. "When anything absurd, forlorn or desperate was to be attempted," one war correspondent wrote, "the Irish Brigade was called upon." They fought bravely at Antietam and Gettysburg, but entered immortality with their stunningly audacious charge up Marye's Heights at Fredericksburg. The Confederate officers and troops actually cheered them for their courage in the attack. The phrase "Fighting Sixty-ninth" was coined by none other than Confederate general Robert E. Lee, who paid tribute to their bravery in his communiqué on the engagement.

The Sixty-ninth made further history in World War I, when it was sent over to France in October 1917 as part of the Forty-second "Rainbow" Division of the American Expeditionary Force. It was recognized for its heroics at Rouge Bouquet, Champagne, Chateau Thierry, and Meuse-Argonne. The brigade commander, Gen. Douglas MacArthur, seriously considered naming its chaplain, Father Francis Duffy, the regimental commander, an unheard-of honor for a priest. Today a statue of Father Duffy stands just south of the TKTS booth in the theater district in what is known as Father Duffy Square, although it is really more of a triangle, but Mayor Mike was always better at algorithms than geometry.

There is a great movie called *The Fighting 69th* as well, starring Pat O'Brien and Jimmy Cagney. A New York poet named Joyce Kilmer (his most famous poem is "Trees") was a sergeant in the regiment and wrote a poem called "When the 69th Comes Back" shortly before he was killed by a sniper while out on patrol:

> . . . *The men who fought at Marye's Heights will aid us from the sky,*
> *They showed the world at Fredericksburg how Irish soldiers die.*
> *At Blackburn Ford they think of us, Atlanta and Bull Run;*
> *There are many silver rings on the old flagstaff*
> *but there's room for another one.*
>
> *The Harp that once through Tara's Halls shall fill the air with song,*
> *And the Shamrock be cheered as the port is neared by our triumphant throng.*
> *With the Potsdam Palace on a truck and the Kaiser in a sack,*
> *New York will be seen one Irish green when the Sixty-ninth comes back.*

And indeed, upon their return the Sixty-ninth were given a hero's welcome.

Speaking from the Philippines, Gen. Douglas MacArthur gave the following address to members and veterans of the Sixty-ninth in New York City via short-wave radio in 1940:

No greater fighting regiment has ever existed than the One Hundred and Sixty-fifth Infantry of the Rainbow Division, formed from the old Sixty-ninth Regiment of New York. I cannot tell you how real and how sincere a pleasure I feel tonight in once more addressing the members of that famous unit. You need no eulogy from me or from any other man. You have written your own history and written it in red on your enemies' breast, but when I think of your patience under adversity, your courage under fire, and your modesty in victory, I am filled with an emotion of admiration I cannot express. You have carved your own statue upon the hearts of your people, you have built your own monument in the memory of your compatriots. One of the most outstanding characteristics of the regiment was its deep sense of religious responsibility, inculcated by one of my most beloved friends—Father Duffy. He gave you a code that embraces the highest moral laws, that will stand the test of any ethics or philosophies ever promulgated for the uplift of man. Its requirements are for the things that are right and its restraints are from the things that are wrong. The soldier, above all men, is required to perform the highest act of religious teaching—sacrifice. However horrible the results of war may be, the soldier who is called upon to offer and perchance to give his life for his country is the noblest development of mankind. No physical courage and no brute instincts can take the place of the divine annunciation and spiritual uplift which will alone sustain him. Father Duffy, on those bloody fields of France we all remember so well, taught the men of your regiment how to die that a nation might live—how to die unquestioning and uncomplaining, with faith in their hearts and the hope on their lips that we might go on to victory. Somewhere in your banquet hall tonight his noble spirit looks down to bless and guide you young soldiers on the narrow path marked with

West Point's famous motto—duty, honor, country. We'll hope that war will come to us no more. But if its red stream should engulf us, I want you to know that if my flag flies again, I shall hope to have you once more with me, once more to form the brilliant hues of what is lovingly, reverently called by men at arms, the Rainbow. May God be with you until we meet again.

Today the Sixty-ninth is no longer Irish but a rainbow of Americans, many relatively new to America, continuing in the great American tradition of assimilation and service.

The parade has become embroiled in many spats over the years. At one point the City decided it was wrong for it to pay for the traditional green stripe down Fifth Avenue on that day and not undertake similar painting for Columbus Day, etc. My cousin Bea MacGuire recruited a group of pals to go out the night before and paint the avenue. The City was not amused.

Cardinal Cooke refused to observe the parade from the doors of St. Patrick's in 1983 when former IRA soldier Michael Flannery was named the honorary grand marshal. He paused and bowed to the cathedral's empty doorway nonetheless. In recent years the dispute has turned to gay and lesbian inclusion in the parade. The parade, managed rather mysteriously by two otherwise unemployed gentlemen in a Queens office, maintained that all were welcome to march regardless of sexual orientation but not to do so as a group since by the church's teaching active homosexuality was "disordered." That policy broke down in 2014 when NBC Universal, which telecasts the parade, threatened to boycott doing so unless a group of its own gay and lesbian employees were allowed to march. The prohibition fell without undue incident, and in early 2016 an agreement was reached that will allow many other LGBT groups to march as well. And Mayor de Blasio (né Wilhelm) graciously condescended to march for the first time since he was elected as well.

The Sixty-ninth Regiment has continued to distinguish itself in our country's service, in World War II, Korea, Vietnam, Iraq, and Afghanistan, and by its devotion to duty and patriotism has continued to earn its pride of place at the head of the line of march each St. Patrick's Day. But there has been one slight change. In the Civil War the Sixty-ninth was 90 percent Irish. In World War I it was 50 percent Irish, and today, as you can see for yourself if you get out onto Fifth Avenue in time to see the regiment and its mascot wolfhounds lead the parade, the Sixty-ninth is indeed a "Rainbow" division of diversity, no more than 20 percent Irish. But every member of the unit is designated an honorary Irishman, of whom Father Duffy said, in describing the non-Irish in the regiment, "They are Irish by adoption, Irish by association, or Irish by conviction."

Whatever their ethnic origin, on the day that all New Yorkers are honorary Irishmen, the sight of those brave men and women marching by is enough to put a lump in the throat and silently say: "God bless America, and God bless the Irish!"

PROFILE:
WATERING HOLES: SARATOGA, SOUTHAMPTON, NEWPORT

Saratoga! The six weeks when all the racing world descends on a sleepy upstate town in the Adirondack foothills and—for a month anyway—forgets to sleep. There are morning workouts to attend, delicious Hand melons to eat at trackside breakfasts, medicinal baths, tennis and golf games in midmorning, elegant lunches on North Broadway's row of Jockey Club members' racing cottages, afternoons of triumph and despair at the elegant old track on Union Avenue, followed by restorative liquids under the Reading Room's towering elms. Then cocktail and dinner parties, yearling sales, and concerts and gala dances before a nightcap at Siro's or the Parting Glass, before starting all over again at five the following morning.

The Documentary History of the State of New York lists the following variations for the place name: Cheratoge, Sarachitoge, Sarachtoga, Saractoga, Saraktoga, Serach-Tague, and many more. Warriors from the Five Nations had been visiting its magically healing springs for centuries before Jacques Cartier first heard of them in 1535. Gentleman Johnny Burgoyne, prince of good fellows, lover of fine jewels and fleet horses, philanderer, indulgent father, frequenter of fashion, statesman, and soldier, was to become Saratoga's biggest loser of all time when in the early autumn of 1777 he led the British Army to the defeat that has been called the "turning point of the Revolution."

Organized horse racing did not begin until August 3, 1863, when pugilist, gambler, and budding politician John Morrissey thought to add it to the cavalcade of resort activities that attracted vacationers from far afield. North-South rivalries and enthusiastic wagering played a large part in these diversions. And so it grew, in the Gilded Age and beyond, into the racing capital of the world, filled with Vanderbilts, Whitneys, Keenes, Sanfords, and Jeromes, and immortal horses with names like Sysonby, Lexington, Pebbles, Regret, Upset (who dealt Man O' War his only defeat in the Sanford Stakes), and Jim Dandy (the victor, at odds of one hundred to one, over Gallant Fox and Whichone in the Travers).

And so it still is today, for a tad more than six weeks of midsummer gaiety. Along the way there are more stakes and steeplechase races than at any track in America, including the Travers, the Whitney for older horses, the Alabama for fillies and mares, the Hopeful and Spinaway for younger colts and fillies, and the A.P. Smithwick and Turf Writers over jumps.

It's impossible to regard this spectacle without being overcome in a sea of memory. On my first visit to Saratoga at fourteen, I was seated on a Trailways bus next to an elderly Jewish gentleman in a seersucker suit and straw boater. I confided that it was my first visit to Saratoga. "How I wish I was making my first visit to Saratoga," he answered. "I've been going for over fifty years."

I asked him if he had known my great-grandfather, an Irishman who, just before the turn of the last century, had plowed some of the profits from his food business into a racing stable. "I liked his groceries better than his horses," the old man groaned before returning to his *Morning Telegraph*.

I should have taken such weltschmerz to heart, but unfortunately the next day I hit the daily double for $106, and have been coming back ever since, until my own fiftieth anniversary at the Spa is now drawing nigh. I can't compete with the stories of another era, such as the uncle who at Siro's removed the film forcibly from the camera of a *Daily News* photographer who had just caught Eddie Arcaro dancing with another of my aunts on the morning he was to ride the favorite in the Travers Stakes.

But there have been moments even in our generation, such as the night Joey Walker and Cabot Lodge sipped champagne at the Spuyten Duyvil out of Jennifer Davis's evening slippers as Bob Field played "Your Feet's Too Big" on the white baby grand. Or the night Molly Wilmot and Jessye Norman almost got into a brawl over whether or not Molly should be smoking in Jessye's presence at a post-concert supper at Siro's (Jessye won). Or the time in the wee hours when my then boss at Macmillan, Ned Evans, tried to take a girl who worked for his racing stable into the all-male sanctorum of the Reading Room second floor. A security guard stopped and evicted them, but an hour later on his perimeter patrol tripped over the duo in the club garden. "Mr. Evans, what on earth are you doing?" "Well, you told me I couldn't take her upstairs."

Finally, there was a night not so very long ago that a group of us finished one of Kay Jeffords's legendary, champagne-filled dinner parties with several additional potions on her porch and ended up mounting a raid next door to skinny-dip under the moonlight in the Phippses' pools. The next day at the track, Cynthia told us with a good-natured giggle that the butler had reported the invasion to Ogden Sr. and asked if he should call the police. "Not yet," Mr. Phipps replied, moving to a forward observation post. "Give me my binoculars first."

In life, inevitably, people like the unsinkable Molly Wilmot, the always kind Kay Jeffords, and Ogden Phipps, whose stable dominated New York racing for many years, go before us. Other great figures of Saratoga who will not be back include the irrepressible bon vivant Teddy Donahue and the much beloved Giants patriarch Wellington Mara, whose father amassed the five-hundred-dollar stake he used to buy the football franchise in 1925 by his toil as an on-track bookie in those pre-pari-mutuel days.

"Well, gentlemen," the ever gracious Mr. Mara would always say after a bit of small talk with old acquaintances before a race, "I'll see you in the winner's circle." Unlike the rest of us, he and the others noted above are already there.

There are new initiates coming into the clubhouse, the grandstand, and even the picnic grounds every year—more than ever before, as Saratoga's attendance surges spectacularly. There is no equal to the excitement you feel in your bones at being one with a huge crowd as a thrilling race begins, and thousands of people simultaneously try to keep track of the infinite changes in position and tactics that the various animals—equine and human—resort to in their efforts to prevail. It has always been that way, and at Saratoga, with its rich collection of grade I stakes, it is only more so.

Some years ago the Saratoga meeting began in classic racing fashion. The first person I ran into at the track turned out to be the brother of a friend recently lost at sea. Knowing that the two of them had not been close in recent years, I simply said, "I'm so sorry." He responded glumly, "Yeah, and he went off the favorite, and not only did he never run, he hurt himself in the stretch, so we may have to send him back down to the farm . . . oh, you mean my brother?"

So it goes at Saratoga, racing's capital and the closest thing upstate New York has to Mardi Gras. With the Saratoga season expanded from four to five weeks in 2016, the old track far outdrew the more modern but oh-so-soulless downstate racing plants, and there was enough drama to go around for an entire year. I can remember an aging Angel Cordero electrifying the crowd when his saddle slipped as his horse bolted from the gate and he lost his leg irons but continued to bounce down the backstretch on the lead. At the top of the lane, he even managed to whip his charge once in a valiant but ultimately futile effort to win the race. On the basis of that performance, when his race-riding days are over, he might well turn to rodeo.

The racing business is in a bad way, and Saratoga racing is as much a tonic for horse folk as its famous waters are for those seeking cures at the spa. The overall quality of racing stock on New York tracks has declined, and half the Thoroughbred farms in the Blue Grass are said to be for sale.

Racing horses has never made economic sense, but the sport is supported by a loyal cadre of horse owners, whose aggregate annual loss before the 1987 change in federal income tax rules was twenty-four million dollars. The new tax laws have made things even harder. Costs have risen sharply, while disposable income is down. In the last twenty years, attendance at tracks has fallen and total betting handles are also declining.

But the Saratoga social scene swims along despite the hard times. Albany author William Kennedy, Broadway producer Rocco Landesman, and eighty-eight-year-old Hall of Fame trainer Horatio Luro were among thousands on the scene each day. Mrs. Walter Jeffords served speckled trout to John McEnroe's mother at her North Broadway house, and Treasury Secretary Nicholas Brady found time to fly up from Washington to watch a couple of days' races.

There were parties everywhere. At Molly Wilmot's benefit for the New York City Ballet, Heather Watts smoked and Peter Martins sipped, and the unsinkable Molly looked on admiringly. "They smoke and drink more than I do, but they're so young and they have such good bodies. So much more fun than that racing crowd—'the Cemetery Club,' I call them." And while Molly was feeling jealous of the younger generation of dancers, Saratoga's undisputed queen was admiring Molly's ever youthful figure. "I hate her for being so thin," Mary Lou Whitney moaned. "I mean, how do you hide the boobs?"

At Saratoga the big questions have always counted. A week later in the meeting, Mary Lou would hold her annual soiree at the Canfield Casino. Three hundred of the Cemetery Club swarmed in at her bidding, dressed in costumes suggested by *Guys and Dolls*, to gamble for charity at tables manned by members of the Saratoga Elks. "I'm not giving my party this year," another Palm Beach heiress was heard lamenting that night. "I'm not up to it." To which came the sympathetic retort, "It doesn't matter. Nobody came anymore, anyway."

During the excitement of Travers Day, I suddenly realized that it was thirty years ago that I had wandered into the press box and seen a diminutive, florid-faced man sipping a vodka and tonic, surrounded by his admirers, the hard-bitten denizens of the fourth estate. It was Red Smith's last visit to Saratoga. He saw Willow Hour win that day. For the fifty years previous he had seen most of the other good ones and the men and women who worked with them. "I love it," he said in a *60 Minutes* interview not long before he died. "It's one of the greatest athletic contests in the world, and I don't think there's a greater collection of characters anywhere than on the back side of a racetrack." He made them come alive: "At lunch Max Hirsch said, 'No thank you' to the waiter with a tray full of martinis. 'I'm running a horse this afternoon. If I drank one of them, I'd probably bet on him.'"

One of Smith's favorite stories was Alfred Vanderbilt's on names: "It isn't easy getting names approved by the Jockey Club. Take my mare Pansy. I just name her foals for the sire and ignore the dam. She produced a foal by Shut Out, so we called him Social Outcast, and another by Questionnaire that we called Query."

Alfred Vanderbilt (1912–1999) was born in London, lost his father in 1915 when the *Lusitania* sank, and was raised in Lenox, Massachusetts. After attending Yale, at twenty-one he took over Sagamore, his mother's six-hundred-acre farm in Glyndon, Maryland, and set about becoming one of racing's leaders for the next seven decades. One of his first horses, Discovery, became the country's top handicap runner, winning both the Brooklyn and Whitney Handicaps three consecutive years, a feat that would be unheard of today. Vanderbilt brokered the famous match race between Seabiscuit and War Admiral in 1938. He won a Silver Star while serving in the navy in the Pacific in World War II and later campaigned such fine horses as Bed O' Roses, Next Move, and his greatest runner, Native Dancer, who went on to become one of the most influential sires of all time.

Vanderbilt was a daily presence at the track and was president of the New York Racing Association (NYRA) during one broiling summer at Saratoga in the late 1960s when he earned the gratitude of his fellow racegoers by ostentatiously removing his sports jacket one sweltering afternoon and encouraging others to do the same.

Young Alfred Vanderbilt spoke about his father, remembering the last time two of his oldest hands had brought up a homebred from Sagamore to race at Belmont Park. "I'd love to have the money Dad spent on funerals." Former *Bloodhorse* editor Ed Bowen remembered the time Jock Whitney paid tribute to Vanderbilt by coming to a costume party at his house dressed as a native dancer. Undoubtedly that would be a microaggression or worse today.

Why do as many as fifty thousand people flock to the venerable wooden Saratoga Racetrack, standing among great elms in the Adirondack foothills? They come because it is beautiful and has a perfect atmosphere for an upstate summer outing. They come because of its history as a place where Indians and settlers gathered to taste the springs and bathe in the healing waters, and where the guerrilla warfare tactics of General Horatio Gates repulsed the British Army and turned the tide of the Revolution. They come to see a city of gingerbread Victorian homes built around the century's turn. But they come most of all for racing.

A day in Saratoga begins at dawn, watching the horses work out on the main track or on Oklahoma, the training track. At 8:00 a.m., when the main track is harrowed and training stops for forty-five minutes, horsemen congregate at the Reading Room, the track, or a local restaurant for a breakfast that cannot be called complete unless it includes one of the succulent, locally grown Hand melons, a delicious hybrid that, happily, ripens in mid-August.

Later in the morning there is ample opportunity for tennis, golf, shopping, or the baths. The races begin at 1:00 p.m. and last until 5:30 or 6:00. Afterwards there is a swirl of cocktail parties and good restaurants to choose from. And although the elegant casinos are long gone, without undue effort one can still last out on the town until just before dawn, when Hatty's Chicken Shack on Phila Street will supply you with a cup of strong coffee before you head out to the track to start all over again.

"People love Saratoga," second-generation trainer Leroy Jolley likes to say, "because it has a beginning, a middle, and an end." Now that the meeting has been extended ten days, not everyone is sure it really does have an end. But that's OK too.

Racing's Rise and Fall

In 2015 the National Museum of Racing and Hall of Fame in Saratoga inducted John Hay Whitney as a Pillar of the Turf. The recognition was long overdue.

Jock Whitney was born in 1904 and over the next seventy-seven years looked after his family's varied business interests; helped produce *Gone with the Wind*; published the late, lamented *Herald Tribune* (where Jimmy Breslin once insisted on buying him a drink so he could tell his buddies at Pep-McGuire's gin joint on Queens Boulevard that he had treated a millionaire); was President Eisenhower's ambassador to the Court of Saint James; and with his sister assembled a magnificent collection of Impressionist and post-Impressionist art.

But racing was always a particular passion for Whitney. After graduating from Yale and Oxford, he received two yearlings as a gift from his father and was elected to the Jockey Club at the age of twenty-four in 1928. In 1934 he formed the American Thoroughbred Breeders' Association. After accepting a captain's commission in the Army Air Corps in 1942, Whitney was captured by German troops while on an intelligence mission in France during World War II. He made a daring escape by jumping from a moving train and, eighteen days later, successfully navigated his way back to American lines.

In 1944 Whitney and his sister, Joan Whitney Payson, inherited their mother's Greentree Stable. Mrs. Payson later became the heroine who brought the National League back to New York City with the Mets in 1961, but she and Whitney raced many Greentree champions as well, including Stage Door Johnny, Late Bloomer, and Bowl Game. Perhaps their best horse was Tom Fool, who won all ten of his races as a four-year-old in 1953, including the Metropolitan, the Suburban, the Brooklyn, and the Whitney and Carter Handicaps, and was named Horse of the Year.

Jock Whitney was the successor to a great racing tradition and, perhaps, with Paul Mellon and Ogden Phipps, the last generation of sporting grandees.

With the founding of the American Jockey Club in 1866, New York became the center of American racing, consistently offering the highest purses and attracting the best runners. Saratoga emerged as the racing capital each August in the early 1860s and has never been challenged. In 1866 Leonard Jerome, the American grandfather of Winston Churchill, purchased the old Bathgate estate in Westchester County and built a European-style course, which he called Jerome Park. In the following years racing in the metropolitan region proliferated, and racetracks were built at Monmouth (1870), Brighton Beach (1879), Sheepshead Bay (1880), and Gravesend (1886), along with the elegant Morris Park in the east Bronx (1889) and the original Aqueduct (1894), with its popular "grandstand as might be seen at a country fair." Would that the architect of the present Aqueduct had embraced the same aesthetic!

With the dawn of the twentieth century, Jamaica Racetrack opened in 1903, Belmont Park in 1905, and Empire City (today's Yonkers Raceway) in 1907. All of these tracks were privately owned, and some of them were highly profitable enterprises. Pari-mutuel betting was introduced in 1940 and soon replaced the often colorful institution of legal, on-track bookies. Handles soared, and with them revenues to the state.

The war effort curtailed racing drastically between 1941 and 1945, but afterwards racing boomed anew. The state's racing facilities were aging, however (as is again the case today), and it became clear that the only way to replace them was through the creation of a new state racing structure. Convinced that private capital could not accomplish the necessary ends under the prevailing tax structure, the Jockey Club proposed the formation of a nonprofit, quasi-public racing association to take over Belmont, Jamaica, Aqueduct, and Saratoga. Whereas from today's perspective a strong argument could be made for reprivatization, at the time the Jockey Club solution was regarded as innovative, and most people involved in the sport believed it was the only way forward.

Following upon the proposal of the Jockey Club study commission, the NYRA, a parastatal agency, was formed in 1954 and bought out the stock of the surviving privately held tracks. It then consolidated racing at Aqueduct, Belmont, and Saratoga and began a program to build new facilities at the first two while upgrading the ancient premises of the third. Enormous plants capable of holding up to sixty thousand fans were constructed at Aqueduct (1959) and Belmont (1965). On good days, that many came out and cheered the exploits of the legendary Kelso, Ridan, Damascus, and other great horses of the era. The sport was established and secure, second only to baseball in the public's heart. New York had the finest racing in the land. The future looked bright.

But during the sixties, while other professional sports—notably pro football—developed sophisticated marketing and promotion programs and greatly multiplied their audiences through the shrewd use of TV, racing seemed almost to disdain its fans. The plutocracy that controlled the sport in New York was unresponsive to changing times, and racing's market share began to wane.

Then in 1971 disaster struck. Off-track betting (OTB), which had been resisted for years, was legalized. The old guard believed that racing was a sport first and a gambling opportunity second: If the public wanted to participate in the sport, the proper place to do that was at the races. So New York state's curious OTB structure was formed, with six separate, autonomous corporations in different regions of the state, each with its own duplicative management structure, overseeing off-track wagering. By common consent it has been an administrative and fiscal disaster.

The arrival of OTB meant the cannibalization of what had been NYRA's exclusive franchise. Despite such superstars as Secretariat, Seattle Slew, Alydar, and Affirmed, on-track attendance plummeted during the seventies and has never been restored. OTB's own operation has been deplorable. Enter a New York City OTB parlor, and one was assaulted by dirt, stench, and rudeness. OTB's operation became one of the most flagrant patronage plums in the state (not an inconsiderable distinction). Furthermore, faced with a declining share of the gambling dollar as lotteries and casino gambling grew, OTB was anything but competitive. It maintained prohibitive "takeouts" reaching 24 percent of each dollar bet, and a punitive "surcharge" on winning bets, both of which drove gamblers away.

Through its resolute mismanagement, NYC OTB failed and had to close. The New York City government may be the only institution in the free world that could run a book, without even having to pay off the cops, and still lose money. Was Johnny Gotti laughing at us?

So horse racing's best days may be behind it, and other sports—football, basketball, NASCAR—have become more popular and profitable, but its history is still there.

When I think of racing, I think of Sunny Jim Fitzsimmons—who rode at the old Aqueduct the day it opened in 1894 and went on to train two Triple Crown winners, Gallant Fox and Omaha, late in life—sitting in the saddling ring, listening to and talking with all who came to pay homage to his stooped body and sagacious mind. I think of Man O' War's groom, Will Harbut, introducing visitors to Big Red on Samuel D. Riddle's farm. "He broke all the records and he broke down all the horses, so there wasn't nothin' for him to do but retire. He's got everything a horse ought to have. He's got it where a horse ought to have it. He's just de mostest horse."

I think of the great steward Francis Dunne joking that if the Japanese really wanted to make a successful sneak attack on the United States they should have come down Belmont Park's old Widener Chute.

I think of little Fred Caposella crying out, "It is now post time," in his big voice from the announcer's booth. I think of the long-ago jump jockey shouting at his colleagues, which included the great amateur steeplechase rider of the thirties, Pete Bostwick: "Get out of my way, you sons of bitches . . . and you too, Mr. Bostwick."

Most of all, when I think of racing, I think of the excitement you feel in your bones and smell in the air at a good racetrack on the day of a great race. Tolstoy caught the flavor of a contest of champions in the magnificent race scene in *Anna Karenina*, of being at one with the huge crowd as a thrilling race begins, and thousands of people simultaneously try to keep track of all the changes in position and racing tactics that the various animals—equine and human—resort to in their efforts to prevail.

I think of stirring performances like Secretariat's record-smashing thirty-one-length win in the Belmont Stakes of 1973, or more poignantly, the courage shown by many a champion trying to stave off what he knows in his heart is certain defeat. Perhaps some people are capable of objectivity at such moments, but as the pounding of hooves overwhelms the roar of the crowd and the field comes swooping down the stretch, I am not one of them. I thought of the horses of my lifetime—Jaipur, Buckpasser, Damascus, Key to the Mint, Affirmed (later disqualified), Java Gold, and Easy Goer—who had impressed me most in winning this race. And I thought of the great ones who came before—Scythian, Kentucky, Barbee, Bersan, Spur, Twenty Grand. It's just de mostest sport, and it doesn't deserve to die a slow death by political mismanagement—not when, with a bit of effort and fight, we could make it moster and moster.

SOUTHAMPTON
Reconsiderations: *The Devil Walks on Water*
This iconic Southampton novel was written by John F. (Jake) Murray (an uncle of Palm Beach and Southampton society figure Hilary Ross) in 1968 but set thirty years earlier in the days leading up to and including the great hurricane of '38.

Briny (Brian) Mitchel, a somewhat arriviste Irish American, is the devil, the protagonist or, more properly, the antihero of the story. Briny is a graduate of "the Priory," as Portsmouth Abbey School was then known, who is now on an insolent, indolent, but not entirely ignorant summer vacation from Princeton, which he loves, though his uncle Aidan Carew, citing canon law, would prefer he go to Georgetown.

Briny is the Peck's Bad Boy of the East End, removing his polo shirt as he watches Midge, the object of his lust, play tennis at the Meadow Club. Other Hamptons locales used as settings in the novel include the Devon Yacht Club, countless shops, and a colorful prewar house of assignation referred to here as Aunt Margaret's, where Briny frequently shacks up with the frustrated wife of a local town cop. Briny is a handsome and hairy-chested bad actor who delights in tweaking convention, insulting his elders, and trying to nail every girl in sight. He discusses sexual mechanics at great length (e.g., the difference between vaginal versus clitoral orgasm) in a way that may have seemed racy when written before how-to books on the subject began outselling the Bible. He is an angry black sheep in search of himself who delights in his alter ego as "the Phantom," speeding by police cars in his sports car and then hiding from them on unpaved tracks deep in the sand dunes.

On the final night of the novel as the hurricane descends, Briny helps start a brawl during a dance at Devon between the "Andovers" and the more recently couthed-up Irish-American contingent. Later he gets set on by the "natives" (aka year-round working-class residents) at Aunt Margaret's when he brings Midge there, but his compliant cop's wife/girlfriend is waiting for him in an upstairs bedroom. Though badly beaten, he somehow escapes back to the house where the night began and seduces a newly arrived Irish maid, a generous soul and well-practiced from her interactions with the County Kerry farm boys back home.

Then, in the climactic scene, as the hurricane crashes inland, Briny tries to leave the maid's room by her window and to walk down the roofline but is unintentionally knocked off it when his little sister opens her shutters. Rather than die in a thirty-foot fall, however, because the storm has burst the dunes and flooded the back of the town, Briny is swept away. He finally gets to his car and drives to Midge's house, "the Wreck," which has been destroyed, and Midge's room above the porte cochere swept out onto Acapogue Pond. Briny swims there and climbs onto the remains of the roof. He knocks and hears Midge knock back faintly, trapped but still alive in an air bubble below. Briny saws and hacks through the roof with his bare hands, extricates Midge, and swims her to safety, all the while imagining them coupling lustfully. Once out of danger, he is utterly exhausted and also realizes the last vestiges of his tuxedo have been shredded. Our quasi-Celtic mythological hero stands before all the wreckage of the world, starkers. But unlike Adam and Eve expelled from the garden, Briny Mitchel is utterly unashamed.

Quite a tale of days long gone by, and much of it based on fact. The *Real Lace* Irish Americans were considered upstarts by the older, established WASP families in Southampton. The Murrays and McDonnells both lost houses in their oceanfront compound during the hurricane of 1938. There was an "Aunt Margaret's" fondly remembered by my father's generation. The clubs are much the same as they were then, and friction still breaks to the surface like a painful hernia between the summer folk and the year-rounders. If you haven't gotten a beach read picked yet for this summer, give Jake Murray's *The Devil Walks on Water* a try!

Southampton remains a vibrant social hub, with the highest concentration of wealth in the country in August. But many of the *Real Lace* families have moved on. Charlotte McDonnell Harris, an outspoken longtime opponent of the "new people," died of COPD. Jack Cuddihy's carriage house, one of the last vestiges of the Murray-McDonnell compound, has been sold since his death. Catherine Murray di Montezemolo, a longtime editor at *Vogue*, died in 2009. Jeanne Murray Vanderbilt died in 2012. Longtime resident Michael Meehan now goes to Europe. Charlotte and Anne Ford remain.

The clubs have slowly changed. When young Howard Dean announced his intention to marry a Jewish doctor, his mother exclaimed, "There goes Maidstone." In January of 2016 Nina Wainwright was married to her husband by a rabbi at the same Maidstone Club.

Property valuations have continued to skyrocket. One *Real Lace* descendant, Hilary Ross, a Murray whose mother, Patricia Murray Wood, for many years wrote "The Beachcomber" column for the Southampton newspaper, is now at the top of the summer social ladder, with her billionaire husband, Wilbur.

NEWPORT
Noreen Stonor Drexel: Portrait of a Lady

An era ended when Noreen Drexel died peacefully on November 6, 2012, after suffering a stroke, just ten days after celebrating her ninetieth birthday in good health, surrounded by family and friends. Mrs. Drexel was the undisputed doyenne of Newport, just as she had been a leading lady until recent years in New York and Palm Beach.

Born the Honorable Noreen Stonor in Henley-on-Thames in England, Mrs. Drexel was the youngest daughter of Lord and Lady Camoys of Stonor Park in Oxfordshire, the Stonors being one of the most ancient families in the peerage, elevated to the barony in the eleventh century. She was privately educated and came to Newport as a teenager with her mother, Mildred Sherman, daughter of William Watts Sherman, on the eve of the Second World War. She was a descendent of Rhode Island's founder, Roger Williams, and of Nicholas Brown, the founder of Brown University.

None of this background prevented Noreen, as she preferred to be called, from undertaking a lifetime of good works. She was a volunteer in three wars—World War II, Korea, and Vietnam—and a tireless advocate, mainly through the Red Cross, of maternal and child well-being and mental health. She was hands-on—a nurse's aide at the Newport Naval Hospital, working on blood drives, helping in the emergency room and on the hospital wards, even driving an ambulance! And all of this was done with the utmost loving, personal kindness. It has been said that the definition of a gentleman is one who always strives to put others at their ease. If that is so, Noreen Drexel was the ultimate lady. She opened her charming Victorian house on Bellevue Avenue to the great and not-so-great. Every year, after presiding over the summer season, she had a reception for the charities she supported, and they were many. Here in Gotham alone, she was active on the boards of Memorial Sloan Kettering, the Hospital for Special Surgery, the Beekman Downtown Hospital, and New York Hospital–Cornell Medical Center and chair of the Women's Division of the Lying-In Hospital of the City of New York. In the 1970s she was appointed to be the representative of the League of Red Cross Societies at the United Nations. In Florida she organized prenatal teaching programs and made childbirth education a major priority. Back in Newport she was the 2011 honoree of the Newport Hospital gala. The hospital's Noreen Stonor Drexel Birthing Center welcomes children to Newport, a city that Mrs. Drexel, through her chairmanship of the Aletta Morris McBean Charitable Trust and other philanthropies, had done so much to improve.

Noreen married John R. Drexel III, a kinsman of Mother Katherine Drexel and a descendant of the founder of Philadelphia's Drexel University, in 1941. They have three children, Pamela, Nick, and Nonie O'Farrell, and seven grandsons.

We first became friends a quarter century ago when Christopher Buckley and I wrote a play about Queen Elizabeth I and the martyred Jesuit missionary St. Edmund Campion. Campion had written and printed his famous pamphlet in defense of the Catholic faith, *Rationes Decem*, at Noreen's childhood home, Stonor Park, which caused a sensation when it was distributed in Oxford and led to his capture and execution not long after. When the play premiered at the Williamstown Theatre Festival, Mr. and Mrs. Drexel made the long trip from Newport to see it, possibly the only time in that decidedly bohemian setting that a couple attended a performance in evening clothes!

In more recent years my sons, Pierce and Rhoads, and Noreen's grandsons—Liam, Fergus, Aidan, and Finnian O'Farrell—have been schoolmates and close friends at Portsmouth Abbey outside of Newport, and Noreen has been their biggest booster at games and other school functions.

Her funeral at St. John the Evangelist Church in Newport on November 10 was presided over by the lady Episcopal bishop of Rhode Island. The governor, Lincoln Chaffee, and past governor, Donald Carcieri, were in attendance, as was Senator Sheldon Whitehouse and many other dignitaries. A large reception was held afterwards at the Pell Center at Salve Regina University, which Noreen did so much to develop and now boasts both Stonor and Drexel Halls. The next day Noreen's body was taken to England for a Catholic funeral mass and burial beside her mother in a village cemetery high in the Chilterns, with a beautiful view of her birthplace, Stonor Park.

"I'm a frustrated nurse!" Noreen liked to exclaim. No one ever gave more, more kindly, or more lovingly, than Noreen, and her example will be her greatest legacy.

Newport has always had its Irish Fifth Ward in addition to its Puritans, swamp Yankees, socialites, and Portuguese. Its colorful mayor, Humphrey Donnelly III, introduced himself to the Queen of England when she visited the city, "Hello there, Queen Elizabeth II, I am Humphrey the Third." Tom Quinn, Peter Kiernan, and Peter Walsh are all prominent citizens today. And even some of the ur-Wasps, such as Tom and Freddy Cushing, were sent forth from "the Ledges," their compound overlooking Bailey's Beach, by their mother to the Priory rather than St. George's, because, in the redoubtable Mrs. Cushing's considered opinion, it was then the better school. The many Goelet cousins, especially John and Ann and Amy, are also active in Catholic affairs during the summer season.

Chapter VIII

Sport

The Yankees

IT IS WELL DOCUMENTED THAT IRISH AMERICANS MADE UP THE majority of baseball players before the turn of the twentieth century, and so it is not surprising that a significant part of the fan base remained Irish American as well.

The first World Series I ever attended was Whitey Ford's opening game two-hitter against the Reds in 1961. I was nine, and I thought I would die of excitement when a movie-star handsome Joe DiMaggio walked by my grandfather's box on his way into the mezzanine press box on the first base side of the field. That was the year Roger Maris and my hero, Mickey Mantle, had dueled for the home run championship throughout the summer until the Mick became hobbled by leg injuries. He ended up with 54 home runs and Roger hit his 61st against Tracy Stallard of the Red Sox on the last day of the 162-game season, thus assuring that an asterisk would always be next to his name since Babe Ruth had hit his 60 homers in 1927 in only 154 games. In addition to Ford, the Yankees had good pitchers like Ralph Terry and Luis Arroyo, the Mariano Rivera of his day. They had a great infield, with Clete Boyer at third (whose brother Ken was a many-time Gold Glove winner at the same position for the Cardinals), Tony Kubek at shortstop, Bobby Richardson at second, and Moose Skowron at first. Hector Lopez played left field, Mickey ranged far and wide when healthy in center, and Maris was an underappreciated, outstanding defensive player in right. Occasionally Yogi Berra, supplanted at catcher by Elston Howard and late in his playing career, but still an extremely dangerous bad ball pinch hitter, would end up in right late in the game as well, and he had the ability to take out ten-foot turf divots while making his signature diving catches. The Yanks won that series four to one and thus avenged the cruel defeat of the year before when Bill Mazeroski hit a ninth inning homer in the seventh game for the Pirates.

In any event, those were glorious years, 1960–1964, when the Yankees won five pennants and a couple of World Series, and my father was wonderfully kind to take me to the Bronx as often as he did, until, aged fourteen, I was finally old enough to take the train and the subway and buy the $1.50 bleacher seat in center field for a Sunday doubleheader—rapture!—all by myself.

Years later, when Mickey Mantle and Whitey Ford were inducted into the Hall of Fame at Cooperstown, my brother and I drove over from Saratoga, and Jane Forbes Clark sweetly got us VIP tickets (I would venture that in her capacity as chairman of the National Baseball Hall of Fame and Museum—not to mention her many other civic, sporting, and conservation activities—Jane has by now spent more time with more Hall of Famers than anyone ever has or will again). We sat on the sun-dappled lawn and listened as Cool Papa Bell, who stole more bases than Ty Cobb—in the Negro Leagues—warmed up the crowd with bittersweet memories of the Kansas City Monarchs and other teams of that time, and of all of the talent that could not be seen in the Majors until Jackie Robinson broke the color barrier with the Brooklyn Dodgers in 1947. Then it was Whitey Ford's turn to speak. He was and is not a tall man, whose mastery consisted not so much in blinding speed but in a bewildering array of off-speed pitches and then, every so often, a sneaky fastball (unusually for a pitcher, he was a dangerous batter as well). "When I was a kid growing up in Long Island City," Whitey began, "all any of us ever wanted to do was to play for the Yankees. The first day I stood on the mound starting a game at the Stadium, I couldn't believe it was true, and I can't believe this is true today either."

There were not many dry eyes in the crowd after that, so when it was time for Mickey Mantle to speak, he held up his plaque and said, "They have a whole lot of my records written down on this thing, but I see they left out the record that will stand longer than any of the others—for most strikeouts." Then Mickey launched, in his folksy Oklahoma way, into a discussion of his somewhat checkered business career since leaving baseball. "I've had my ups and downs, but now I have a business called Mickey Mantle's Country Fried Chicken. My partner takes care of all the business, and all I had to do was come up with the slogan; and the slogan I came up with—Merlin (his long-suffering wife) doesn't want me to tell you this—is 'To get a better piece of chicken, you'd have to be a rooster.'" That brought down the house.

My children were able to celebrate the 2009 Yankees with a mature team of stars like Andy Pettitte, Mariano Rivera, Derek Jeter, Alex Rodriguez, and Hideki Matsui, an admirable and worthy successor to the great Yankee teams of the past. And the Mets struggled valiantly but were outplayed by Kansas City in the 2015 series. But interest in baseball shows signs of declining as kids used to playing video games and operating three screens at once lose patience with a three-hour game. For that matter, so do grownups who have trouble operating only one screen. In the old days the Stock Exchange would close at two, and Wall Streeters would hustle uptown to the bars of their clubs for a quick snort and then go on to the Stadium for the game. It doesn't happen like that anymore, although spectators who do go pay fantastic amounts for tickets, food, and assorted trinkets. Racing has been in decline for fifty years, and baseball may soon join it.

FOOTBALL: THE GIANTS!
Rooting for the Giants is a multigenerational religion in my tribe. The team's founder, Tim Mara, was a bookie who often plied his trade at my great-grandfather's Empire City Race Track in Yonkers. In 1925 he plunked down five hundred dollars for the New York franchise in the new National Football League. At the time the Giants were one of only five franchises, and today we are the only one of those five still to exist. "Anything in New York is worth $500," Big Tim reasoned shrewdly, and that investment is worth over a billion today.

My father went to grade school at Loyola with Jack and Wellington Mara, and the early lore of the Giants—Red Grange, the first 1927 championship, the 1934 "Sneaker" championship game in the snow against the Bears, Pearl Harbor day, the sudden-death loss to Johnny Unitas and the Colts in the 1958 championship game—was passed along and constantly reanalyzed as the sports equivalent of Torah commentaries among my five brothers and me.

Along the way there were many successes as well. Under the legendary coach Steve Owens, we won eight divisional and two league championships. Our MVPs over the decades have included Mel Hein, Frank Gifford, Charlie Conerly, Y.A. Tittle, and Lawrence Taylor.

The first game I ever attended was at the Polo Grounds. Afterwards Dad took us up to the Harry M. Stevens catering office for some refreshment. When we got there, the voice of the Giants on television in that era, Chris Schenkel, had preceded us, and the day's proceeds were being counted, the bank notes laid out on a long table and the silver whirring in a coin-counting machine. "What'll it be?" asked the Stevens patriarch, "Mr. Frank," lugging some bottles out of the safe. As Red Smith wrote, "This is the first place I've seen where the money's out in the open but the whiskey's in the safe!"

Later the Giants moved to Yankee Stadium, and my brother Schuyler drove us in there on a freezing rainy Sunday just before Christmas in 1961 to watch Sam Huff, Andy Robustelli, and Roosevelt Grier neutralize Jimmy Brown and sew up the divisional title against Cleveland in a ferociously fought 7–7 tie. Our seats were in the front row in the end zone near home plate. In those days, after a victory, you could still run out onto the field and take down the wooden goalposts, saving splinters for souvenirs. I kept mine for thirty years, until I gave them to my nephews, but the shoe I lost getting trampled as I ran happily through the excited mob that day has never resurfaced, and when we got back to Long Island, Mother was not nearly as amused as my older brothers were.

Speaking of television, today's younger generation would be amazed to learn that there was a seventy-five-mile blackout of TV coverage for NFL home games in those years, so as not to cannibalize stadium attendance. The result was that motels up and down the upper Connecticut Turnpike sold their rooms for ten times the normal rate on Sundays as Giants fans flocked to them to watch the games on grainy black-and-white TVs with rabbit ears. When I related this to my son Pierce, he said, "When I was little and watching old programs on TV, I used to think that all of life had been lived in black and white."

From the middle sixties on, the Giants endured a heartbreaking decline during a long-simmering family ownership feud, only to come storming back under the leadership of Coach Bill Parcells and General Manager George Young in the 1980s. Our first Super Bowl victory was over the Denver Broncos, 39–20, at the end of the 1986 season. Then the Super Bowl victory we won four years later, 20–19, when the Bills' last-second field goal went just a tad wide, got most of the credit for causing my wife and sister-in-law to go into labor the next week, so I remain grateful to the team on many counts.

Moving to the Meadowlands was, of course, a large step forward in 1976, although every time I took my kids as they grew up, the weather was around zero, the wind swirled crazily, and their vocabularies were enlarged in undesirable ways. Wellington Mara lived to a venerable age and became known as the "Conscience of the NFL" until his death in 2005. It still needs one, as the ongoing concussion scandals demonstrate.

And who can ever forget the 2007 season, where under a maturing Eli Manning we came storming through the stretch to finish 10–6; beat Tampa Bay, Dallas, and Green Bay in the playoffs; and went into the Super Bowl as twelve-point underdogs against the 18–0 New England Patriots? Somehow we managed to hang in the game for the first three quarters against the Patriots' confident and furious assault, and then things began breaking our way, first with a circus catch by David Tyree on his helmet and then Plaxico Burress's reception of Eli's winning touchdown with less than a minute to play. The defense held on to win another Super Bowl, vindicating the disciplined yet often creative coaching style of veteran Tom Coughlin. The normally low-keyed managing owner, John Mara (Wellington's son), called it "the greatest victory in the history of this franchise, without question."

After a disappointing end the season before, the Giants came alive in September 2011, stomping Michael Vick and the Philadelphia Eagles and then making a thrilling fourth-quarter comeback to beat the Arizona Cardinals thanks to a cool-handed Eli and great catches by Victor Cruz and Hakeem Nicks. Then, on November 6, Eli led the Jints to a victory over New England that was reminiscent of our Super Bowl upset in 2007, with the defense shutting Brady down and Jake Ballard making key catches almost as acrobatic as Tyree's.

The Giants struggled to make the playoffs, beating the Dallas Cowboys in Week 17 to clinch the NFC East, but then excelled in the playoffs of January 2012, beating the Atlanta Falcons 24–2 and the Green Bay Packers 37–20. In the NFC championship game on January 22, they beat the San Francisco 49ers 20–17 in overtime on a field goal by Lawrence Tynes. Finally, in Super Bowl XLVI, the underdog Giants beat the New England Patriots 21–17.

Nowadays the Giants have a pricey new stadium, and the operations crew has by now learned how to keep the lights in it on. Now that my kids are old enough to get to the game on their own, most of my viewing is done from the couch, and I'm inclined to keep it that way until grandchildren come along. But if I were sure there would be another blackout, I might sally forth. The Harry M. Stevens Company is long gone, alas, but I like to think the ghost of "Mr. Frank" would emerge from his safe one more time with a little liquid encouragement for the electricians and the rest of us.

After the death of Jack Mara, the Giants have been jointly owned by the Maras and the Tisch family, with John Mara being the managing partner for football operations. The team's value has increased in those years, but the death of Ann Mara, Wellington's widow, in 2015 has complicated the ownership structure, and the Giants' performance on the field has raised questions as well.

For the last four seasons, the Giants have failed to make the playoffs, and in 2016, after the Giants' defense proved the worst in the NFL, it was finally time to say goodbye to Tom Coughlin, a good man and a once great coach. Young offensive coordinator Ben McAdoo now has a chance to prove himself as head coach, and the Maras and the Tisches loosened General Manager Jerry Reese's purse strings in the 2016 off-season so he could resign Jason Pierre-Paul and hire several other high-quality defensive players for Steve Spagnuolo to deploy.

Hope springs eternal. Let's *go*, Giants!

James Butler and grandchildren.

Thomas A. Edison (center), with Grandpa Murray (to his right), Walter P. Chrysler (to his left), and friends and relations.

Mother Butler of Marymount, worldwide Mother General of the Religious of the Sacred Heart of Mary.

Priory faculty in 1965, high-water mark for the monastery.

Father Hilary on the farm at Portsmouth—"the Good Shepherd."

Wedding of Genevieve Travers to Dr. Samuel B. Moore, the last of the lavish pre-War weddings.

Groom and groomsmen at Schuyler MacGuire's wedding to Dean Tyndall, 1968.

T. Murray McDonnell, Jacqueline Onassis, the author, Father Vincent Dwyer, and Caroline Kennedy at Megan McDonnell's wedding in Peapack, New Jersey, mid-1970s.

Christopher Buckley, Katy Close and family at their wedding, 2012

William F. Buckley Jr. at his National Review desk with Bible: ever faithfully.

William F. Buckley Jr. with David Niven and the future St. John Paul the Great at the Vatican.
THE BUCKLEY FAMILY

New York Times and *Commonweal* editor,
Peter Steinfels.

Casey Carter, a Carroll descendant and head of Philadelphia's Faith in the Future Foundation.

Peter Flanigan with Senator James L. Buckley, two old Washington hands, taken at Flanigan's birthday celebration a month before his death in 2013.

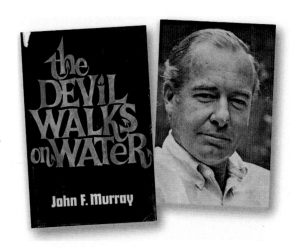

The Devil Walks on Water:
Southampton novelist Jake Murray.

Jay, Jimmy, Anna, Sean, and Sheila Buckley.

PROFILE:
THE MARAS AND ROONEYS: FROM RACING TO PRO FOOTBALL

The Rooney family has owned the Pittsburgh Steelers since the team's inception in 1933. After emigrating from Ireland in the 1840s, the Rooneys established their U.S. roots in Pittsburgh in the 1880s, and have been active in sports ever since.

Art Rooney, the paterfamilias, owned the team until his death in the late 1980s. He paid twenty-five hundred dollars to bring the then Pittsburgh Pirates into the NFL. He was also a professional gambler and generous philanthropist, especially to the Church. Stories are told of him picking up priests in Pittsburgh to give them a ride, and, when he let them out, reaching into a grocery bag stuffed with cash from his racetrack winnings to make an offertory to their church. Following Art's death, ownership of the Steelers transferred to his first-born son, Dan Rooney, former United States ambassador to Ireland. In recent years, Art Rooney II has run the team.

Like the Maras, the Rooneys have been loyal owners, employing only three head coaches since 1969, the fewest number of any team in American professional sports during that era. This approach has resulted in six Super Bowl victories.

The Rooneys are now related to the New York Giants Mara family. Actresses Kate Mara and Rooney Mara are daughters of Chris and Kathleen Mara (née Rooney). Their maternal grandfather, Timothy James "Tim" Rooney, has run Yonkers Raceway, the former Empire City Race Track owned by James Butler, in Yonkers, New York, since 1972. Dan Rooney's Sports Pub is a popular venue there, part of what is now called Empire City Casino, where slot machines and other gambling are available.

The Rooneys also own an interest in the Palm Beach Kennel Club, a greyhound track, which Pat Rooney Sr., one of Art's sons, moved to Florida to run in 1984. Three other sons are also seasonal residents. One of Pat's daughters, Bridget Rooney Koch, had a son, Liam, with actor Kevin Costner and is now married to 1962 America's Cup champion and wine collector William Koch, a son of Koch Industries founder Fred C. Koch, who now concentrates his energies on a college preparatory school he founded, Oxbridge Academy of the Palm Beaches.

Other family members work in the hospitality and restaurant industries, and Tom Rooney is a Republican member of the House of Representatives for the Sixteenth District, which includes parts of Palm Beach County.

To understand the connection between the Rooneys' Yonkers Raceway and the original Empire City Race Track, it is worth recalling the story of *Real Lace's* James Butler and Matt Winn, the "Father of the Kentucky Derby."

MATT WINN: FATHER OF THE KENTUCKY DERBY

The Run for the Roses, as the Kentucky Derby is known (for the blanket of flowers bestowed upon the back of the winner), was founded by Colonel Meriwether Lewis Clark Jr., a grandson of William Clark of the Lewis and Clark expedition. He had traveled to Europe in 1872 and visited the Epsom Derby in England and the Grand Prix de Paris at Longchamps. Returning home to Kentucky, he organized the Louisville Jockey Club, and on May 17, 1875, in front of a crowd of ten thousand people, a colt named Aristides defeated fourteen other three-year-olds to win the first Derby.

The track encountered financial difficulties, and its success was not secured until 1902, when Colonel Matt J. Winn put together a syndicate of local businessmen to acquire Churchill Downs. As recounted in his memoir, *Down the Stretch*, Winn was a lifelong Louisvillean and was proud of its position on the Ohio River as the Gateway between the North and South. But in the 1860s and 1870s when he was growing up, it was, for all its hustle and bustle, still a primitive town with no water supply. At various street corners were water wells where people would go with buckets, fill them with water, and haul them home. "As a boy, that was one of my principal chores, and Saturday was a day I never looked forward to. . . . Saturday was bath day." Matt Winn saw the first Derby at the age of thirteen, standing atop his father's grocery wagon in the infield.

Mule-driven streetcars came, then the railroad, and in due course even the telephone. But in the rural parts of Kentucky where Winn often traveled as he built his business, first in groceries and then as a merchant tailor, there was no money, only barter, and the country folk often paid in skins they had trapped or with moonshine.

Under Matt Winn's management Churchill Downs broke away from the Western Turf Association and prospered, and the Kentucky Derby became the preeminent stakes race for three-year-olds in North America throughout Winn's long life (he died in 1949, having attended the Derby for three quarters of a century). And so it has remained.

There is a New York connection between Colonel Winn and horse racing. Once Matt Winn had reorganized Churchill Downs and put the Kentucky Derby on its path to preeminence, he was asked by grocery magnate James Butler to do the same with Butler's recently acquired track, Empire City in Yonkers. Empire had been a trotting track originally, but with the closing of Jerome (named for Leonard Jerome, the American grandfather of Winston Churchill) and Morris Parks in the Bronx, Butler wanted to provide a venue for racing fans to enjoy the sport in Westchester County.

The problem was that racing in New York state was controlled by the Jockey Club, organized by August Belmont, Leonard Jerome, Harry Knapp, John Sanford, and other WASP grandees. They liked racing as it was at Jamaica and Belmont Park on Long Island and upstate in August at Saratoga Springs. When an upstart Irishman like James Butler applied for racing dates in competition with Saratoga, they wasted no time in turning him down. A Chicago horseman, Big Ed Corrigan, introduced Butler to Matt Winn.

"You're a fighter," Butler said. "And I'm a fighter. I want you to join with me."

Winn answered, "So you want to race at Empire City, Belmont or no Belmont, Jockey Club dates or no Jockey Club dates?"

"That's right," Butler answered. "Fact is, I started to put on a meeting, but the horsemen, jockeys, bookmakers, the whole kaboodle, turned me down. They said if they operated at Empire without a Jockey Club OK, they would be blacklisted at all the other New York tracks."

Winn suggested Butler get a license from the Jockey Club, and Butler immediately remonstrated, "Haven't I just been telling you I can't get such a license. They won't give it to me."

"You went to them," Winn replied, "and they wouldn't give it to you. Now you have to go into court and get an order from a judge directing the Jockey Club to give you a license to operate a racetrack. A license won't get you dates from the Jockey Club, but before you can run a racetrack, you must have a track owner's operating license."

Butler accepted Colonel Winn's suggestion and went to court. After a long and bitter battle with the Jockey Club, he won the right to a license. But he still had to get dates for a race meeting from the Jockey Club, which meant another fight.

Years later Winn recalled, "I knew that August Belmont and the Jockey Club gang would put up a fight to stop us, and why not? They had enjoyed a monopoly in New York State for thirty-five or forty years. Jim Butler and I, on the other hand, had the right to break into New York racing, if we could."

Matt Winn devised an ingenious strategy.

When the regular Eastern campaigners wouldn't desert the Jockey Club and the established tracks, I knew the only way I could put on a meeting was to persuade the western and the southern horsemen, bookies etc. to go along with us. But it was no sure thing. So I rounded up the operators of the tracks in New Orleans and the tracks other than Churchill Downs in Kentucky. I talked to owners and bookmakers too. I proposed a circuit: Empire City in August, then to Kentucky, then to New Orleans for winter racing, back to Kentucky for the spring of the year, and north in August to Empire City. That way they knew that even being blacklisted by the Jockey Club couldn't stop them from racing all the year 'round.

The fight was covered gleefully in the newspapers of the day. Butler and Winn won a lower court ruling, and the starchy August Belmont made the Jockey Club's opposition crystal clear in a formal announcement: "We have great solicitude that the holding of the Empire City meeting will not be in the best interests of racing, and we believe that the Supreme Court of New York will overturn the Appellate Court's decision to grant racing dates."

To the Jockey Club's surprise, however, the Supreme Court did not overturn the lower court's ruling giving Empire City racing dates. And yet putting on the meet at Empire still faced many hurdles. The stands needed repairs. The grounds were overgrown with weeds. The racing strip was in poor condition. Some of the barns needed to be rebuilt. But in August 1907 the Little Track That Could opened in direct competition with Saratoga, with seventy-six entries on a card of six races, and more than ten thousand downstate racing fans thronged through the gates. The meeting went on to a rip-roaring success, and finally the Jockey Club conceded defeat.

Winn recalled:

On the tenth day of the meeting I was rather amazed to see Harry Knapp, a Jockey Club member and August Belmont's lieutenant, enter my office. "I came here to express Mr. Belmont's congratulations on the fine and formful meeting you are running here," Knapp said. "When the Saratoga meeting is over and Mr. Belmont is back in New York, he would like to meet with Mr. Butler and you about dates for Empire City next year, under Jockey Club supervision."

And so the battle ended, and the Empire City race meeting went on for another four decades, though not without an interruption from 1910–1913 when anti-gambling reformers succeeded in banning racing from New York. Winn's and Butler's response was to buy Laurel Racecourse outside of Washington and to race there. But Winn recognized that to save the sport they needed a southern circuit as well. As an ever resourceful entrepreneur, he came up with an idea.

"I talked to Jack Follansbee, who runs the Hearst mining interests in Mexico, and Albert Terrazas, whose father is the cattle king of the entire country," Winn told Butler. "They have some property near the center of Juarez we could use. There are no signs of any anti-racing laws in Mexico. We could have winter racing there far beyond the reach of the reformers."

James Butler's answer was characteristically blunt: "Then what the hell are we waiting for?"

The Juarez Jockey Club was formed, and the track was named Terrazas Park. The clubhouse was built with concrete with silver tailings. Harry M. Stevens, the hot dog king, took the restaurant concession.

We opened in Juarez in December of 1909 and continued racing there until 1917. In those days El Paso was the last frontier of the old West, full of gambling houses. The houses in the red light district were like palaces. There was boxing, bull fights, aristocrats and brigands, the 400 and ladies of the night, all together.

Pancho Villa and his men rode into town one day and Villa asked for uniforms with real brass buttons for his band to play at the track. We were happy to comply. One day Villa bet $50 on a tip and watched the race from the judges' stand. Two horses crossed the finish line closer than a frugal Scotsman's pocketbook. The other horse won the race, and Villa's sidekick, the butcher seethed, "It is wrong," and drew his pistol. There was an awful moment of silence. Then Villa twirled his own revolver and said, "My horse did not win. The other one won."

Post time for the Derby on the first Saturday in May is 6:32 p.m. They say that Colonel Matt Winn still watches the Derby, though from a seat with a better view than he had in the infield in 1875.

Racing has taken its lumps in the last half century as other sports, notably football, took better advantage of the opportunity television presented and grew in popularity. The world moved farther away from an equine, agricultural society, and the Thoroughbred breed showed signs of declining. Horses were bred for sprints, not stamina; they raced fewer times and broke down more often, probably because of the advent in America of frequent medication, some of which was intended to build muscle but at the expense of bone. In Europe, Hong Kong, and other drug-free jurisdictions, Thoroughbreds continued to run longer and more often.

If one could choose a time when the sport in America climaxed, it could well be Secretariat's completion of the Triple Crown in 1973.

Secretariat's Triple Crown: Forty Years On

In the spring of 1973, Secretariat won the Kentucky Derby and the Preakness in record times and entered the Belmont Stakes as the prohibitive favorite to become the first Triple Crown winner in twenty-five years. A son of Bold Ruler and Somethingroyal, Secretariat was bred by Virginia horseman Christopher Chenery. Mr. Chenery died on January 3, 1973, and never got to see his greatest horse's triumphs, but Secretariat was campaigned brilliantly by his daughter, Penny Tweedy, who during her father's declining years expertly managed the family's Meadow Stable.

The Phipps family owned Bold Ruler, and rather than charge stud fees for breeding to him preferred to breed twice and to claim one of the foals for its own breeding program. Thus, after Somethingroyal was bred twice to Bold Ruler, in the fall of 1969, Ogden Phipps and Mrs. Tweedy tossed a coin in the office of New York Racing Association president Alfred Vanderbilt Jr. Phipps won and chose to keep a weanling filly from the pair, meaning that Meadow Stable would retain the unborn foal that Somethingroyal was then carrying. The filly was called the Bride, and in the elegant formulation of sportswriter Red Smith, "She couldn't beat a fat man." The colt was foaled on March 30, 1970, at 12:10 a.m., a bright red chestnut with three white socks and a star with a narrow blaze. He was called Secretariat.

Secretariat won the Eclipse Award for Two-Year-Old Champion Male Horse and began his three-year-old year with an easy win in the Bay Shore Stakes at Aqueduct. In his next race, the Wood Memorial, however, he was upset by his own stablemate, Angle Light. It was later determined that Secretariat suffered from a painful abscess in his mouth that day.

The entry of Secretariat and Angle Light went off at three-to-two favorites in the Kentucky Derby the first Saturday of May. Secretariat broke last, moved up on the field in the backstretch, overtook Sham for the lead, and pulled away to win the Derby by two and a half lengths in the still record time of 1:59.4.

Two weeks later Secretariat won the Preakness Stakes in Baltimore, again by two and a half lengths over Sham, and again in a record time of 1:53. (The Derby is run at a mile and a quarter and the Preakness at a mile and three sixteenths.)

Thus, excitement was high when Secretariat came to Belmont Park on June 9 in a bid to become only the ninth Triple Crown winner and the first in a quarter century. Only four horses dared to enter against him, and, as "The Sidewalks of New York" was played during the post parade, Secretariat was a one-to-ten favorite. My brothers and I had driven my gallant but ailing father across from the south shore for what would be his last day at Belmont Park. I can still remember the first roar that greeted "Big Red" (Secretariat and Man O' War shared the same nickname, and in most polls are rated as the numbers one and two Thoroughbreds ever to race) as he walked through the tunnel and pranced up the main track to warm up.

Belmont Park was crammed with nearly seventy thousand fans from all walks of life that day. Racing friends from around the country streamed back from the paddock and stopped to say hello as they passed my father's box. The tension mounted, and as the starting gate sprung open, another roar rose from the crowd. Secretariat and Sham set a fast early pace and opened ten lengths on the field. After six furlongs Sham began to tire and Secretariat opened a larger and larger lead. CBS television announcer Chick Anderson yelled into his mike, "Secretariat is widening now! He's moving like a *tremendous machine!*"

A tremendously powerful but also *beautiful* machine. At the finish Secretariat, trained by Lucien Laurin and ridden by Ron Turcotte, had won by thirty-one lengths in an unbelievable time for a mile and a half of 2:24, both records that have never been eclipsed. The iconic photo of the always gracious Mrs. Tweedy exulting in victory with arms upraised over her head is one of the most stirring images in racing history.

I have strong memories of that day. In many ways it was the climax of a golden era for the Sport of Kings, and the interconnected network of families that maintained racing as a sport rather than a business, today too often dominated by drugs for the innocent but ever courageous animals involved.

I remember Secretariat's great victory gratefully, because of my father's bravery in getting out to Belmont Park that day to watch him run. And I am further grateful that the lunkheaded celebratory spree I went on after watching that magnificent performance—including a beautiful twenty-first birthday dinner dance in Mt. Kisco and an equally enjoyable deb party back on Long Island—ended up with my taking out a Long Island Lighting Company utility pole at four thirty the next morning after missing a turn trying to get home, but not doing any more damage to my younger brother and me than what it took a quick visit to the emergency room to repair.

The car, however, was another story, and the bad news was it belonged to my older brother, with whom I was flying off to Ireland, Scotland, and England that very night. Relations were frosty for a few days, but ultimately the memory of Secretariat's brilliant Belmont melted the ice, and by the time we got to the Curragh, we were hoping to see yet another champion. But ones like Secretariat are few and far between.

Seattle Slew and Affirmed also won the Triple Crown in the 1970s, and then came a long dry spell that was only broken in 2015. I felt fortunate to be there.

American Pharoah Wins the Triple Crown

The morning of June 6 dawned with heavy skies and intermittent rain on Long Island, but none of that deterred over ninety thousand racing fans from pouring through the gates of Belmont Park in hopes of seeing American Pharoah win the Belmont Stakes and become the first Triple Crown winner since Affirmed in 1979. They were not disappointed.

The thirteen-race card included ten graded stakes, and excitement built throughout the afternoon. Even the Trustees' Room, where the Jockey Club's Stuart Janney presided over his customary table, had an excited buzz, and the Turf and Field Club was a raucous throng from early on. Beautifully dressed young men and women came pouring off the Long Island Rail Road trains and through the clubhouse gates, the guys wearing Mad Men hats and the gals favoring ever-higher platform heels. The crowds were still pouring in at four thirty in the afternoon when Honor Code turned back Tonalist, last year's Belmont winner, in the Metropolitan Mile. Racing fans from around the country swarmed the enormous old Belmont plant, and paddock sightings included Billy

Turner, masterful trainer of 1977 Triple Crown winner Seattle Slew; Ian Highet; Shel Evans; Kaleem Shah; Bill Farish; Van Cushney; Frank Loughran; Charlie Fenwick; and Bill and Renee Lickle with their beautiful granddaughters.

As anticipation of the big race rose a, group of my college friends, including bloodstock agent Kip Elser from Camden, South Carolina, and Louisville lawyer John Egan, ventured out from the Champagne Room and took their places standing on benches close to the rail about three hundred yards down from the starting gate. The roar as American Pharoah came out onto the track was terrific, but only half as loud as that which accompanied the starting gate springing open.

The horses went by us in a blur, but Pharoah was already clearly in the lead. After honest fractions, Materiality fell back on the far turn and Frosted and Keen Ice came on, but American Pharoah, beautifully trained up to the race by Bob Baffert, dug in and began to pull away, and then came the loudest, most prolonged roar of all. His final quarter was just as fast as Secretariat's record-breaking performance in 1973, and as Victor Espinosa raised his clenched fist crossing the finish line, wondrous things began to happen.

Up in the press box, Joe Drape of the *New York Times* reported the next day, hard-boiled members of the fourth estate cheered and wept. A lady standing next to me I had never met before gave me a spontaneous hug. John Egan's pretty and enthusiastic daughter, Stewart, just down from her freshman year at Choate Rosemary Hall and on her first trip ever to Belmont Park, threw her arms around me as well. "You'll tell your grandchildren about this," I assured her. It was that kind of a day, and just what the Sport of King needs—even better than a new king of racing, a Pharoah.

CHAPTER IX

In the Public Arena

IN 1980 THE NUMBER OF AMERICANS SELF-IDENTIFYING AS IRISH AMERican exceeded forty million, whereas in 2010 that number had dipped beneath thirty-five million. There are several possible explanations for this apparently counterintuitive decline. It may reflect severely diminished immigration (from a peak of 914,119 in the decade of 1851–1860 to a nadir of 11,940 in 1971–80; but from 1981–90 that number rose to 31,969). Ongoing assimilation into the broader culture may also be a factor, as may be the growing phenomenon of intermarriage.

And yet the persistence of large numbers of Irish Americans in public and political life is indicative of an ongoing resilience in this domain. As late as the 1960s, to choose one example, 42 percent of the New York Police Department were Irish Americans, and it remains notable that the commissioners of that department in the last three decades have included William Bratton (twice) and Raymond Kelly.

Prominent Irish Americans in high public office in recent years include President Ronald Reagan; Vice President Joe Biden; associate Supreme Court justices Anthony Kennedy and Sandra Day O'Connor; U.S. Ambassador to the United Nations Samantha Power; Speaker of the House Paul Ryan; Virginia governor Terry McAuliffe; and Senators Christopher Dodd of Connecticut, Susan Collins of Maine, Pat Toomey and Bob Casey Jr. of Pennsylvania, Tim Kaine of Virginia, Patrick Leahy of Vermont, and Maria Cantwell of Washington. Although the Irish tend to vote roughly equally for Republicans and Democrats, Ronald Reagan was an exception to this rule and won many working-class Democrats to his coalition. Since John F. Kennedy, every president has claimed some Irish heritage, though in Jimmy Carter's case this is purely Scots Irish, and no documentation has been found to authenticate Bill Clinton's claim on this score. Barack Obama's maternal ancestors came to America from a small village called Moneygall in County Offaly.

CULTURE

In popular culture James Cagney, Walt Disney, John Ford, Judy Garland, Spencer Tracy, and Irish-born actress Maureen O'Hara are all Irish Americans, as is Mia Farrow via her mother, Maureen O'Sullivan. Singer Judy Collins and George Clooney, a nephew of Rosemary Clooney, are also Irish Americans.

Comedians include Jackie Gleason, George Carlin, Bill Murray, Will Ferrell, Chris Farley, Stephen Colbert, Conan O'Brien, Bill Maher, and Jimmy Fallon. As for musicians, there are Bing Crosby, Mariah Carey, Katy Perry, and Taylor Swift.

On the wrong side of the law were "Bugs" Moran, Legs Diamond, and Whitey Bulger.

In literature, in addition to Fitzgerald and James T. Farrell, there was Eugene O'Neill, who won the 1936 Nobel Prize in Literature. There was also Flannery O'Connor and, more recently, Thomas Flanagan (*The Year of the French*), Cormac McCarthy (*All the Pretty Horses*, *No Country for Old Men*, and *The Road*), poet laureate Billy Collins, novelists Peter Quinn and Alice McDermott, and political journalist Peggy Noonan (who in her memoir of the Reagan years, *What I Saw at the Revolution*, credits *Real Lace*'s Mary Jane Cuddihy MacGuire with helping her to find an apartment when she moved from Washington to New York). John Patrick Shanley (*Moonstruck* and *Doubt*) has written masterpieces for the stage and screen, and Thomas Cahill wrote the best-selling popular history *How the Irish Saved Civilization*.

Gregory Wolfe, editor of *Image*, writes:

Over the years Image has featured many believing writers, including Annie Dillard, Elie Wiesel, Christian Wiman, Marilynne Robinson and Mark Helprin. But these writers of religious faith and others are not hard to find elsewhere. Several prominent American authors— Franz Wright, Mary Karr and Robert Clark—are Catholic converts. Nathan Englander and Jonathan Safran Foer last year published "New American Haggadah," a contemporary take on the ritual book used by Jews on Passover.

In short, the myth of secularism triumphant in the literary arts is just that—a myth. Yet making lists of counterexamples does not get at a deeper matter. It has to do with the way that faith takes on different tones and dimensions depending on the culture surrounding it.

We live in a postmodern world, where any grand narrative is suspect, where institutions are seen as oppressive. So the late Doris Betts could say that for all her admiration of Flannery O'Connor, her own fiction had to convey faith in whispers rather than shouts. Indeed, one of the most ancient religious ideas is that grace works in obscure, mysterious ways. But obscure is not invisible.

In sports Irish Americans comprised a third of early professional baseball players, and Nolan Ryan was a worthy successor to that tradition. Quarterbacks John Elway and Tom Brady are both Super Bowl champions. Jimmy Connors and John McEnroe were leading players at the dawn of the Open tennis era. Texan Ben Hogan was a great golfer of Irish extraction, although today there are several outstanding *Irish* Irish players on the tour, such as the Ulsterman Rory McIlroy.

In short, Irish Americans continue to influence American politics and culture strongly, and a useful exercise is to survey developments that have occurred in the last fifty years in two of the more public families Stephen Birmingham wrote about in the original *Real Lace*, the Kennedys and the Buckleys.

PROFILE:
THE KENNEDYS AND THE BUCKLEYS

In the original *Real Lace*, Stephen Birmingham lavished a good bit of copy on the Kennedys, but with an intent to portray them as nouveau riche parvenus who were not quite the social equal of what he called the First Irish Families (FIFs). In one passage he quotes the then Senator John F. Kennedy, who was briefly engaged to Charlotte McDonnell, riding in an elevator at the Waldorf-Astoria to a Catholic function with Anna Murray McDonnell and asking her, "Do you know I almost married your daughter?"

"Yes," she responded evenly. "And I'm so glad you didn't."

There is a historical problem with this version. Yes, Uncle Tom Murray regarded Jack Kennedy as a "moral roustabout" and his father as "a crook and thorough bounder." However, the truth is that the first Kennedys to arrive in America, Patrick Kennedy and Bridget Murphy, actually *preceded* many of the *Real Lace* families when they landed in 1849. Their son, P.J., entered business and politics, and he and his wife, Mary Hickey, were the parents of the "Founding Father," Joseph P. Kennedy, who married Rose Fitzgerald and launched their famous line, which others have called "America's Royal Family."

It was thus wonderfully ironic when *Real Lace* was reissued as an e-book by Open Road Media that the cover photograph was a montage of the Kennedys, not the Murrays or McDonnells or Ryans or Bradys. But from a marketing point of view it made perfect sense, given the family's celebrity, its longstanding tradition of public service, and also its ongoing talent for attracting notoriety.

Although New York governor Al Smith, the first Irish Catholic to run for president, lost to Herbert Hoover in 1928, in large part brought down by the anti-Catholic Ku Klux Klan, Smith, the "Happy Warrior," deserves credit for laying the foundation of what would become

Franklin Delano Roosevelt's New Deal coalition. During the 1932 presidential election, Joe Kennedy worked tirelessly for FDR and contributed generously to the campaign war chest. After Prohibition ended in 1933, Kennedy traveled with FDR's son James to Scotland to secure liquor distribution rights that would make both of them rich. Roosevelt rewarded him by naming him head of the Securities and Exchange Commission, perhaps in part because of Kennedy's trading skill in profiting from the Great Crash of 1929. Despite their close working relationship, Roosevelt and Kennedy were wary of each other. Given his Irish background, Kennedy was reluctant to commit American youth to fight a war in Europe for the British, and his posture earned him the reputation of an isolationist, which he had to defend even as he was named ambassador to the Court of Saint James. His controversial remark, "Democracy is finished in Britain, and may be here," during the Battle of Britain in 1940 resulted in his resignation under pressure as ambassador.

The death of Joe Jr., whose plane exploded over Suffolk in 1944 as part of Operation Anvil, on whom his father had pinned his hopes for the next generation, was a cruel blow, as was, in 1948, the death of his daughter, Kathleen Kennedy Cavendish, Marchioness of Hartington, also in a plane crash, this time over France. A further sadness in the 1940s was Joseph P. Kennedy's decision to lobotomize his daughter Rosemary in hopes it would stabilize her mood swings and erratic behavior. The radical operation on the brain left her unable to walk or speak very intelligibly, and she remained institutionalized the rest of her life. According to some reports, she would shrink from her mother when Rose visited, apparently blaming her for permitting the operation.

But the family's influence grew through the 1950s after Jack Kennedy entered the Senate, married the glamorous Jacqueline Bouvier, and successfully ran for president against Richard Nixon in 1960. One of his brothers, Robert, became his attorney general, and his younger brother, Ted, was elected senator from Massachusetts in Jack's place in 1962 at the age of thirty, the minimum age required by the Constitution of the United States.

Tragedy had continued to dog the family. In 1955 George and Ann Skakel, Ethel Kennedy's parents, were killed in a plane crash in Oklahoma. The following year Jacqueline Bouvier Kennedy gave birth to a stillborn daughter, Arabella. And in 1958, prefiguring a later scandal, fifteen-year-old Francis Medaille, a son of Ethel's cousin Betty Skakel Medaille, strangled and then pushed seven-year-old Kathleen Hegmann to her death from their New York apartment building.

On August 9, 1963, Patrick Bouvier Kennedy died two days after his premature birth. And three months later, on November 22, 1963, Lee Harvey Oswald assassinated the president in Dallas, plunging the nation into an extended period of mourning.

The following June, Teddy Kennedy was pulled from the wreckage of a plane crash by his fellow senator, Birch E. Bayh, and spent weeks recovering from a broken back, a punctured lung, broken ribs, and internal bleeding. One of his aides and the pilot were killed, and Kennedy walked with a lopsided gait ever afterwards.

After Senator Eugene McCarthy narrowly lost to Lyndon Johnson in the 1968 New Hampshire primary, Robert Kennedy, by now a U.S. senator from New York, entered the presidential race as well. Johnson announced he would not run again, and Kennedy ran strongly against McCarthy and Vice President Hubert Humphrey. Following his victory speech after winning the crucial California primary on June 5, 1968, Kennedy exited the celebration through the Ambassador Hotel kitchen, where Palestinian Sirhan Sirhan awaited and assassinated him.

Finally, to round out the terrible Kennedy tragedies of the 1960s, late on the night of July 18, 1969, after leaving a party, Teddy Kennedy drove his car off a bridge on Chappaquiddick Island. Kennedy extricated himself and escaped, but his young colleague, Mary Jo Kopechne, was drowned. By his account, Kennedy dove back into the water seven times to try to save Kopechne, but he did not report the accident to the police until the following day, by which time the body had been found.

Kennedy pleaded guilty to leaving the scene of an accident and on national television called his failure to report the accident immediately "indefensible," though he denied that alcohol had played any part in the car careening off the bridge. The Kennedys paid the Kopechne family hush money, and a grand jury chose not to indict. Kennedy asked the voters of Massachusetts to advise him on whether he should remain in office, and, receiving an outpouring of support, decided to do so.

In November of that year, Joseph P. Kennedy, who had been confined to a wheelchair and unable to speak since a disabling stroke in 1961, died at eighty-two.

The Kennedy "Curse," if such it was, skipped to the next generation in the 1970s. In August of 1973 Joseph P. Kennedy II, oldest son of Bobby and Ethel, was the driver of a car that crashed and left his passenger, Pam Kelley, paralyzed. Later that year, in November, Ted Kennedy Jr. had his right leg amputated due to bone cancer. In early 1974 Athalia Lindsley, a former fiancée of Joseph P. Kennedy Jr., was brutally murdered on the front steps of her home in St. Augustine, Florida, a crime that remains unsolved. On October 30, 1975, Martha Moxley was bludgeoned to death with a golf club. Almost twenty years later, in 2002, Kennedy cousin Michael Skakel was convicted of her murder. He was granted a new trial in 2013 and was released on bail.

Teddy Kennedy: A Flawed but Dedicated Public Servant

The youngest of the nine Kennedy children, and, at best, an indifferent student, Edward Moore Kennedy could not have anticipated the role that destiny would thrust upon him. He worshipped his maternal grandfather, John F. "Honey Fitz" Fitzgerald, a former Boston mayor and U.S. congressman, who may have supplied the early inspiration for his entry into politics, although his father and brothers undoubtedly played a part as well.

Teddy Kennedy came to Portsmouth Priory School briefly and, apparently, not very happily during the years that his brother Bob was a student there. His mother, Rose Fitzgerald Kennedy, was a longtime oblate of the monastery. Thus, after the senator's death, it was interesting to note an item in connection with the announcement that the Kennedy Compound in Hyannisport would become a museum: "Rose wanted to turn the place over to the Benedictine monks before she died," Benedict

Fitzgerald, the late Kennedy matriarch's personal attorney, told author Ed Klein for his book *Ted Kennedy: The Dream That Never Died.* "I drew up the legal papers for her on my front porch. But when Ted found out about it, he ripped the thing in half. There was no way he was going to have the place turned into a monastery."

Instead, the Kennedy Compound will be converted into an educational center and museum as a tribute to the late senator Edward Kennedy.

Edward Kennedy played football at his next school, Milton Academy, where his headmaster described him as "absolutely fearless. He would have tackled an express train to New York if you asked . . . he loved contact sports." He played tennis as well and, during summers, began his lifelong love of sailing, which would become an increasing consolation to him in the latter half of his life.

Kennedy played football at Harvard, too, but was caught cheating when he asked a friend to take his Spanish examination for him and expelled. He entered the army for a four-year hitch, which was reduced to two years when his father intervened, and was discharged as a private first class after twenty-one months. Kennedy reentered Harvard in the summer of 1953 and improved his study habits. His gregarious personality helped win him membership in the Owl final club as well as Hasty Pudding, the theatrical club, where he would begin to burnish his gift for oratory. He played football and caught a pass to score the only touchdown in Harvard's 21–7 loss to Yale his senior year. He graduated with an A.B. in history in 1956, barely making the top half of his class.

His law school career at University of Virginia followed a similar arc. Kennedy got mostly C's, said he had to study four times as hard as others, and was charged with reckless driving and driving without a license. He married Joan Bennett in 1958 and was admitted to the Massachusetts Bar in 1959.

After working on his brother's election, Ted won a special election to fill Jack's seat, defeating George Cabot Lodge II, and began his forty-seven-year tenure in the U.S. Senate, eventually becoming known as "the Lion of the Senate." "If your name was Edward Moore instead of

Edward Moore Kennedy," his opponent Edward McCormack told him during a debate, "your candidacy would be a joke." But he won easily.

He and his brother Robert worked hard to achieve immigration reform with the Immigration Act of 1965, which ended the system of national quotas that had traditionally favored Europeans. Ironically, this would prove detrimental to the Irish, and in later years he worked to refine this defect.

Teddy and Joan had three children—Kara, born 1960, Ted Jr., born 1961, and Patrick, born 1967. By the late 1960s, however, their marriage was strained by Ted's womanizing and Joan's struggle with alcoholism. I have a memory of seeing him walk into the breakfast room of the Heart of Palm Hotel after Sunday morning mass in about 1966, resplendently handsome in a dark suit. He cast his eyes around looking for someone he could not find and left quickly.

In his long career in the Senate, Kennedy championed many progressive causes including voting rights, immigration reform, and the creation of the National Teacher Corps. His view of the Vietnam War went from hawk to dove, especially after Gene McCarthy's challenge to LBJ provided an opening for Bobby Kennedy to launch his presidential campaign, which Ted worked hard and effectively to support. He then had to endure the nearly unbearable grief of seeing another brother shot down and killed.

In the 1970s Kennedy's strong opposition to abortion waned, and he became an increasingly ardent advocate of a woman's right to choose. He also supported national health insurance and school busing. In September of 1974 he made a surprise appearance at an anti-busing rally in Boston to plead for peaceful dialogue. He was bombarded with tomatoes and eggs hurled by the angry, mostly white crowd and retreated.

While talks of a Kennedy presidential candidacy were always in the air, the memories of Chappaquiddick were still strong and Teddy's sense of obligation to his family was deeply felt. He won reelection to the Senate in 1976. Teddy's prominence in Washington declined when Jimmy Carter became president, and Carter and he never forged a close relationship. Moreover, Kennedy and his wife Joan officially separated in 1977.

Kennedy's and Carter's different approaches to a national health plan caused a rupture between the two, and in August of 1979, buttressed by polls showing him a clear winner, Kennedy decided to challenge Carter for the 1980 Democratic presidential nomination. For a prominent senator to challenge a sitting president of his own party was an extraordinary, if not unprecedented, act, and once again called Kennedy's judgment and prudence into question. Why could he not have waited?

Instead, Kennedy launched into the campaign, aggressively courting labor unions and the rest of the old Kennedy political machine. Campaign disorganization, a less than persuasive interview on the CBS network with Roger Mudd on Chappaquiddick, and lingering questions about his personal life detracted from his message. At a St. Patrick's Day parade in Chicago, hecklers yelled, "Where's Mary Jo?" and in the next day's Illinois primary, Carter trounced him, winning 155 of 169 delegates. Thus, the very state that had proven decisive in JFK's victory over Nixon in 1960 (Mayor Daley had held back the count of the Cook County votes until after the other statewide returns had come in, and Papa Joe Kennedy was reputed to say, "Don't buy one more vote than necessary; I'll be damned if I'm going to pay for a landslide!") had left him in a mathematically impossible position to secure the nomination. Kennedy soldiered on nevertheless and won ten primaries to Carter's twenty-four. At the convention he launched a last-ditch effort to change the convention rules and free delegates from being bound by primary results. It failed the first night, and Kennedy withdrew. His convention speech ended with the poignant words: "For me, a few hours ago this campaign came to an end. For all of those whose cares have been our concern, the work goes on, the cause endures, the hope still lives, and the dream shall never die."

Kennedy's support of Carter during the election campaign that fall against Ronald Reagan was lukewarm, and Carter bitterly blamed him for his defeat in November. For Kennedy the unexpected loss of the Senate meant that he was in the minority for the first time in his career. He became the ranking member of the Labor and Public Welfare Committee, reaffirmed his commitment to liberal causes, and became a highly visible opponent of Reagan foreign policy, opposing interventions in Central America and weapons systems including the B-1 bomber, MX missile, and the Strategic Defense ("Star Wars") Initiative. In 1981 he and Joan announced they were getting a divorce.

In the ensuing years Kennedy's personal life again came into question as frequent episodes surfaced of heavy drinking and womanizing. He and Senator Chris Dodd of Connecticut were twice involved in 1985 incidents in Washington restaurants, one of which involved forcing themselves on and groping a shocked waitress. In 1987 Kennedy and a young female lobbyist were the subject of newspaper articles when they were surprised in the back room of a restaurant partially undressed.

In 1984 and 1988 Kennedy again considered but decided against running for president. "The presidency is not my ultimate goal," he said. "Public service is."

His ferocious, even vicious, opposition to Robert Bork's nomination to the Supreme Court in 1987 changed the way Washington worked. Controversial nominations now became bitterly contentious, and efforts to conciliate across the aisle were less and less successful. Sadly for our democracy, this trend has continued into the present day.

Kennedy's housing legislation in the late 1980s and Americans with Disabilities Act of 1990 (especially important to him given his sister Rosemary's and son Ted's handicaps) were important achievements, as was the Civil Rights Act of 1991.

Nonetheless, Kennedy's personal life diminished his reputation. He was photographed by European paparazzi having sex on a motorboat in 1989. His presence with William Kennedy Smith in Palm Beach nightclubs and at the Kennedy compound when Smith was accused of rape, though found innocent, was the subject of innuendo about an aging, hard-drinking Irish womanizer. *Newsweek* said Kennedy was "the living symbol of the family flaws." His reputation prevented him from being as effective as others hoped he would be in opposing Clarence Thomas's nomination to the Supreme Court.

In 1991 Kennedy met Victoria Reggie, a Washington lawyer, and they began dating. In an unusual mea culpa at the JFK School of Government that fall, Kennedy said:

I am painfully aware that the criticism directed at me in recent months involves far more than disagreements with my positions. It involves the disappointment of friends and many others who rely on me to fight the good fight. To them I say, I recognize my own shortcomings—the faults in the conduct of my private life. I realize that I alone am responsible for them, and I am the one who must confront them.

Kennedy and Reggie were married in 1992, and she helped usher in a new period of stability and tranquility to his private life.

A disappointment of the early Clinton years was Kennedy's enthusiastic support for Hillary Rodham Clinton's health care plan and its signal failure.

In 1994, in the first sign that the Kennedy fortune was not infinite, Ted took out a second mortgage on his Virginia home in order to supply badly needed funds in his campaign against a young challenger, the telegenic young businessman Mitt Romney.

Rose Kennedy died in 1995 at the age of 104 after many years of being out of the public eye. The passing of this matriarch of the family dynasty and her lifelong example of indomitable faith caused Kennedy to recollect himself spiritually, and he began attending Mass more frequently again.

He also recommitted himself to the Irish peace process, a cause that he had been involved in since 1970. In January 1998 he traveled to Ireland and spoke directly with nationalists and unionists, urging them to come to terms so that both their communities could flourish. In April of that year, the Northern Ireland Peace was finally signed.

With the death of John F. Kennedy Jr. and his wife Carolyn Bessette in a plane crash off Martha's Vineyard in 1999, Teddy's role as the family patriarch was reinforced, and he conscientiously carried on that role with his Kennedy, Shriver, Lawford, and Smith nieces and nephews.

In his later years Kennedy exerted his influence by endorsing Barack Obama for president in 2008 despite pleas from both Clintons not to do so. They were enraged and embittered by what they viewed as a betrayal, but Kennedy proclaimed that it was "time again for a new generation of leadership." In return, Obama made universal health care a priority of his administration, and he kept his word.

On May 27, 2008, Kennedy suffered a seizure at the Kennedy compound in Hyannisport and was diagnosed with a malignant glioma, a kind of cancerous brain tumor. Initially told the cancer was inoperable, he consulted experts and was operated on at Duke University Medical Center, subsequently receiving intensive chemo and radiation therapy. Although weakened and his balance affected, he made an appearance in the Senate that summer to break a Republican filibuster and electrified the Democratic National Convention that summer. He pledged to be present at President Obama's inauguration in January of 2009, but suffered a seizure at the lunch at the Capitol afterwards. Many honors came to him in the coming months, and he was able to throw the ceremonial first pitch at Fenway Park for the Boston Red Sox season opener that April, as his grandfather and inspiration, "Honey Fitz," had done to open the park in 1912.

His health deteriorated. In July 2009, Kennedy was awarded the Presidential Medal of Freedom by President Obama. Sadly, he was too sick to attend the ceremony, nor could he attend the public funeral of his sister, Eunice Kennedy Shriver, when she died at the age of eighty-eight that August. Kennedy died fifteen months after his original diagnosis, on August 25, 2009. His body lay in repose at the John F. Kennedy Library in Boston, and on August 29 his funeral mass was celebrated at Our Lady of Perpetual Help Basilica in Boston. Four former presidents attended, and President Obama delivered the eulogy. He was buried at Arlington National Cemetery, near his brothers Jack and Bobby.

During his long Senate career Teddy Kennedy shepherded more than three hundred of his bills into law. For all of his faults and shortcomings, he was a giant of public service, which decades before he had proclaimed his true vocation.

The *New York Times* obituarist wrote:

He was a Rabelaisian figure in the Senate and in life, instantly recognizable by his shock of white hair, his florid, oversize face, his booming

Boston brogue, his powerful but pained stride. He was a celebrity,
sometimes a self-parody, an implacable foe, a man of large faith and
large flaws, a melancholy character who persevered, drank deeply and
sang loudly. He was a Kennedy.

Other Family

Edward M. Kennedy was not the only member of his family to find himself in the uncomfortable spotlight as the 1980s continued.

In 1984 David Kennedy, a son of Bobby and Ethel, died of a cocaine overdose in a room at the Breakers Hotel in Palm Beach.

In April of 1991 William Kennedy Smith, a son of Stephen Smith and Jean Kennedy Smith, was arrested and charged with the rape of a young woman at the Kennedy estate in Palm Beach. Smith had spent the earlier part of the evening drinking with his Uncle Ted and cousin Patrick Kennedy in night spots around town. In addition to the victim, a relative of the O'Neill General Tire family, another young woman present and three others were willing to testify that Smith had also forced himself upon them in the late 1990s, but they had not reported the incidents. Their testimony was disallowed. Smith was acquitted of all charges.

Smith went on to earn his medical degree at Georgetown, to marry, and to carry out impressive work with the victims of land mines in several countries. However, sexual assault charges filed by female colleagues have bedeviled Dr. Smith on at least two further occasions, one of which he settled out of court.

Jacqueline Kennedy Onassis led a private life in New York working as an editor at Doubleday and was active in municipal arts causes such as the preservation of Grand Central Terminal when it was threatened by developers. In November of 1993 she fell from a horse while fox hunting in Middleburg, Virginia, and was unconscious for an hour. An inflamed lymph gland was detected. The following January she was diagnosed with non-Hodgkin's lymphoma, a blood disease. Though doctors were initially optimistic, the cancer proved aggressive. She returned home from the hospital (where at one point former president Nixon was also being treated) in May of 1994, a crowd of well-wishers greeting her outside her

Fifth Avenue apartment, and died peacefully the following night. Her funeral mass was celebrated at the Church of St. Ignatius Loyola, where she had been baptized, and her estate was valued at forty-two million dollars. Her companion of her last twenty years, mining magnate Maurice Tempelsman, is said to have increased the value of her estate many times for her daughter Caroline's benefit.

On New Year's Eve of 1997, Michael LeMoyne Kennedy, another son of Robert and Ethel Kennedy, died in a skiing accident in Aspen, Colorado. Earlier that year he had been suspected of statutory rape after his affair with a sixteen-year-old babysitter was alleged to have started when she was just fourteen.

Perhaps most tragically, on July 16, 1999, John F. Kennedy Jr. died when his plane crashed into the Atlantic Ocean under foggy conditions. His wife and sister-in-law were also on board and killed. Pilot error and "spatial disorientation" were cited in the accident. Little "John John," who had saluted his father's coffin as it passed in 1963, was the owner and publisher of *George* magazine. His wife and he were said to be in a turbulent marriage, and there were rumors of cocaine abuse as well.

In September 2011 Kara Kennedy Allen died of a heart attack while exercising in a Washington health club. She had suffered, but recovered from, lung cancer nine years earlier. She was a television and film producer until her early death.

On May 16, 2012, Mary Richardson Kennedy, second wife of Robert Kennedy Jr., hanged herself on the grounds of her home in Bedford, New York. She was said to be depressed, in part because of the details of Bobby's multiple affairs she had discovered in her husband's diaries.

In July of 2012 Kerry Kennedy, another child of Bobby and Ethel, sideswiped a tractor trailer on Interstate 684 while under the influence of a sleeping pill that she had mistaken for her thyroid medication. She was acquitted on all charges. Kerry Kennedy is the former wife of Governor Andrew Cuomo of New York. Their marriage was ended by the discovery of an affair between Kennedy and McDonald's franchise heir and society polo player Bruce Colley, whose own mother was found murdered in her North Salem estate in late 2015.

Bishop Tobin of Providence publicly called another Kennedy, Representative Patrick Kennedy of Rhode Island, to "conversion and repentance" in 2009 after the congressman sided with abortion advocates in voting against the Stupak amendment, which bars the use of federal funds in paying for most abortions in the House's health care reform legislation. Following the vote Bishop Tobin issued a public letter to Representative Kennedy in which he ripped the congressman's statement that "the fact I disagree with the hierarchy on some issues does not make me any less of a Catholic."

"That sentence certainly caught my attention and deserves a public response, lest it go unchallenged and lead others to believe it is true," wrote Bishop Tobin. "And it raises an important question: 'What does it mean to be a Catholic?' Opposition to abortion, of course, is not based on a sectarian doctrine accepted only by the Catholic Church. 'Thou shalt not kill' is a moral imperative written into Mosaic law and advanced separately by Hippocrates long before the Church was established on earth."

After the letter was published in the November 12 edition of Bishop Tobin's diocesan newspaper, he and Representative Kennedy postponed a meeting they had scheduled to discuss the subject.

Patrick Kennedy served as U.S. representative for Rhode Island's First Congressional District from 1995 until 2011. When he retired in 2011, it was the first time since 1947 that there were no members of the Kennedy family in national public office. He has been an advocate for health care while also battling drug and alcohol abuse. After crashing his car into a police barricade on Capitol Hill at 2:45 a.m. on May 4, 2006, he also sought treatment for OxyContin addiction at Mayo Clinic. In 2009 he checked into another facility and said that his recovery was a "lifelong process." He now resides in Brigantine, New Jersey, with his wife, Amy, and three children.

Ted Kennedy Jr. is a lawyer and member of the Connecticut State Senate. His son, Edward M. Kennedy III, a student at Choate Rosemary Hall, at age eleven announced his intention to run for the U.S. Senate in Massachusetts one day.

Patricia Kennedy Lawford divorced Peter Lawford, moved to New York, and died in 2006. She, too, battled alcoholism and was increasingly private in later years. She had four children.

Christopher Lawford has been an author and actor. He began abusing drugs at Middlesex School and contracted hepatitis C. After his cousin David's death in 1984, however, he sought help and has been sober since. He and his first wife had three children. He remarried in 2014 in Hawaii to Mercedes Miller, a yoga teacher. He left the Catholic Church after his uncle Bobby was killed in 1968 and, while praising his grandmother's faith, has said, "That's just not something that speaks to me. I have my own tradition. I go to an ashram. I meditate. I chant. I do all that kind of stuff." He has appeared in more than twenty films and is the author of a book, *Symptoms of Withdrawal: Memoir of Snapshots and Redemption*. Christopher's sister, Sydney, a sometime model and marketing executive, is married to television producer Peter McKelvey. They and their family now live in Washington, D.C. Victoria Lawford married Robert Pender Jr., and they have three children. Robin Lawford is a marine biologist.

Jean Kennedy Smith, the last surviving of the Kennedy siblings, was named American ambassador to Ireland by President Clinton and served from 1993 to 1998. She has also been an advocate for the arts. In addition to Dr. William Kennedy Smith, she has a son, Stephen, a former assistant district attorney in the Bronx who now works for the Conflict Management Group. She also has two daughters: Amanda, a doctor, and the author of *Hostage to Fortune: The Letters of Joseph P. Kennedy*; and Kym Maria, a travel agent in New York.

Ethel Kennedy is now eighty-nine years old. Her children have been active but also troubled. Her eldest child, Kathleen, was lieutenant governor of Maryland from 1995 to 2003 and ran unsuccessfully for governor in 2003. Joseph P. Kennedy II served in the U. S. House of Representatives from 1987 to 1999 and founded the Citizens' Energy Corporation to provide discounted heating oil to low-income families. He married Sheila Rauch in 1979. They had twin sons, Matt and Joe, and were legally divorced in 1991. However, when Joseph Kennedy asked the Archdiocese of Boston for an annulment of this marriage so he could remarry Beth Kelly in the church, Joe's ex-wife, Sheila, an Episcopalian, opposed it. When she found out the annulment had been provisionally granted without her knowledge, Sheila Rauch wrote a book, *Shattered Faith: A Woman's Struggle to Stop the Church from Annulling Her Marriage*. Rauch appealed directly to the Holy See, and the original decision was overturned by the highest appellate tribunal of the Roman Catholic Church, the Roman Rota, in 2005. However, Rauch was not informed of this decision until 2007.

Robert Kennedy Jr., born in 1954, is an attorney specializing in environmental law and activism and president of the board of Riverkeeper Alliance, dedicated to protecting waterways worldwide. He is also the author of five books. Like so many others in his family, Kennedy has struggled with drug abuse. In 1984 he was fired from the New York District Attorney's office for it. Earlier he had been charged with heroin possession in South Dakota. He was sentenced to community service after rehab, which he performed on behalf of Riverkeeper, his introduction to the organization. He has been married three times, most recently in 2014 to actress Cheryl Hines, and now lives in Malibu. He has two children from his first marriage to Emily Black, one of whom, Kick, was the maid of honor to Christopher Buckley's daughter, Cat, at her wedding at Chelsea Piers in May of 2016. He also has four children from his marriage to the late Mary Richardson Kennedy. On May 12, 2010, Kennedy filed for divorce from Mary. Three days later she was charged with drunk driving. The following day Mary was found dead at her Mount Kisco home. Deeply distressed and depressed by Bobby's multiple infidelities and divorce action, she had hanged herself. In September of 2013 the *New York Post* released excerpts from Robert Kennedy Jr.'s diary from 2001, in which he detailed multiple affairs and outspoken opinions about public figures. Kennedy did not dispute the authenticity of the diary but insisted it had been illegally stolen from him.

Courtney Kennedy Hill worked at Children's Television Workshop and was formerly a representative for the United Nations AIDS Foundation. She has been married twice and legally separated since 2006. She has a daughter from her second marriage named Saoirse Hill and lives in Bethesda, Maryland.

Christopher Kennedy is chairman of Joseph P. Kennedy Enterprises, former chairman of the board of trustees of the University of Illinois, and the former president of Merchandise Mart properties, the commercial real estate entity built and controlled by his grandfather. He lives in Chicago and has four children with his wife of thirty years, Sheila.

Max Kennedy is a lawyer and the author of two books, one of which is *Making Gentle the Life of This World: The Vision of Robert F. Kennedy and the Words That Inspired Him*. He lives in New York with his wife Victoria and three children.

Douglas Harriman Kennedy, named in honor of Averell Harriman, is a journalist who has long worked at Fox News. He is married to Molly Stark and has five children.

Rory Kennedy is a documentary filmmaker with a particular interest in social issues. In 2011 she produced and directed *Ethel*, about her mother, and in 2014 *Last Days in Vietnam*. Both premiered at the Sundance Film Festival. She is married to Mark Bailey and has three children. They live in Brooklyn but in 2013, like Bobby Jr., purchased a home in Malibu.

Eunice Kennedy Shriver, who died in 2009, married Sargent Shriver, of an old Maryland Catholic family, who became John F. Kennedy's first director of the Peace Corps. In 1962 Eunice founded Camp Shriver on their Maryland farm, which in time evolved into the Special Olympics. She had a lifelong devotion to children's health and disability and was a fiercely pro-life Democrat.

Her son Bobby Shriver is an attorney, a former investor in the Baltimore Orioles, and the producer of several television programs and films. He has been chairman of the California State Parks and Recreation Commission and a member of the Santa Monica City Council. He lost his 2014 campaign to become Los Angeles county supervisor. He married Malissa Feruzzi in 2005, and they have two children.

Maria Shriver is an American television journalist, author, and former first lady of California. Tom Brokaw introduced her to Austrian bodybuilder and actor Arnold Schwarzenegger in 1977, and they married in 1986. They have four children. They separated in 2011, and two days later Schwarzenegger admitted he had fathered a child with a longtime household employee, Mildred Baena. Shriver filed for divorce two months later. She is the author of six books, several of which have been bestsellers.

Tim Shriver is the chairman of the Special Olympics. A longtime educator with an interest in disabilities, he is married to Linda Potter and has five children. They live in Chevy Chase, Maryland.

Mark Shriver was a member of the Maryland House of Delegates from 1995 to 2003 and is now the senior vice president of strategic initiatives at Save the Children. He is married with two children.

Anthony Shriver heads Best Buddies International, which offers programs for adults and children with disabilities. He is married to Alina Mojica. They live in Miami and have five children.

While all of the Kennedy children have shown an interest in public service, Caroline Kennedy came to it later than some, but has embraced it as fully as any. A sometimes shy girl whose life was upended by her father's death, she returned to New York and attended Brearley and Convent of the Sacred Heart before going to boarding school at Concord Academy. After completing the Sotheby's art course in London in 1975–76, she matriculated at Radcliffe College and won her A.B. in 1980. She then worked at the Metropolitan Museum of Art in its film and television department, where she met her future husband, Edward Schlossberg. They married in 1986. She won her law degree from Columbia in 1988, finishing in the top 10 percent of her class. Caroline and Ed have three children—Rose, Tatiana, and Jack. Rose graduated from Harvard in 2010 and took a master's from the Tisch School at NYU in 2013. She works as a videographer and in 2016 created, co-produced, and starred in a Web series called *End Times Girls Club*. Tatiana has worked at the *New York Times* as a reporter. Jack graduated from Yale in 2015, wrote for the Yale *Daily News*, and has said he is interested in a career in politics.

Caroline has written, co-written, or edited eight books, including several collections of poetry, one of which was a compilation of her mother's favorites and the other an anthology of children's poems.

Although she preserved her family's privacy admirably while her children grew up and in the aftermath of John Jr.'s tragic death, Caroline took a more public posture in January of 2008 when she published an op-ed in the *New York Times* endorsing Barack Obama, called "A President Like My Father." In December 2008 Kennedy expressed interest in filling the Senate seat being vacated by Hillary Clinton, who had been appointed secretary of state, but after being widely criticized for inexperience and inability to articulate her views effectively, she withdrew from consideration in January of 2009. Governor Paterson then announced his selection of Rep. Kirsten Gillibrand to fill the Senate seat.

In July of 2013 President Obama announced Caroline Kennedy as his nominee to be United States Ambassador to Japan. She was confirmed by unanimous consent and sworn in by Secretary of State Kerry on November 12. She has been a conscientious and popular envoy there, and given her lifelong record of personal rectitude and exemplary behavior, it will be interesting to see if there will be further chapters ahead in her life of public service.

The Buckleys

Whereas the Kennedys sought a public life, and many of them public office, in the Buckley family it was initially William F. Buckley Jr. who pursued a public life in galvanizing and guiding the conservative cause from the mid-1950s until his death in 2008. He did run, rather tongue in cheek, for mayor of New York in 1965. When asked what he would do upon being elected, he famously answered, "Demand a recount." He also spent several months as a U.S. observer at the United Nations, but when, in 1981, newly elected president Ronald Reagan offered him the coveted ambassadorship to the Court of Saint James in London, Buckley declined. Bill Buckley preferred to retain his independence and autonomy in the public arena via his magazine, *National Review*; his television show, *Firing Line*; his syndicated newspaper column; his speeches; and his more than fifty books.

His older brother, James Lane Buckley, was born in 1923, graduated from Yale in 1943, entered the navy, and was discharged as a lieutenant in 1946. After graduating from Yale Law School in 1950, he spent his early career furthering the family's oil interests as a vice president and director at its holding company, Catawba. Thereupon he became more and more drawn to public service, initially through his brother Bill's mayoral campaign in 1965.

In 1968 James Buckley ran for the United States Senate from New York against liberal Republican Jacob K. Javits and lost. In 1970 he ran on the Conservative Party line, facing liberal Republican Charles Goodell (father of the present NFL commissioner, Roger Goodell) and Democrat Richard Ottinger. When the liberal vote split, Buckley won an upset victory with only 39 percent of the vote.

In the Senate he proposed the Human Life Amendment in 1974, which defined the word "person" in the Fourteenth Amendment to include the term "embryo." His enacted legislation includes the Family Educational Rights and Privacy Act and the Protection of Pupils Rights Act. In the spring of 1974, as the Watergate scandal grew, Buckley was the first Republican to call on President Nixon to resign. Nixon resisted but ultimately did resign on August 9, 1974.

In his 1976 reelection bid, Buckley at first looked well positioned in facing liberal representative Bella Abzug of Manhattan. But when Daniel Patrick Moynihan, the United States ambassador to the U.N., made a late entrance into the Democratic primary and defeated Abzug, Buckley could no longer rely on getting moderate votes. In an earnest yet good-humored campaign marked by Buckley in their first debate addressing Moynihan as "Professor," Pat Moynihan chortled, "There! Now let the mudslinging begin." He defeated Buckley 54 percent to 45 percent.

In the first Reagan administration, James Buckley served as undersecretary of state for security assistance, favoring aid to Pakistan to blunt the Russian invasion of Afghanistan. He then served as president of Radio Free Europe and Radio Liberty from 1982 to 1985. In 1985 he was appointed by President Reagan to the United States Court of Appeals for the District of Columbia Circuit. He became a senior, or semiretired, judge of that court in 1996, and his place was taken by John Roberts, now chief justice of the United States.

Although modest and mild-mannered in person, he has continued to espouse a consistent, firm conservative philosophy, warning of the dangers of arrogating powers to the federal government properly reserved by the Constitution to the states and advocating the principle of subsidiarity, that is, letting issues and disputes be decided at the local level rather than by a centralized government far removed from the people most affected.

At ninety-two, a widower who faithfully attended his wife Anne in her years of decline after a tragic car accident (she died in 2011), he remains mentally and physically vigorous and deeply engaged in the issues he has championed throughout his long public life. In 2010 he published his third book, *Freedom at Risk: Reflections on Politics, Liberty and the State.*

James Buckley remains notable for being the only American to serve at the highest levels of all three branches of government—executive, legislative, and judicial.

After his death in 2008, the first conference on Bill Buckley was held at Portsmouth Abbey in the summer of 2009. *The Catholic William F. Buckley Jr.* focused on a crucial aspect of Buckley's life and thought, which had been underreported in the mainstream media.

Former presidential speechwriter Clark Judge called Buckley's greatest creative act the introduction of a Catholic sensibility into the main currents of American political thought.

He showed the acuity of his technical understanding of finance in The Unmaking of a Mayor. *The appendix collects the position papers he wrote for his candidacy, including one on New York's fiscal situation. In 1975, when New York went bankrupt, politicians and journalists alike—including, for example, the much-celebrated Ken Auletta, chronicler of the bankruptcy—insisted that no one could have predicted the crisis. They conveniently forgot—if they had ever bothered to know—that Bill Buckley had diagnosed its causes and forecast its coming a decade earlier.*

Bill had read Hayek, von Mises and Friedman. Their writings influenced his commentaries long before they were widely known within the American intelligentsia.

To them, Bill added a moral understanding of markets. He argued that the free market was best for achieving social justice. He

challenged the notion—popular again today—that government pro-
vides a wider and fairer distribution of wealth and a more humane
material standard of living. He noted that market-oriented countries
did much better on all these scales than socialist ones and that the freer
a country's markets the more socially just its economy.

Clark Judge concluded his remarks: "Through the application of Catholic moral sensibility and Catholic styles of discourse, his teaching clarified during pivotal decades the political thought of the United States—and, I believe, will continue to clarify that thought for as long as there is a United States."

At the same conference, James Buckley provided insight into his family's faith. His grandfather, John Buckley, had emigrated from Canada to Texas and become sheriff of Duval County. (There is a history of Irishmen in Texas going back to Hugh O'Conor, known as "Capitan Colorado" for his red beard, who was governor from 1767 to 1770.) The original William F. Buckley was John's son and had graduated from the University of Texas with a law degree.

Our parents had an unusual history, unusual at least for Americans.
To begin with, they had actually witnessed religious persecution and
had sacrificed for their faith. At the time of their marriage, my father
("Will" Buckley) had been living in Mexico for a dozen years where
he practiced law and engaged in oil and land development, and their
first home was in the Mexican city of Tampico.

At that time, priests were being executed and the celebration of the
Mass was forbidden by the local authorities. Our mother used to tell us
of receiving telephone calls from friends advising her that a plumber
or a carpenter would be visiting their home at a particular time—code
for the fact that a priest would be going to that house at that time to
say a clandestine mass. And it was in substantial part because of my
father's very public denunciation of the Church's persecution that he
was expelled from Mexico, had his properties confiscated, and, at age

forty, had to begin his life all over again. That, he knew, was the risk of speaking out, but he felt he had to.

But it was my mother who set the spiritual tone in our home. Hers was not an oppressive piety, and she was far more than a daily communicant. She simply radiated her belief in, and dependence on, a caring God whose love she totally and unaffectedly reciprocated. My mother's faith was such an inherent part of her persona that although her obituary in National Review didn't dwell on her spirituality, Bill couldn't avoid allusions to it. And so the obit was peppered with such statements as "There were rules she lived by, chief among them those she understood God to have specified"; "Her anxiety to do the will of God more than ritual"; "Her grief was profound, and she emerged from it through the solvent of prayer, her belief in submission to a divine order"; and "She never complained because, she explained, she could never repay God the favors He had done her, no matter what tribulations she might need to suffer." And our mother had her share of tribulations.

Given my father's sacrifice for his faith, given our mother's example of a life sustained by it, given our love and respect for our parents, it would have been an unseemly act of filial arrogance for Bill to repudiate the beliefs that had permeated and sustained our home. This, I believe, explains the absolute conviction reflected in Bill's statement that he had never, ever, entertained any doubts about his Catholic faith.

Now that nearly a decade has passed since his brother Bill's death, we can perhaps better trace the arc of his protean life and thought.

In 1965 New York City mayoral politics were enlivened by the insurgent candidacy of Conservative Party aspirant William F. Buckley Jr., who believed that the choice between Democrat Abraham D. Beame and Republican John V. Lindsay was a distinction without a difference and that the public was entitled to a forthright voice in favor of financial restraint, reduced crime, and improved education.

In making his case, Buckley combined rhetorical brilliance and frequent wit, the latter of which quality won me over, then a thirteen-year-old nascent newspaper junkie on Long Island. His frequent put-downs of the oracular editorial page of the *New York Times* and his appeals to his debating opponents not to interrupt him, as in, "Could we please have a little more quiet from the zoo over there?" were a welcome departure from the dreariness of conventional campaigns. Bartle Bull, former publisher of the *Village Voice*, remembers with delight a debate during the campaign when Buckley repeatedly mispronounced John Lindsay's name as "Lindley." When asked what his position would be on the all-important issue of fluoridation, Buckley raised his eyebrows and drawled, "I know about as much about fluoridation as Mr. Lindley knows about economics."

So, despite Buckley's failure to win and demand a recount in that election (in the end he won about 10 percent of the vote but, more importantly, respect for positions that had previously not been considered seriously by the mainstream media), you can imagine my delight a year later when I discovered that Bill's son Christopher would become my classmate and, as the years went on, dear friend.

My first interaction with Bill came at a parents' weekend dinner a year or two later when I was the waiter assigned to serve Father Peter's best claret to the Buckley table. As I finished filling his wineglass and began to move on, Bill said, "Not so fast," and, finishing his water, added, "Fill this one too." When I had done that, he held up his coffee cup, and when that was filled, he asked me to follow the same arrangements for Mrs. Buckley. The other parents at the table appeared nonplussed. I, on the other hand, realized immediately that I had just learned a lesson of life-changing proportions. (When I reminded him of this interaction in a birthday note decades later, he responded that, though he did not recall the event, it sounded "inherently credible.")

Over the course of his eighty-two years, Bill taught many lessons, most of them far more profound than the one someone as superficial as I was able to digest that night (on the JV football field, about an hour later, if memory serves).

Upon his death in March 2008, the major media were full of his achievements as an author, editor, TV host, etc., all from the secular point of view to be expected from such organs. It was left to George Weigel of the Ethics and Public Policy Center to state the obvious point that Bill "belonged on any serious list of the five most publicly consequential Catholics in the 20th century."

This was evident in his first book, *God and Man at Yale* (1951), when he wrote: "I believe the duel between Christianity and atheism is the most important in the world. I further believe that the struggle between individualism and collectivism is the same struggle reproduced on another level."

In *Nearer, My God* (1997), Bill wrote of his own Catholic schooling at St. John's, Beaumont, the Jesuit school near Windsor, in England:

I had been, notwithstanding the distance from home, very happy there, and I knew absolutely—about this there was simply no doubt— that I had a deep and permanent involvement with Catholic Christianity. They say about alcoholics that they are never "cured," but I am a senior citizen and my faith has never left me, and I must suppose that Father Sharkey and Father Manning and Father Payne had something to do with it; they and the closeness I felt, every morning, to the mystical things that were taking place on the altar.

In the same book he wrote about visiting Lourdes:

They are in Lourdes because of this palpability of the emanations that gave birth to the shrine. The spiritual tonic is felt. If it were otherwise, the pilgrims would diminish in number; would, by now, have disappeared, as at Delphos, which one visits as a museum, not a shrine. What it is that fetches them is, I think, quite simply stated, namely a reinforced conviction that the Lord God loves His creatures, healthy or infirm; that they—we—must understand the nature of love, which is salvific in its powers; and that, although we are free to attempt to divine God's purpose, we will never succeed in doing so. The reason is that we cannot know (the manifest contradictions are too disturbing) what is the purpose behind particular phenomena and therefore must make do with only the grandest plan of God, which treats with eternal salvation. Our burden is to keep the faith: to do this (the grammar of assent) requires the discipline of submission, some assurance that those who are stricken can, even so, be happy; and that the greatest tonic of all is divine love, which is nourished by human loves, even as human love is nourished by divine love.

And Bill believed that we must respond to divine and human love in our turn, though few can do so with the prodigious discipline and productivity that he did. As he wrote in a speech he gave in 1988:

To fail to experience gratitude when walking through the corridors of the Metropolitan Museum, when listening to the music of Bach or Beethoven, when exercising our freedom to speak, or, as happened to us three weeks ago, to give, or withhold, our assent, is to fail to recognize how much we have received from the great wellsprings of human talent and concern that gave us Shakespeare, Abraham Lincoln, Mark Twain, our parents, our friends. We need a rebirth of gratitude for those who have cared for us, living and, mostly, dead. The high moments of our way of life are their gifts to us. We must remember them in our thoughts and in our prayers; and in our deeds.

Reading Bill was an excellent way to improve vocabulary—from *animadversions*, through *chiliastic*, *saprophytic*, and *tergiversations*, to *viscidity*, it was best to have a dictionary close at hand. If one were confronted with a handwritten note from him (he wrote one to the author of every *National Review* piece in addition to dictating over two hundred letters a week to readers, controversialists, and friends), it was also advisable to have a magnifying glass—even a soothsayer—such was the scale of the illegibility.

At the overflowing memorial mass at St. Patrick's Cathedral in New York on April 4, 2008, Father George Rutler said in his homily:

His indignation at the wrong ways of men was not savage like that of Jonathan Swift, for it was well-tempered and confident of victory.

He fit Newman's definition of a gentleman as one who is "merciful toward the absurd."... Since William's death many people have told how he brought them to belief in God, and there are those who became priests because of him. His wide circle of friends encompassed those of different beliefs, but its width was the measure of his own unfailing confidence, in the Holy, Catholic, Apostolic and Roman Church ... Our friend knew that Communism was worse than a social tyranny because it was a theological heresy. His categories were not right and left but right and wrong. What graces he had to change a century came by his belief in Christ who changed all centuries.

In his eulogy, Henry Kissinger reminisced upon the sailing competition enjoyed each summer for fifteen years on Long Island Sound between Bill and Peter Flanigan. Peter's boat won every race, including the last one, when Bill insisted on skippering it.

Dr. Kissinger also reflected on discussions he and Bill had on the relationship between knowledge and faith, how Bill's brand of conservatism was not concerned with utopias but "the liberation of the human spirit, which is a deeper and more eternal undertaking than causes geared to political timetables." His voice breaking with emotion, Kissinger concluded:

We will forever remember how we were sustained by Bill's special serenity, the culmination of a long and very private quest. The younger generation, especially of his collaborators whom he so cherished, was inspired by the inward peace Bill radiated, which he was too humble and, in a deep sense, too devout to assert except by example. In the solitude of parting, all of us give thanks to a benign Providence that enabled us to walk part of our way with this noble, gentle, and valiant man who was truly touched by the grace of God.

In his own remarks Christopher Buckley noted that the rector of the cathedral had told him that the mass, with magnificent music by Bach (the Second Brandenberg, *Firing Line*'s longtime theme song), Palestrina, Albinoni, and Tomas Luis de Victoria and stirring hymns—Bunyan's

He Who Would Valiant Be, Jerusalem the Golden, and *I Vow to Thee My Country*—would in effect be a dress rehearsal for the papal mass two weeks hence when Benedict XVI would visit New York. "I think that would have pleased him," Christopher added. "Though doubtless he would have preferred it the other way around."

Christopher also recalled that his father was once asked in an interview in *Playboy* magazine (Why did he consent to such an interview? "So as to communicate with my sixteen-year-old son.") what he would want for an epitaph: "I know that my Redeemer liveth."

"Only Pup," Christopher concluded, "could get the Book of Job into a Hugh Hefner publication."

Perhaps the best way to conclude a reflection on his faith is with Bill's own words, delivered on April 4, 1965, to the New York Police Department Holy Name Society communion breakfast, an event that helped propel him into the mayoral election later that year:

Every age in which values are distorted, an age like our own in which truths are thought either not to exist, or as to exist only as quaint curios from the dead past, the wrath of the unruly falls with focus on the symbols of authority, of continuity, of tradition.

It is no accident at all that the police should be despised in an age infatuated with revolution and ideology. It is no surprise that the Catholic Church should in our time have been singled out for the brunt of the organized hatred of the principal agents of revolution— the Church with its unyielding devotion to eternal truths which resist the plastic manipulations of the willful revolutionaries. Who are the enemy? The agencies of order and tradition. The truths of Christianity. The guiding lights of our tradition. The loyalty to our country and to our traditions. The laws that were bequeathed to us, given to us as what T.S. Eliot called "the Democracy of the Dead": These are the enemies of the calls whose restlessness of soul is ultimately a sign of spiritual anemia, of a rootlessness that expressed itself in a resentment of the old values. . . .

You must know that you will be hated for doing your duty, and be reviled by those who misrepresent you. But bear this in mind, that there are the two worlds of which I speak [roughly speaking, the world that makes the newspapers and the world that doesn't], and though the voices of the one sometimes seem so very much noisier than the voices of the other, that other world, the world of sensible men and women, looks on you with pride and gratitude.

Sustained by the implicit gratitude of the people, you are also sustained no doubt during this holy season by the knowledge of the silence with which the Author of all values walked during His own days on earth.

William Francis Buckley Jr. founded *National Review*, wrote fifty-five books and thousands of columns, hosted hundreds of *Firing Line* television shows, and became recognized as the founder of the modern conservative movement. Many of Buckley's early colleagues in writing and work—his brother-in-law, L. Brent Bozell, James McFadden, Erik von Kuehnelt-Leddihn, Wilmoore Kendall, and Russell Kirk, to name but a few—were or became Catholics.

As George Nash wrote in *The Conservative Intellectual Movement in America Since 1945*, "Buckley and his colleagues believed that education, to be worthy of the name, must lead students to the sure knowledge of the permanent truths."

And yet Bill Buckley, though blessed with an impervious faith, was not always predictable in his Catholic views. He resisted the reforms that came out of Vatican II, preferred the Latin Mass, and did not suffer what he considered to be the bishops' foolishness in their pastoral letter on the economy at all gladly. *America* magazine called for his excommunication when he employed Garry Wills's characterization of a papal encyclical on an *NR* cover: *Mater si, Magistra no!* But he also questioned the church's teaching on birth control, early on called for Cardinal Law's resignation, and was the first to confess that he was no theologian.

At the first conference dedicated to his life and thought after Buckley's death, Peter Flanigan reminisced about his sailing friendship with

Buckley, whose nickname amongst his nautical inclined friends was "Captain Crunch."

It is extremely fitting that we are gathered here on the shores of Narragansett Bay, the Mecca of U.S. sailing, and at Portsmouth Abbey, a center of Catholic learning, to celebrate the life of Bill Buckley.

I spent more time with Bill at sea than on land. I was never on one of his ocean-crossings on a large new boat, but we did sail together on small boats—his and mine—from the Bahamas to Newfoundland, from three-week cruises to overnight escapes. From reading his books and articles, many of you know the details of these adventures. But what does not generally come through in these writings is his carefree, almost devil-may-care approach to skippering a boat.

Bill was careful and precise with the written word and serious ideas, but with a boat it was otherwise. No matter the weather, he would let sail. No matter the crisis, he was having fun. He never saw a dock he didn't charge, planning to go into reverse at exactly the right moment, but often miscalculating, which resulted in a fearful "thump." He scorned a GPS or a Loran electronic navigator system, opting instead for celestial navigation with his sextant. After taking a star sight, and doing the required mathematical equation, he would delightfully declare that we were "Oops," in the middle of the Sahara Desert.

All this was, of course, the ever entertaining and amusing Buckley. Serious things were treated seriously, and for Bill, religion was the most serious of all. He publicly proclaimed his belief in the Catholic faith in his books and articles. I recall a long article in the New Yorker *on a typical day in the life of Bill Buckley. He relates how, after a hectic schedule, he falls into bed and, as he has since childhood, says a Rosary. Imagine—praying a Rosary to our lady in The New Yorker. He was an extraordinary public witness.*

Near the end, when the time for the lighthearted, less important things had passed, Bill's faith became ever more important. Always the conservative, he greatly preferred the Latin Mass, and had a priest friend, a former National Review *staffer, celebrate one for him on Saturday evenings. When his emphysema had become so bad that every step was an enormous effort, and when his friends urged him to stay home, he insisted on attending that mass. I recall a Saturday just before he died when he slowly, painfully struggled up the few steps to the chapel, and throughout the service his labored breathing accompanied the Latin prayers.*

In one of his most poignant meditations on faith, Buckley wrote:

I have always thought Anatole France's story of the juggler to be one of enduring moral resonance. This is the arresting and affecting tale of the young monk who aspires to express his devotion to the Virgin Mary, having dejectedly reviewed, during his first week as a postulant at the monastery alongside Our Lady of Sorrows, the prodigies and gifts of his fellow monks. Oh, some sang like nightingales, others played their musical instruments as virtuosi, still others rhapsodized with the tongues of poets. But all that this young novice had learned in the way of special skills before entering the monastery was to entertain modestly as a juggler. And so, in the dead of night, driven by the mandate to serve, walking furtively lest he be seen and mocked by his brothers, he makes his ardent way to the altar with his sackful of wooden mallets and balls, and does his act for Our Lady.

This account of the struggle to express gratitude is unsurpassed in devotional literature. The apparent grotesquerie—honoring the mother of the savior of the universe, the vessel of salvation, with muscular gyrations designed to capture the momentary interest of six-year-olds—is inexpressibly beautiful in the mind's eye. The act of propitiation; gratitude reified.

Of this passage E.J. Dionne, the progressive opinion journalist at the *Washington Post* and also a Portsmouth alumnus, wrote in 2009:

Who, in the end, can escape loving this man who spent his own life as a juggler—of words, of ideas, of friendships, of commitments, of adventures. God granted Bill Buckley life, and in doing so, blessed the rest of us, and that is why we are here, in witness to our gratitude.

Bill Buckley was famous for making friends across ideological divides. His longtime skiing adventures with John Kenneth Galbraith are but one of many examples, as was his friendship with the doomed congressman Allard Lowenstein. While he was completely open to such friendships with the Kennedys, on at least two of the occasions he endeavored to connect, things did not turn out as he had foreseen. In the first the Buckleys invited Teddy Kennedy to their chateau in Switzerland near Gstaad for dinner, and after a raucous evening Bill and Teddy went down into the basement to paint, one of Bill's artistic avocations.

By the time they emerged, the other guests had departed, and Teddy had no way to get home, so Buckley lent him a car on the understanding that Teddy would return it the next day. Several days later, Kennedy having by then left town, the Buckleys were able to locate and recover it, but WFB was not amused.

Years later in New York, Jackie's sister, Lee Radziwill, asked Buckley to come talk to her because she was suffering from questions about her faith. Buckley, of course, obliged, but during the course of the interview began to suspect that Radziwill had something more seductive in mind and withdrew. Although ever the gentleman, he was sufficiently unnerved by the experience to tell a few close friends, and the story quickly got around town, possibly with the formidable Mrs. Buckley's active assistance!

At the same conference Lee Edwards recalled Buckley's gift for the witty aperçu. "Above all, Bill Buckley was the master of the one-liner who could sum up any issue or put down any one with just a few well-chosen words."

After the Chernobyl nuclear meltdown in the 1980s, he wrote: "The Soviet Union has finally contrived to give power to the people."

Of the CIA he wrote: "The attempted assassination of Sukarno last week had all the earmarks of a CIA operation. Everyone in the room was killed except Sukarno."

He once suggested an advertising campaign for the *New York Times*. Beneath a smiling Fidel Castro would appear the words, "I got my job through the *New York Times*."

Neal Freeman, Buckley's campaign manager, producer, and syndicator, recalls another example of Bill's rapid response one-liners:

> *Some years back my good Catholic wife gave me the best Christmas present I ever received—a copy of my FBI file. I don't know if the lacuna still exists, but at the time, under an obscure provision of the Freedom of Information Act, you could obtain a redacted copy of everything the Bureau had bothered to remember about you. Included in this so-called raw file were transcripts of Agent interviews conducted during field audits—those elaborate inquiries into a candidate's suitability for Federal appointment. These files made for fascinating reading: all of the interviewees had been sworn to tell the truth but, at the same time, had been promised permanent confidentiality. The raw file, indeed. Well, come Christmas morning I read through what I immediately recognized as Bill's interview—complete with the Agent's misspelling of* mutatis mutandis—*and I came to the final, omnibus, fanny-covering question: Would I, candidate Freeman, be likely to embarrass the Administration? Replied witness Buckley, under oath: "I should think that the reverse is much more likely."*

Bill's wit was sharpened by being married to the formidable society matron Patricia Taylor Buckley. At their spacious maisonette on Park Avenue and 73rd Street (now owned by Mark and Kimberly Rockefeller), and at their country house overlooking the Long Island Sound in Stamford, Connecticut, Mrs. Buckley presided over a never-ending salon of the great and near great, hosting a never-ending series of lunches, receptions, and dinners. Neal Freeman recalls:

> *To those of us who knew her in the Sixties, she was Patsy. By the Seventies, when she was emerging as a powerhouse fashionista, it was Pat; and by the Eighties when she had become an arbiter of*

cosmopolitan taste and trend, it was, always, "the chic and stunning Pat Buckley." Down through the decades Patsy had been a constant presence at National Review *board and editorial dinners. Her custom was to descend the marble staircase of the maisonette after her guests had assembled in the foyer, make the entrance grande, and then perambulate, working her way around the room with a witty word and an air-kiss for each of us. We would then go in to dinner, Patsy hosting one table, Bill the other. During the first course, Bill would move around the tables handing out slips of paper with after-dinner speaking assignments. On one memorable evening, my slip read simply, "After Henry." I didn't recall meeting anybody named Henry at the reception, so I looked around the tables and saw, sitting next to Patsy, a man who looked very much like Henry Kissinger.*

We finished Patsy's magnificent dinner—Beef Wellington, it frequently was in those days—Bill tapped his wine glass and then introduced our special guest, instructing him to "crystallize" his views on the current international situation. We all enjoyed it when Bill would issue instructions to princes and Presidents. Almost invariably, they would immediately and meekly comply. Well, Henry Kissinger got to his feet and began to unwind this sweeping tour d'horizon, fully Kissingerian in scope, weaving historical, military and economic apercus into a fine geostrategic tapestry. As he did so, I sat staring glumly at my slip of paper, a young NR director whose knowledge of foreign affairs might charitably be described as cursory; a young NR director praying that God, even a Catholic God, might breathe a little inspiration my way. Kissinger concluded to thunderous applause and just as I rose to speak, Patsy Buckley said in that voice that could cut through harbor fog—"Henry, you're making no sense at all. Thank God we've got Neal here to straighten this all out." Only my Episcopalian genes restrained me from dashing across the room and kissing her sloppily on the face.

Like Pat Buckley, Neal Freeman is an Episcopalian, which makes his memory of Bill Buckley all the more arresting:

To those close to him, however, what was most striking of all was Bill's devotion to his Church. I travelled with him in five different decades and I can report that, while he could not always be relied upon to find a decent restaurant, or an hygienic restroom, or a surgeon who spoke English, he could always find a place to profess his faith. On a rocky coast, in an urban hellhole, even in a Communist wasteland—wherever his travels took him, he would identify some semblance of a Church outpost and make his pilgrim's way there to worship his Saviour.

I leave it to you licensed professionals to determine whether Bill Buckley was a good Catholic. What I can say with authority is that, for the rest of us, he made Catholicism look resplendently good.

When Buckley came to speak at Portsmouth in the late 1960s, he mentioned that boarding school food had not changed since he was at Millbrook. I have a clear memory of Bill's evident devotion at Mass then, as well as on every occasion I saw him in church.

Patricia Taylor Buckley, on the other hand, was somewhat different. She descended on Father Leo in her then ultra-chic wardrobe of North African pajamas and demanded that the fourteen-year-old Christopher be moved from his lodgings in St. Benet's to somewhere more suitable—the Breakers would do quite nicely, thank you. Years later, when, then a grad student at Cambridge, I thought to economize by spending the week before Christmas on an Intourist trip to Moscow and Leningrad, whom did I meet but the Buckleys leading the *National Review* staff through the Kremlin. "*Jamie,*" Pat demanded in her timid way, "*how dare you come to Moscow* without a proper overcoat? You go buy one this very afternoon," which would have been an inspired suggestion had not the only thing emptier than the Muscovy shops of that era been my wallet.

It wasn't until many years later that the Catholic Pat Buckley revealed herself to me. I was lunching with my brother Pierce near his office at Tiffany when Pat rushed in, and stopped quickly to say she was late to join her party but that we were on no account to leave the restaurant without coming over after we finished our meal. We did so, and

Mrs. Buckley called out, "Jamie, I see that the pope created sixty-three new cardinals today." "Well," I answered, "I did read something about that in the paper, but I think the number was twenty-four." "*Jamie*," she said in her most menacing way at my impudence in contradicting her. There was a nanosecond of tense silence until one of her lunch partners, renowned ecclesiologist and costume jewelry king Kenny Jay Lane, helpfully defused the situation. "No, Pat dear, there are sixty-three only if you count their children."

In *Losing Mum and Pup*, Christopher recounts seeing his father for the first time after his mother's death:

> *I went to his study. Pup was red-eyed, puffy-faced, out of breath, in rough shape. He was gradually suffocating from emphysema and had just lost his wife of five decades. We embraced.*
>
> *That afternoon, Pup was going to Mass. I said I'd come. Normally, I didn't. Normally, when in Connecticut on a Sunday, I would discreetly make myself scarce around this time, when he would gather up the Hispanic staff and drive to St. Mary's Church, where a priest would say a private Latin Mass for them. Today, however, I reckoned, was not a day to skip church, so I went with them. Pup wept throughout the Mass. Afterward he told a friend who was there that he was "so pleased" that I had attended.*
>
> *Pup and I had engaged in our own Hundred Years' War over the matter of faith. Our Sturmiest and Drangiest times were over religion. Pup had the most delicious, reliable, wicked, vibrant sense of humor of anyone I knew, yet his inner Savonarola was released at the merest hint (to use his term) of impiety. Finally, exhausted, I adopted—whether hypercritically, or cowardly or wisely—a Potemkin stance of being back in the fold. My agnosticism, once defiant, had gone underground. I no longer had the desire to nail my theses to his church door. By now I knew we didn't have much time left, and I didn't want to spend it locking theological horns, making him heartsick with my intransigence.*
>
> *When I was younger and periodically confessed to him my doubts about the One True Faith, he dealt with it in a fun and enterprising*

way: by taking me off to Mexico for four or five days, during which we would read aloud to each other from G.K. Chesterton's great work of Catholic apologetics, Orthodoxy. *. . . we'd drive up into the hills of Cuernavaca and Taxco and sit on narrow balconies overlooking the zocalos, drinking margaritas and reading Chesterton aloud to each other. Not a bad way to restore one's faith, really. Four or five days of this and I was content to shrug off my doubts about the Immaculate Conception or the Trinity. They were some of the best days I ever had with him.*

Some months later . . .

He summoned me one afternoon to his bed and said to me, a look of near-despair on his face, "Oh Christo, I feel so bloody awful."
"I know you do, Pup," I said. "I'm so sorry. I wish . . ."
"If it weren't for the religious aspect," he said, "I'd take a pill."
The religious aspect. Here we were venturing onto thin ice. This was not the time to break what remained of his heart by telling him though I greatly admired the teachings of Jesus, I had long ago stopped believing that he had risen from the dead.

But let us contrast that for a moment with the message Christopher sent Bill on his birthday as they sailed the Pacific on *Sealestial* after a period of estrangement, as recounted by Bill joyfully in 1992 in *Windfall*: "My prayer—and it will be that, a prayer—will be for you, my dear and beloved Pup."
And finally:

Yesterday, I was driving behind a belchy city bus on the way back from the grocery store and suddenly found myself thinking, not for the first time, about whether Pup is in heaven. He spent so much of his life on his knees in church, so much of his life doing the right thing by so many people, a million acts of generosity. I'm—I shouldn't use the word—dying of curiosity: How did it turn out, Pup? Were you right after all? Is there a heaven? Is Mum there with you? (Grumbling, almost certainly, about the "inedible food.") And if there is a heaven and you are in it, are you thinking, Poor Christo—he's not going to make it. And is Mum saying, Bill, you have to speak to that absurd creature at the Gates and tell him he's got to admit Christopher. It's too ridiculous for words.

Even in my dreams, they're looking after me. So perhaps one is never really an orphan, after all.

Christopher Buckley's memoir of his parents received praise and criticism, the latter taking him to task for filial impiety in making public unflattering details of his parents' declining years. Joan Frawley Desmond summed up this line of argument by writing in *Inside Catholic* that Christopher himself had not always behaved well, and that he might have written a better book had he gained the perspective of another five years. Christopher's English teacher Father Damian Kearney dismissed that argument by observing, "Buckley was smart to write the book now. In five years no one would have cared."

The book is trenchant, unsparing but loving, and often hilarious, as in the description of a titled English lady houseguest hanging on "as tenaciously as a monomaniacal abalone" to Bill's despair, or the recounting of Bill's wish that his and Pat's ashes be entombed forever in a cross that adorned their Stamford lawn, whatever the religious inclination of the house's future owners might be. It is also an only child's cri du coeur about growing up in what must have often seemed to be a three-ring circus. As Christopher once said to me, "One of my earliest memories is wondering what country we came from."

Of course, what the book leaves out is the many years that Christopher (the name itself, as Father Julian pointed out in his homily at Christopher and Lucy's wedding, means "Christ bearer") was himself a devout Catholic. Certainly during the years in the late 1980s when we collaborated on a play about Elizabeth I and St. Edmund Campion, he was a convinced believer and conscientious practitioner of his faith. At some point after *Campion* was produced in 1987, however, he read a book review that referred to the "alleged" resurrection of Jesus Christ, and a seed of doubt entered into his mind that is still there.

And yet I find it interesting that nearly every other posting that he made to his blog at *The Daily Beast* was church-related. At Christmas he still FedExes ice cream to the monks of Portsmouth in gratitude for their prayers, at his request, for a loved one.

So Christopher, it seems to me, is on a journey, and whether he follows in the path of Catholic literary sons like Auberon Waugh or Wilfrid Sheed or undergoes a new conversion we cannot know.

What I do know is that we, beset as we *all* are by our own sins and doubts, must travel beside him on that voyage with love and prayers that he, and all of us, reach our ultimate safe harbor.

Family Update

John Buckley, the eldest Buckley brother, ran Catawba, the family's oil holding company. It was forced to enter into a consent decree with the SEC in 1981 alleging that investors in other Buckley oil companies had been defrauded so that the fully family-owned Catawba could pad its coffers. He died in 1984 of what his brother James called "an abdominal ailment." His brother Reid, however, wrote that the cause was excessive drinking.

Patricia Buckley Bozell, widow of Brent Bozell, died in 2008. She had helped Bozell launch *Triumph*, a conservative Catholic magazine. Among her ten children was L. Brent Bozell III, who founded the Media Research Center watchdog group, dedicated to exposing liberal bias in the mainstream media.

Jane Buckley Smith died in 2007 after many years of active service in civic affairs in Sharon, Connecticut. Her son Cameron is a businessman who remains active in New York and Sharon. Another son, Bruce, lives in Princeton, and she also leaves four daughters and grandchildren.

Priscilla "Pitts" Buckley, longtime managing editor of *National Review*, died at age ninety in 2012. "She was head and shoulders the favorite aunt of nieces and nephews," said James Buckley. "She never married, but she had a huge family. She was too busy having a good time to get married."

Reid Buckley died in 2014 at eighty-three. A colorful and sometimes caped figure, he was a novelist and proprietor of the Buckley School of Public Speaking in Camden, South Carolina. His son Hunt was a classmate of Christopher Buckley's and mine at Portsmouth and today practices law in Mexico City. Reid also had three other children and four stepchildren.

Carol Buckley, the only surviving daughter of her generation, lives quietly in Newburyport and has three children.

Peter Buckley, the eldest son of James and Ann Buckley, has been a successful investment banker and now lives in Aiken, South Carolina.

His brother Jay is an executive with GTech in Rhode Island. Among other duties he has helped Eastern European and other countries develop lotteries.

Caitlin Buckley, Christopher's daughter, recounted several instances of Pat Buckley offering her instructions on table manners at Pat's memorial service at the Temple of Dendur in the Metropolitan Museum of Art. In *Losing Mum and Pup*, Christopher recounted a scene at the dinner table with Caitlin and her friend Kick Kennedy, in which Pat Buckley, in an imaginative moment, claimed to be an alternate juror at the trial of Kick's cousin once removed, Michael Skakel, for the murder of Martha Moxley. Caitlin Buckley married Michael Leavey in May of 2016.

Jay and Sheila's daughter, Anna, graduated from the Georgetown School of Nursing and is a physical therapist in Austin.

In April of 2015, Sean Buckley, a son of Jay and Sheila Buckley, a graduate of Portsmouth Abbey, and student at Georgetown, wrote an op-ed in *The Daily Beast* announcing he was coming out as a gay conservative.

If you had asked me a few years ago if I supported the freedom to marry, I'd have been one of many young Republicans at the time who'd have given you an unequivocal "no."

As the grandson of former Conservative Party New York Sen. James L. Buckley and great-nephew of National Review *founder William F. Buckley Jr., I believed that gay rights were inherently anti-conservative and anti-Catholic.*

But I began to reexamine my views after acknowledging a part of myself that I'd suppressed for years—I am gay.

My family is loving and compassionate but they have been active in the fight to keep marriage limited to heterosexual couples. Because of their influence and the views expressed by so many in my religious community, I grew up with an extremely negative view of gay people. . . . I was taught a "hate the sin, love the sinner" approach to moral issues while always being told to respect those with whom I disagreed. But given that you can't separate yourself from who you love, teaching someone to hate their sexual orientation inadvertently teaches them to hate themselves. For me, this led to an intense self-hatred and a reflexive rejection of anyone that resembled the part of me I was so desperately trying to fight.

As early as high school I felt that my current university, Georgetown, had betrayed its Catholic faith by supporting an LGBTQ organization. But as the fact that I'm gay became increasingly difficult to deny, I struggled to identify with a conservative political community that disdains who I am, and a gay personal community that largely disagrees with what I believe.

Because I refuse to sacrifice my faith in God or conservative values, I had to find a way to reconcile these conflicts through a conservative lens.

American conservatives hold many different views but there are some core principles that help guide us toward specific policy prescriptions. Conservatives reject the idea of moral relativism and believe there are certain eternal truths regardless of time, place, or culture. We believe the collection of laws and institutions in place today are an amalgamation of human trial and error pursued in the effort to reach those universal truths. Finally, conservative thought demands recognition of our fallible human nature amid the understanding that we are all limited in our pursuit of truth and virtue.

Progress is good, but as Russell Kirk, one of the fathers of American conservative thought, put it: "change and reform are not identical." As history has made abundantly clear, no country or culture is immune to bad ideas taking hold. Recognizing this, conservatism suggests we should slow the pace of change, especially in times of intense public disagreement. Under this framework, I understand why many conservatives in the U.S. are unnerved by granting the freedom to marry to same-sex couples. Just a few years ago, I stood with them.

But in the past decade, never mind the last century, attitudes and responses towards gay people as individuals and a community as a whole have drastically changed.

Before 2003, it wasn't legal for two loving, committed individuals of the same sex to enter into what has been the most fundamental building block of our society—marriage. Today, gay and lesbian couples have the freedom to marry in 37 states, with the number poised to keep growing.

A clear majority of Americans now understand that being gay is not a choice. Gradually, this understanding is also extending among conservatives. And over 60% of millennial evangelical youth now support the freedom to marry.

Historically, marriage was primarily considered an economic and political transaction between families. As such, it was too vital of an institution to be entered into solely on the basis of something as irrational as love. It was not until the dawn of the Enlightenment in the 18th century that the idea of marrying primarily for love arrived. Those who opposed this shift saw it as an affront to social order, and rejected it as a dangerous change in the definition of marriage—similar to the arguments today.

But we've evolved, and learned that marriage matters for other reasons. At its core the institution of marriage hinges on two individuals committing to one another in life, for life, on a bedrock of love and self-sacrifice, which results in a better environment for raising children.

Above all else, the greatest gift our parents can give us is to teach us how to love—an emotion that gives the human experience both the purpose and meaning that is so critical to a happy and healthy life. I count this as one of the greatest gifts my parents have given me, and hope one day to give the same to my kids. Conservatives are right to argue that the best environment to raise children is within a marriage. However, it has nothing to do with the gender of their parents but instead the love they have for one another.

Most people would agree that the shift from marriage focused on political considerations to marriage built on love was for the best.

What they may not consider is that at its core, this shift was in recognition of a universal right to follow one's heart. In this, granting the freedom to marry to all loving couples is not a shift from the central tenet of marriage, but instead a fulfillment of its most basic ideals.

Gay couples today are building families and raising children. If we as conservatives care about preserving marriage and family, we must include gay people in the equation.

As a Young Conservative for the Freedom to Marry, *I believe that individuals have the power and ability to make decisions for themselves better than any government can. For conservatives who likely agree, I ask: why does this suddenly change when it comes to whom one loves and chooses to marry? This is a fight specific to the LGBT community, but it is also a fight for the rights of individual self-determination—a cause conservatives should always be ready and willing to fight for.*

As the Supreme Court prepares to consider whether all loving couples should have the freedom to marry, it is time for conservatives to recognize that just as individual liberty should not depend on a person's gender or race, it should not depend on whom a person loves, either.

Sean's father, Jay, posted on Facebook how proud he was of his son, and all of his relatives have been compassionate and supportive. I have no doubt Bill Buckley would have been the same, even if he could not quite offer his complete approval. (This was the case with Bill's close friend Marvin Liebman, when he published his 1992 book *Coming Out Conservative*). What Sean's well-reasoned and well-written manifesto does reveal is that the long-held Buckley family gene for independence of mind has carried successfully into a new generation.

In its June 2015 decision, the Supreme Court upheld the right of same-sex couples to marry.

CHAPTER X

Vatican II

An Age of Anxiety

In *REAL LACE* several members of the McDonnell, Murray, and Cuddihy clans expressed disappointment that the Second Vatican Council introduced doubt and confusion into their lives as Catholics precisely at a time when divorce, once thought unthinkable, was on the rise, and when traditional ethics and morals were being questioned throughout American society.

The 1960s were a time of tremendous social upheaval, beginning with the civil rights movement, proceeding into protests against the Vietnam War and increasing radicalization, and culminating in the series of assassinations—John F. Kennedy in 1963, Martin Luther King and Robert F. Kennedy in 1968—that seared a nation.

The Second Vatican Council, which lasted from 1962 to 1965, was certainly not intended to be seen as part of this fabric. Called by Pope John XXIII to "open the windows of the Church to the world," it was the twenty-first ecumenical council of the Catholic Church and the second to be held at the Vatican. The first had been held nearly a century before but had been cut short when the Italian army entered the city of Rome at the end of Italian unification and presaged the fall of the Papal States.

Various calls for social, scientific, and technological change were made by theologians leading up to the council, but according to Pope Paul VI, who concluded the council after John XXIII's death, the primary results were the renewal of consecrated life, ecumenical outreach toward other religions, and the call to holiness for all, including the laity. (Previously the church had been defined as being made up of the bishops, priests, and religious; henceforth it was considered to comprise all "the people of God.")

For many the most apparent result of the council was the widespread use of vernacular languages rather than Latin during the Mass. There was also a reduction of ornate clerical regalia, the revision of Eucharistic prayers (resulting in some appalling translations into English), the abbreviation of the liturgical calendar, the ability to celebrate the Mass facing the people as opposed to facing the altar (*ad orientam*, or east, toward Jerusalem), and the opening to modern aesthetic change encompassing liturgical music and art. While fine in theory, this became a source of embarrassment as dumbed-down liturgies, folk masses, saccharine songs replacing the majesty of Gregorian chant, and horrendously ugly art and architecture became the norm for generations of churchgoers, none of which had been intended by the council fathers.

Rather than promote growth in the Body of Christ, these misguided reforms and other liberal initiatives had the effect of loosening discipline and increasing dissent. Priests defected to marriage or a gay lifestyle; nuns threw off their habits in favor of social work or left their vows entirely. Applications to seminaries and convents withered, the result being, at least in the case of the seminaries, that rectors and their bishops felt compelled to accept unqualified candidates in order to "keep their numbers up." This and the emergence of a "lavender mafia" (a network of gay-sympathizing seminary superiors) had the effect of demoralizing those seminarians who were heterosexual. In time, this would prove disastrous as bishops ignored early reports of priestly sexual abuse, then merely shuffled abusers to different parishes where they could continue to abuse victims, and, finally, bought into misguided therapy programs in the hopes that serial sex accusers could be "cured" and returned to active, and often abusive, ministries. Instead they should have been locked away in institutions where they could do no more harm, defrocked altogether, and reported to criminal justice authorities.

If the hope was to renew the church, therefore, the results suggest the council was a failure, at least in the decades after it. Yes, women were included as auditors. Yes, significant outreach to other religions, especially Judaism, was launched and Catholic theology and liturgy were revised to reflect that the church no longer held the Jewish people as a whole responsible for the death of Christ. Yes, the amount of Scripture read during the Mass was significantly expanded (a sore point for Catholics given greater Protestant emphasis on and familiarity with the Bible), but overall the result was a weakening of the institutional church.

As Michael Novak put it:

> *Everything "pre" (Vatican II) was then pretty much dismissed, so far as its authority mattered. For the most extreme, to be a Catholic now meant to believe more or less anything one wished to believe, or at least in the sense in which one personally interpreted it. One could be a Catholic "in spirit." One could take Catholic to mean the "culture" in which one was born, rather than to mean a creed making objective and rigorous demands. One could imagine Rome as a distant and irrelevant anachronism, embarrassment, even adversary. Rome as "them."*

Pope Benedict XVI tried to recapture what he and other conservative theologians believed to be the true spirit of the council by proclaiming a "Year of Faith" in 2012–13. He quoted St. Pope John Paul the Great that the texts of the council "have lost nothing of their brilliance" if properly read and understood. "I feel more than ever in duty bound," Benedict wrote, not long before he took the unprecedented step of retiring from the papacy, "to point to the Council as the great grace bestowed on the Church in the twentieth century; there we find a sure compass by which to take our bearings in the century just beginning."

This view of the council has been traced to the idea of the "Development of Doctrine" as adumbrated by the Blessed Cardinal John Henry Newman, who was beatified in 2010 by Pope Benedict in an outdoor mass near Birmingham, England, Newman's home oratory. The "hermeneutic of continuity," as it is sometimes called, implies that the church develops its ideas and doctrines slowly and consistently, sometimes over the course of centuries, but remains the authentic deposit of faith forever. It is an attractive theory and may well prove true in the fullness of eternity.

As Ian Ker, Newman's biographer, said at a Portsmouth Institute conference on Cardinal Newman organized just weeks before the beatification in 2010:

> *Those who participated in or lived through the Second Vatican Council are less likely to understand the true meanings and significance of the Council's teachings than posterity. The "idea" of Vatican II, if Newman is correct, will grow "more equable and purer and stronger" as the "stream" moves away from the "spring," and "its bed has become deep, and broad and full." Far from taking place in a historical void, the Second Vatican Council met at a time of enormous upheaval in Western society, a time of optimistic euphoria but also a time of great moral and spiritual devastation.*

If so, it will be fascinating to see how future generations perceive the council. But in the immediate wake of the council and the social and economic changes that flowed from the late 1960s on into the early twenty-first century, at least in America and Europe, the barque of Christ became an increasingly beleaguered vessel.

CHAPTER XI

The 1960s

High-Water Mark

IN THE 1960S THE CHURCH IN AMERICA WAS AT ITS HIGH-WATER MARK in terms of serving priests and religious, schools, hospitals, social services, and other charitable works. New parishes were still being built to serve growing suburban populations, and the influence of powerful members of the hierarchy was strong. Nowhere was this truer than in New York City, where Francis Cardinal Spellman held enormous sway over not only the religious but also the civic life of the City.

Operating from the chancery in one of the Villard Houses across Madison Avenue (today the Palace Hotel) from St. Patrick's Cathedral and the cardinal's residence, the cardinal's office was called the Powerhouse, in part because of its spiritual strength, but also because of the extensive financial and real estate portfolios it held—churches, rectories, convents, schools, hospitals, houses, and other buildings throughout Manhattan, the Bronx, and the counties north of New York City. The other Villard House was the home at the time of Random House publishers, and in that faraway time one could drive into the Villard Houses' courtyard and park one's car. However, the archdiocese controlled the parking spaces and would only allocate one space to Random for its head, Bennett Cerf.

This exasperated other senior Random House executives, so when opportunity knocked one day in the form of Cardinal Spellman walking across the courtyard and personally presenting a manuscript of his poetry to editorial director Jason Epstein for consideration, Epstein took immediate advantage. After a somewhat truncated editorial meeting on the merits of the cardinal's verse, an offer to publish it was made contingent on the allocation of three additional parking spaces; and so publishing history was made!

Upon Cardinal Spellman's death he was succeeded by Terence Cardinal Cooke, who had served as Spellman's secretary. A less extroverted personality, Cooke worked quietly. Until his death from leukemia in 1983, he opened nine nursing homes; began Birthright, which offered women alternatives to abortion; and founded the Inner City Scholarship Fund, which provides financial aid for inner-city Catholic schools, as well as an archdiocesan housing program for low-income families, an outreach ministry for African Americans, and the archdiocesan newspaper.

Nonetheless, at the time of his death, urban parishes and schools were beginning to struggle as the percentage of Catholics in some neighborhoods declined, and when it came time to appoint a successor, Pope John Paul II looked beyond the New York archdiocese and chose John Cardinal O'Connor, a Philadelphian who had worked for many years as a priest in the military vicariate before becoming bishop of Scranton. O'Connor spoke Spanish, wore a Yankees hat in public, and became extremely popular with New Yorkers, including then mayor Ed Koch. Like Cooke, Cardinal O'Connor came from working-class roots and, though theologically conservative, was socially liberal. However well-intentioned, his management put severe strain on the archdiocesan finances, because he hated to close parishes or schools, even those whose Catholic populations had been decimated and were operating at deep deficits. When it became time, after O'Connor was diagnosed and died of brain cancer, to name his successor in 2000, Pope John Paul II chose Edward Cardinal Egan, originally of Chicago and later bishop of Bridgeport. He and O'Connor had not gotten along during Egan's tenure under him as vicar for education in the late 1980s, and Cardinal O'Connor lobbied in his last weeks against Egan's appointment. But Edward Egan had spent many years in the Vatican as a canon lawyer on the Roman Rota and was known as a manager rather than a public personality. Ultimately the Pope decided he was the right man for the job at the time.

SOCIETY OF THE SACRED HEART

One of Stephen Birmingham's chapters in *Real Lace* is entitled "Sons of the Priory, Daughters of the Sacred Heart," and certainly Sacred Heart schools have had a profound influence on educating young women in America over the past hundred years. They continue to do so today, sometimes including young men now as well.

The Society of the Sacred Heart was founded in the turmoil of post-Revolutionary France by St. Madeleine Sophie Barat. Its history is the story of strong and dedicated women true to the society's motto, *Cor unum et anima una in Corde Jesu* ("One heart and one mind in the heart of Jesus"). Sister Madeleine Sophie and her companions set out to give women a classical education (not common in their day) and to offer religious studies and practical skills. St. Rose Philippine Duchesne first brought the society to the Americas—to St. Charles, Missouri—in 1818. In the first half of the twentieth century, the society reached into all continents and opened colleges as well as schools. In the mid-twentieth century, Sabine de Vallon brought the society "face to face with the realities of today." The Society of the Sacred Heart carried out the mandates of Vatican II by defining itself as an "apostolic community," removing the rule of the cloister at the General Chapter of 1964. A simplified habit was adopted, gradually to be dropped in favor of contemporary dress, and major initiatives were begun in education, missionary activity, and social justice. A special chapter in 1967 concluded that the society should adopt every means of education as needs arose, from university campuses to inner city and vacation camps.

There was a profoundly serious theological and sociocultural basis to the Sacred Heart ethos, as Birmingham explained: "To her pupils the Reverend Mother reads this doctrine:"

> *The child of the Sacred Heart understands that her role is central to the design of creation. If she be not among those few called to the perfect life of religion, it will be her task to guide the souls of her own children. Her special influence depends upon her distinctively feminine qualities: tact, quiet courage, and the ability to subordinate her will to another's gracefully and even gaily. Filled with the tranquility of inner certitudes, she does not disperse her energies in pointless curiosity, in capricious espousal*

of new theories, in the spirit of contention. Long years of silence, of attention to manners and forms, have instilled in her that self-control without which order and beauty are impossible. Her bearing is the outward shape of that perfect purity which is her greatest beauty, and which models itself on the ideal womanhood found in the Mother of God. She who can bear the small trials of daily discipline will not falter at those crises in life which require fairness and fortitude.

But already there were signs of stress in this value system as the 1960s closed and women, including sisters and students of the Sacred Heart, began to question their place in society, their sexuality, and much more.

Michelle Coppedge's mother, Bridget Coltman Joyce, was born in Wellington, New Zealand, and sent to a Sacred Heart school in Auckland at the age of seven. Coppedge was sent by her parents in Pasadena to board at the Sacred Heart school in Atherton, near San Francisco, when she attained the ripe old age of twelve. Michelle recalls:

The old motto of noblesse oblige was no longer used and instead we were impressed with the idea that it was an honor to serve. There was never any sense of aristocracy, superiority or class distinction, quite the opposite. At the same time, there was still a sense that Sacred Heart schools the world over were running on the same system. The biggest difference at Atherton was between the day students and the boarders. The boarders were expected to live as did novices in the convent, practicing the Great Silence from saying Grace after dinner to the following day's breakfast.

There was Primes, a kind of assembly, every week. The Mother Superior sat on the stage, presiding. If one's name was read out for an infraction one was expected to step out of line, curtsy, say, "Thank you for correcting me," and go to the back of the line. The idea was to instill poise at all times.

It all changed after 1968 when the order reconsidered its mission and ventured out into the world. There are less than half the number of convents today as there were then.

PROFILE:
PORTSMOUTH AGAIN: FROM PRIORY TO ABBEY

Just as the church in New York was reaching the zenith of its power and influence and the Sacred Heart schools were at their peak, "Father Diman's School" in little Portsmouth, Rhode Island, was also forging ahead.

After Father Hugh Diman's death in 1948, Portsmouth Priory continued to evolve. A split within the monastery as to whether it should continue to operate a successful and highly regarded school or to become a more contemplative religious house was decided in favor of the former, but resulted in several monks departing to found a more prayer-focused monastery at Mount Saviour in upstate New York, including the prior, Dom Gregory Borgstedt.

By 1949–50 the school numbered 140 boys. Evelyn Waugh, sportswriter Red Smith, and Thornton Wilder were among the speakers who lectured there. A new dormitory, St. Bede's, and a new gymnasium were constructed in the early 1950s, significantly ameliorating the facilities.

Dom Peter Sidler was named the acting prior until the abbot president of the English Congregation decided on appointing Dom Aelred Graham, a monk of Ampleforth Abbey in Yorkshire, the permanent prior. His books, *Catholicism and the World Today* and, later, *Zen Catholicism?*, brought added national recognition to Portsmouth, as did his eight-thousand-mile lecture tour of the United States. He became a spokesman for Portsmouth's belief that it should prepare boys for Catholic *and* non-Catholic universities, a practice almost unique among Catholic schools at the time.

Aelred Graham also appointed a new headmaster, another Aelred, the popular and urbane St. Louisan Dom Aelred ("Barney") Wall, who had himself been a student in the school. The monastery added several new novices, the school grew to 175 students, and applications soared from all over the country. In 1957 Father Aelred Wall resigned to found the Monastery of Christ in the Desert in Abiquiu, New Mexico, where the Stations of the Cross were designed by a neighbor in that remote southwestern countryside, the artist Georgia O'Keeffe. He was replaced as headmaster by Dom Leo van Winkle, also an alumnus, who had been awarded his Ph.D. from Yale in chemical engineering and gone on to work on the Manhattan Project in Los Alamos during World War II.

Under Father Leo van Winkle's leadership, the school climbed to new academic heights. An entirely new upper campus, designed by MIT dean of architecture Pietro Belluschi, working closely with Fathers Hilary and Peter, came into being. The centerpiece of this was the new church, monastery, and dining hall complex. The church was immediately recognized as a mid-twentieth-century modernist masterpiece, patterned after the great Justinian Revival Church of San Vitale in Ravenna, commissioned in St. Benedict's lifetime. It was octagonal in shape but built primarily of redwood and fieldstone in the lower half with a clerestory of stained glass up above. The height of the building, which dominates the campus, is enhanced by a slender spire crowned by a cross. Inside there is a sense of soaring verticality as one looks up at the great animated birch arches that support the tower blending with the beauty of the colored light streaming through the stained glass.

Shafts of light falling from an opening above the altar irradiate a crucifix hanging high above the celebrant. This crucifix, supported by myriads of thinly drawn gold wires strung in a pattern by Richard Lippold, which he called "the Trinity," seems at high mass to float on clouds of incense rising from the thurible swung below. As John Walker, longtime director of the National Gallery, wrote: "It is as though God's grace, transmitted along a web of shining beams of light, is drawn to the altar by the head and outstretched arms of the crucified Christ. When the church is filled with boys and monks singing, the effect is sublime and unforgettable."

More buildings followed in the sixties, including a science building, an auditorium, an administration building, and an indoor hockey rink, followed in the seventies by three new residential houses, a classroom building, and a library.

Under Father Leo's leadership academic standards remained high, college placement was outstanding, and admissions swelled so that only one out of every six applicants gained a place in the school. What distinguished Portsmouth Priory in this era was a highly educated and gifted monastic faculty, many of whom were qualified to teach at the college or university level. Instead they devoted their learning and teaching efforts to a group of secondary school boys. Needless to say, their vows of poverty reduced the school's operating costs considerably in relation to its northeastern boarding school peers.

A number of outstanding lay faculty burnished the school's reputation as well, including historian Thomas Brown, who, after leading the Priory history department for some years, went on to teach at Boston College; and William ("Uncle Billy") Anton Crimmins, a charismatic Anglo-Irish-American who taught and coached for a dollar a year, school-mastering by day and enjoying the delights of Newport society by night. He later helped to found *Monumenta*, an exhibition of contemporary environmental sculpture on Aquidneck Island, and the Newport Music Festival, which continues to this day. Crimmins was beloved for coming to the rescue of boys in trouble. When the rather stern Father Leo threatened to withdraw the scholarship of Bill Maher, who grew up in Yorkville, the son of a brewery manager and a secretary, and went on to become a judge in New York state, Crimmins said, "I'll take care of his tuition." When Lawrence Doyle, a North Carolinian, was caught out trying to buy liquor in the village of Portsmouth using the ID card of a sailor on the Newport Naval Base, he ran cross country through the cow pastures back to the school, evading the police who came looking for him. By the time he got back to his dorm, his clothes were ragged and muddy. Knowing his housemaster would report him for being outside the dorm without permission if they were discovered, he called Crimmins, who immediately sped over in one of his twin Camaros from his seaside mansion in Middletown and collected them. By breakfast the next morning they were back, laundered and ironed impeccably.

As the school's reputation rose, influential churchmen came to pay their respects. Cardinal Spellman visited in the 1950s. When Bishop Terence Cooke was notified by Rome that he would be appointed Spellman's successor, he came to Portsmouth and submitted to an interview with Father Wilfried Bayne, at that time the country's leading heraldic scholar, who would design Cooke's coat of arms. At the end of their dialogue, Father Wilfried, an aristocratic and occasionally acerbic New Orleanian, asked the soon-to-be cardinal if he had any special requests. Cooke, whose father was a chauffeur, replied, "Yes, my mother always said we were descended from the great kings of Ireland, and I would like to see that in some way reflected."

"Nonsense," answered Father Wilfred. "Every Irish American says that, and there's not a word of truth to it!"

When in 1967 it came time for Dom Aelred Graham to retire back to his home monastery at Ampleforth in Yorkshire, the monks of the now independent Portsmouth Priory elected a new superior from among their own, the profoundly spiritual twenty-nine-year-old Baltimorean and classicist Dom Matthew Stark. The priory was raised to an abbey and Dom Matthew became the first abbot. There were twenty-six monks in the community, with a median age of forty-six. The school was thriving. The future looked bright.

Father Hilary

Perhaps the most influential monk of this period at Portsmouth was Father Hilary Martin. Descended from an Ulsterman father and French mother, he eschewed high office in the monastery but managed to exert power by dint of the family money that he brought with him, his powerful personality, and his many friends, whom he was more than happy to call upon for assistance with his ambitious building projects.

In a dinner at the Brook Club in New York some years ago, Father Damian Kearney made the following remarks:

Father Hilary, as we all know, was a man of many talents and interests as well as a man of contradictions. He was a monk vowed to stability, but one who traveled often and to many countries; we are reminded that one of Chaucer's pilgrims was a monk. His intellectual growth never stopped; the wide range of his literary interests showed a mind that was active to the end; he was a progressive and liberal in the best sense, and was always able to retain the friendship of his conservative friends. He appreciated the world of the past but he was able to blend it with the present, insisting on the need to look to the future. Anyone of you who took his Art and Civilization course or accompanied him on a cultural quest to Europe is able to echo the truth of this assessment. . . . My first contact with Father Hilary was as a third form student in the early 1940s (during the war) in a Christian Doctrine course he taught on St. Luke's gospel. We were a rowdy lot, and he was just beginning to teach at this level. One of the students who gave him a particularly hard time was a cynical Frenchman who had transferred from Exeter to Portsmouth and questioned every bit of doctrine brought up—a budding Voltaire. In his sixth form year he inherited the ancient title of Duc d'Uzes and became the premier peer of France. He must have retained something valuable from the school because, in a newspaper interview at the time of his marriage to a wealthy American heiress, he gave it and his teachers the highest praise. Although I failed to appreciate this Scripture course at the time, the love of Luke's gospel has been a valuable part of my spiritual as well as cultural development. Like d'Uzes, I learned far more than I thought.

Father Damian went on to recount Father Hilary's role in buying and running the priory farm for nearly thirty years, shepherding the flock of sheep, acquiring art for the abbey's and school's collections, and choosing Pietro Belluschi to design the new church and campus. He closed by paying tribute to Father Hilary's legendary and very Benedictine practice of hospitality, his environmental stewardship, his success as a teacher and housemaster, and most of all, his gift for friendship.

Among many, many examples of this was the fact that it was Father Hilary who was asked to give religious instruction to Janet Jennings Auchincloss, Jacqueline Kennedy's half-sister, when she was engaged to be married to Lewis Polk Rutherfurd and wished to be received into the church. And, having successfully completed this mission, Father Hilary was on the altar assisting the pastor of St. Mary's Newport and Monsignor Whelan, a Princeton friend of Winthrop Rutherfurd, father of the groom, during the wedding ceremony as a crowd of five thousand jammed the streets outside before a reception for six hundred at Hammersmith Farm. Among the junior attendants that day were Caroline

Kennedy and John F. Kennedy Jr. Among the ushers was Cyr A. Ryan, of the Portsmouth class of 1960.

One of Father Hilary's favorite protégés would surely be Shirley Carter Burden Jr. of the class of 1959. And the feeling was reciprocated. When Father Hilary died in 1980, Burden wrote:

When I entered St. Bede's in 1955, a terrified, homesick Third Former . . . the nuns had clearly not prepared me for a monk like Dom Hilary: a monk who performed Caesarians on pregnant sheep, who had rare Picasso etchings in this room, who said "Dear boy" and "Come" when you knocked on his door. This was no Mr. Chips. He did not aspire to be one of the boys. He had firm view and high standards and was decidedly intolerant of bad manners, narrow-mindedness, cruelty, rock and roll and television. He understood adolescence but did not indulge it. Like God, he expected a great deal from us.

Father Hilary demanded more, but he gave more. He understood the importance of ritual and invested even routine occasion with ceremony. An annual Christmas party with real eggnog (or so we believed) after which Father Hilary, dressed in a Santa Claus suit, presented each of his dear boys with a special present—a map of St. Philomena's perhaps, or in my case, a toy telephone so I could stay in constant contact with my parents (after 25 years I am still too mortified to call home) . . .

Hilary's commitment to our education was not confined to teaching, nor, I am happy to say, did it end with graduation. Every other summer he would embark with a group of boys on a two-month tour of Europe. I was a member of the 1959 tour and it proved to be the biggest bargain of my life . . . Our parents' modest $1200 investment paid for everything—round-trip airfare, the worst hotels and best restaurants, even a $200 dividend at the end of the trip. We met Berenson at 'I Tatti' and had tea with Harold Acton at 'La Pietra.' We drank beer in Munich, new wine in Orvieto, Chateau Petrus and Chateau D'Yquem at Lucas Carton in Paris. We listened to Mozart on a summer night in the open courtyard of the bishop's palace in Dubrovnik, and were too young and boorish to appreciate *it all. But the seed had been planted. Our own limited view of the world had been enlarged—and enhanced—by the privilege of seeing it through Hilary's eyes.*

To say that I learned about the world from a Benedictine monk sounds like a contradiction, but it's true, and I never stopped learning from him . . . I suppose, for that matter, that Hilary himself was a contradiction. A man with firm views and high standards who was not rigid, who taught, above all, the importance of tolerance and understanding and human tragedy. An outspoken conservative in liturgical matters who was liberal about everything else. A patrician, whose hero was Mother Teresa. An Anglophile, who wanted the Battle Hymn of the Republic played at his funeral. A man of the world who became a monk, and who seemed to appreciate the world all the more for having left it. Hilary Martin was many things, but like Augustine, the saint he admired most and whose work he taught so brilliantly, he never lost sight of his true priorities. There was never any doubt about what came first—his God, his vocation, his values— the same values he sought to pass on to us. Better than anyone I have ever known, he demonstrated that it is possible to love God and the world. I am grateful to him for that, more grateful to him than I can say for his friendship, which nourished me for nearly 25 years. In the beginning I was intimidated by Hilary Martin but, like so many other "Dear Boys," I came to love him, and I will miss him very much.

Students

The student body at Portsmouth was of course all male, 90 percent boarding (as opposed to 70 percent today), and representing a national geographic reach, from such cities (or the more affluent suburbs of same) as Boston, Providence, New York, Washington, Miami, Memphis, New Orleans, Chicago, Detroit, San Francisco, and Los Angeles. At least five members of my class were sons of alumni, their fathers having attended in the early days of the school in the 1930s. There were only 220 in the school in those years, as opposed to more than 360 today, but it was an often colorful group. There were Astors, Bacardis, Buckleys, Burdens, Bloomingdales, La Farges; a son of the actor Claude Rains; the grandson of Fort Worth newspaper magnate Amon Carter; and great-grandsons of Michael Henry de Young, Henry K. Flagler, Leo Tolstoy, and Stanford White. And in due course they have gone on to fulfilling careers in architecture, agriculture, banking and other financial businesses, communications, journalism, law, medicine, new technology, politics, publishing, and other pursuits. Christopher Buckley went to Yale and became a presidential speechwriter and satirical novelist. E.J. Dionne went to Harvard, won a Rhodes Scholarship to Oxford, and has had a distinguished journalistic career at the *New York Times* and the *Washington Post*. He is also a senior fellow at the Brookings Institution. Nion McEvoy owns Chronicle Books in San Francisco and McEvoy Ranch, a producer of fine olive oil and wines, in northern Marin County, and, as a collector of photography and other art, is active on the boards of SFMOMA and chair of the Smithsonian American Art Museum. Denis Hector is associate dean of the University of Miami School of Architecture. William Maher went to Fordham Law School at night and ended up as a long-serving New York state judge. Terry McGuirk was CEO of Turner Entertainment Group and is now CEO of the Atlanta Braves. Roman Paska is an internationally acclaimed puppeteer and former head of the Institute of Puppet Theatre in Charleville, France. Gregory Hornig is a distinguished neurosurgeon in Kansas City, who as a resident at George Washington University Hospital earned a footnote in medical history when he was called upon to insert a Foley catheter into President Ronald Reagan after he was shot by John Hinckley Jr. in 1981. And so it goes . . .

Souvenir of the Late Sixties

I have my own very personal memory of Portsmouth at the end of the sixties . . .

In the summer of 1969, between my fifth and sixth form (junior and senior) years, I had my most intimate experience of the monastery at Portsmouth. I returned from a visit to California where I had attended dozens of concerts at the Fillmore in San Francisco and watched Neil Armstrong walk on the moon on a forty-foot screen at Disneyland while high in the air on the Moon Ride, a sliver of moon in the night sky shining down on Anaheim. I stopped off at my classmate (today Notre

Dame's longtime PR guru) Michael Garvey's house in Springfield, Illinois, where we joined a sit-down civil rights demonstration in the governor's office in solidarity with the people of downstate Cairo and were promptly ejected by state police. When the news of Chappaquiddick broke, Michael's father, Hugh Garvey, the proprietor of the estimable Templegate Press, quoted Judge Learned Hand: "They saith not a Pater Noster there." Upon reaching Long Island the following week, I asked my parents' permission to go camping upstate with some friends and to hear "a little music." I believe the ticket to Woodstock cost fifteen dollars, and none of us setting out to it had any idea of the monumental event (and mess) it would become.

The Tuesday following the concert's mud-soaked finale found me getting off the bus at the top of Cory's Lane and walking down to the Portsmouth Abbey School gates to make up a disastrous 39 in my Math 3 final the previous June. Father Hilary was away on his annual vacation in Italy, but I was well cared for by the other monks.

For the next two weeks, I was expertly and elegantly tutored through the course by Dom Geoffrey Chase, lovingly supervised by math department head Dom Andrew Jenks, who saw to it that the exam I retook had 105 points in it, just in case I needed the extra insurance. For those two weeks I lived life on the monastic model, taking all my meals in the refectory and, along with Dr. Frank Lally (my father's housemaster and history master in the 1930s, he had left the nursing home in Fall River to which he had retired to live in the monastery, which he found more congenial), attending daily mass and vespers. It was a curious contrast to Woodstock, both countercultural lifestyles, one energized by a search for a new way and the other stabilized by fourteen centuries of a seventh-century saint's strict but loving rule.

I studied math all morning, then swam in the bay and ate lunch in silence in the monastery as a book was read aloud by one of the monks. After twenty minutes of recreation afterward in the calefactory, in which conversation ranged from the day's news to astronomy, archaeology, cartography, eschatology, and the relationship of alchemy to medieval theology, there was Little Hour, another period of prayer. In the afternoons I had a shorter math tutorial and would then be free to play tennis with

Father Bede and read on my own, often down by the boathouse in my swimming trunks, where Father Damian would be doing the same. After vespers and dinner there was another short recreation period, and I got to know a bit of the monks' life stories. Father Wilfried had lived in Greenwich Village near e.e. cummings and danced with Pavlova. He was now a Dragon Rouge—the highest honorific awarded to a herald—and one of the country's foremost heraldic artists. Brother Basil had an encyclopedic knowledge of the royal families of Europe and occasionally dashed off to New York to compete in high-level bridge tournaments. And so forth . . . I wanted to know what drew them to that life, and in a way, I wanted to be drawn to it too.

"Monasticism is a protest," Abbot Matthew had preached to us the previous spring, "Not a protest against anything, but a protest *for* God and the things of God."

When I left the monastery to fly back to New York (in a small Newport Aero plane, as it happened, alongside Jimmy and Candy Van Alen, on their way to the second U.S. Open at Forest Hills, where Van Alen's tiebreaker system would be deployed), I wondered if, of all the countercultural adventures I'd had that summer of 1969, those two weeks of study and silence at Portsmouth hadn't been the most amazing of all. And the words of St. Benedict resonated in my ears:

Seek peace and quiet; be much more of a listener than a talker; listen with reverence; if you must speak, speak the truth from your heart. In other words, walk in the presence of God under the guidance of the gospel, in order to see him who has called us to his kingdom. To start with, ask God for the help of his grace; then never give up.

Chapter XII

Gratitude

Philanthropy among Irish-American families has long been a way of giving back. Broadcaster Daniel Burke, for example, was for many years chair of the board of New York–Presbyterian Hospital and a director of the Partnership for a Drug Free America, and his longtime business partner Tom Murphy has been extremely philanthropic as well. The MacArthurs and Galvins of Chicago and the McKnights of Minneapolis are just three with long-established records of admirable charitable giving.

MacArthur Foundation

John D. and Catherine T. MacArthur were quiet philanthropists in their lifetime, giving primarily to organizations in cities where they lived: Chicago and Palm Beach. Their business interests included the immensely successful Bankers Life and Casualty insurance company and real estate holdings concentrated in Florida, New York City, and Chicago.

On October 18, 1970, the documents establishing the John D. and Catherine T. MacArthur Foundation were completed. Mr. MacArthur intentionally left the business of what to fund to the foundation's first board of directors. "I made the money; you guys will have to figure out what to do with it," MacArthur told the board. This direction presented the foundation's first board with the task of shaping a forward-looking organization that could change with society's evolving challenges.

When John died of cancer on January 6, 1978, the foundation assumed his assets, estimated at one billion dollars. Since 1978 the foundation has made grants totaling more than five billion dollars around the world. The foundation's early programmatic focus was on the MacArthur Fellows, support for public radio, investment in peace and security, mental health, and the environment.

The second decade saw rapid expansion and experimentation, fueled by growing assets as Mr. MacArthur's real estate holdings were liquidated. New Chicago-based ventures included a leadership role in school reform and support for vigorous neighborhood development efforts. The foundation launched the Population Program, with field offices in Mexico, Nigeria, Brazil, and India. Shortly after the collapse of the Soviet Union, the foundation opened an office in Moscow in support of its work to strengthen universities and policy institutes in the sciences and social sciences.

In its third decade the foundation deepened investment in some of its most promising areas of work, including human rights and international justice. From 2009 to 2014 the foundation's granting practices emphasized strengthening American democracy.

Today, MacArthur is one of the nation's largest independent foundations, with assets of approximately $6.3 billion and annual giving of approximately $220 million. In addition to the MacArthur Fellows Program, the so-called "Genius Grant Awards," the foundation continues its commitments to the role of journalism in a responsible and responsive democracy, and the strength and vitality of its historic headquarters, Chicago.

MacArthur is one of the nation's largest independent foundations and supports organizations in about fifty countries.

ROBERT W. GALVIN FOUNDATION
Founded in 1953 by Motorola's longtime CEO Bob Galvin, this foundation focuses on education, the arts, children, and social services. While it is smaller than MacArthur (about fifty million dollars in assets), it remains highly thought of in Chicago and continues to fund innovative and effective programs in education and other areas.

McKNIGHT FOUNDATION
The McKnight Foundation makes grants in support of regional economic and community development, Minnesota's arts and artists, early literacy, youth development, Midwest climate and energy, Mississippi

River water quality, neuroscience and international crop research, and community-building in Southeast Asia. For more than sixty years, its primary geographic focus has been the state of Minnesota.

The foundation was established in Minneapolis in 1953 by William L. McKnight and his wife, Maude L. McKnight. One of the early leaders of 3M, William rose from assistant bookkeeper to president and CEO in a career that spanned fifty-nine years, from 1907 to 1966.

In 1974, shortly after his wife's death, William L. McKnight asked their only child, Virginia McKnight Binger, to lead the foundation. In 2015 Meghan Binger Brown was elected chair of the board of directors, becoming the foundation's seventh chair since it was established in 1953.

The McKnight Foundation has granted more than two billion dollars. The foundation had assets of approximately $2.1 billion and granted about $88 million in 2015.

In addition to these long-established charitable organizations, the tradition of Irish-American philanthropy has continued in the past forty years. Three of those who have used their hard-won treasure to do great good are Chuck Feeney, Tom Monaghan, and Peter Flanigan.

CHUCK FEENEY

Chuck Feeney came from a modest background in New Jersey and was the first member of his family to go to college, at Cornell, like Tom Murphy of Capital Cities/ABC. With a partner, Robert Miller, he founded Duty Free Shoppers, a duty-free business selling cigarettes, alcohol, and luxury items to tourists in airports and elsewhere, in time becoming a leading global retailer. In 1996 Louis Vuitton Moët Hennessy (LVMH), the French luxury goods group, bought DFS for $1.63 billion.

Feeney founded the Atlantic Philanthropies in 1982, and later transferred much of his wealth to the foundation. Atlantic has made grants totaling more than seven billion dollars, supporting health, education, and social projects.

In 2011 Atlantic gave $350 million to help build the campus for Cornell University's new high-technology Cornell-Technion campus on Roosevelt Island in New York City. It aspires to spearhead the creation of an East Coast Silicon Valley.

In 2015 Feeney attacked dementia and related neurodegenerative disorders, giving $177 million to establish the Global Brain Health Institute at UC San Francisco and Trinity College, Dublin. Feeney, whose family traces itself to County Fermanagh in Northern Ireland, has given more than $1.5 billion to Irish causes.

For many years Feeney sought to remain anonymous in his giving, but when a legal dispute with his former partner threatened to expose his philanthropy, he went public. He is bashful, prefers dressing informally, and gives few interviews, but does agree to speak to emphasize his philosophy of "giving while living," which has inspired many others, including Warren Buffett and Bill Gates.

Atlantic Philanthropies is scheduled to make its final round of grants in 2016 and to close down operations completely by 2020, when Feeney will turn ninety.

TOM MONAGHAN

The wealth Tom Monaghan amassed from selling Domino's Pizza enabled him to concentrate on good works, and in the years since he has demonstrated a particular interest in church-related philanthropy (Monaghan is a member of Opus Dei and is a Knight of Malta).

He first established the Ave Maria Foundation, to focus on Catholic education, media, and community projects. He next formed Legatus (or "commander" in Latin), an organization for Catholic CEOs. It holds conferences at luxurious resorts around the country and has included prelates and presidents among its speakers, who urge its members to play a powerful and virtuous role in their companies and communities. I have attended two of these comfortable gatherings in Bermuda and Dana Point, California; the attendees attend Mass as well as play golf, and, while sociable, are serious about their higher purpose.

In addition, Monaghan established a group of elementary schools, the Spiritus Sanctus Academies, and the Ave Maria School of Law and Ave Maria University in Collier County, Florida, thirty miles east of Naples in a planned community of the same name.

The town of Ave Maria has grown more slowly than planned. The contemporary church at its center is architecturally undistinguished, even ugly, and there have been internal disagreements on academic governance that led at least one senior administrator, Father Joseph Fessio, S.J., to resign. But Monaghan doggedly perseveres in his mission.

YOUNG PHILANTHROPISTS

In addition to Chuck Feeney and Tom Monaghan, other new Irish-American businessmen and philanthropists have emerged in recent decades.

Sean Fieler is managing director of Equinox Partners. Fieler has served as president of the Chiaroscuro Foundation and on the boards of the Witherspoon Institute, the Institute for American Values, and the Dominican Foundation.

Thomas Healey, a former Goldman Sachs partner and undersecretary of the treasury who now teaches at the Kennedy School of Government, has been active in promoting Catholic education and in urging Catholic institutions to become more transparent, data-driven, technologically up to date, and better governed. He has also called for tuition tax credits to assist them where appropriate.

Two of Peter Flanigan's sons have become active in philanthropic causes. Bob Flanigan has supported FOCUS, the Fellowship of Catholic University Students, a fast-growing campus evangelization group that now has branches around the country including at secular strongholds such as Columbia and New York Universities. His brother Tim, a doctor and Roman Catholic deacon, has championed Anna Halpine's World Youth Alliance, an advocacy group dedicated to the dignity of the human person and to basic human rights and necessities.

Casey Carter's Faith in the Future Foundation is another example of educational innovation. Carter, a descendent of Daniel Carroll II of Rock Creek (1730–1796), tried his vocation at Portsmouth Abbey for several years after graduating but ultimately left monastic life in favor of a successful career editing *Crisis* magazine and promoting and managing charter schools.

At Philadelphia archbishop Charles Chaput's request, in 2013 Carter became head of Faith in the Future, a first-of-its-kind foundation that operates the largest independent Catholic school system in the world. It is an independent not-for-profit 501(c)(3) separate from the Archdiocese of Philadelphia. Today it has direct operational oversight responsibility for seventeen high schools and four schools of special education. Once progress is made on its initial scope, the reach of its work should extend to support the 156 archdiocesan elementary schools as well. The archdiocese owns its high schools and schools of special education. That means it is able to grant direct operational control of those schools to the foundation. However, at the elementary level, where parish and regional schools are still overseen by pastors, the role of the foundation is to support these schools through the Office of Catholic Education. This joint venture is a unique combination of civic management matched to Catholic mission.

Faith in the Future aims to make Catholic education affordable for any family that desires it. All across the country, since the year 2000, more than two thousand Catholic schools have closed. Most have been priced out of business. Quite simply, tuition has become a significant barrier to entry for many families. Fortunately, in Philadelphia, the cost of Catholic education is among the very lowest in the United States. Still, it remains out of reach for thousands of parents forced to keep their children in failing public schools whose only redeeming characteristic is their free cost.

Faith in the Future aims to create a financially self-sustaining network of schools. It hopes to make high-quality educational seats available to an increasingly larger number of families each year.

Today its seventeen high schools serve 14,219 students in buildings with capacity for 28,000 students or more. Its growth strategy focuses on creating a unique selling proposition for each school so that it can expand in all segments. By taking a product portfolio approach to the systems as a whole, and by managing the system for the first time as a system, Faith in the Future will create economies of scale and achieve network benefits across the schools not realized before.

In its early years of operation, Faith in the Future has exceeded its goals, and Casey Carter remains optimistic about achieving success in Philadelphia and then moving on to replicate his strategy in other locations around the country.

PROFILE:
PETER FLANIGAN AND STUDENT SPONSOR PARTNERS

One of the best-known and most innovative educational philanthropists of the last thirty years is Peter Flanigan, who, in his telling, while winding down his investment banking career at Dillon Read and UBS, determined to find a new interest that would keep him away from what he dreaded—a life of golf in the morning, bridge in the afternoon, and martinis at night. Instead he founded Student Sponsor Partners.

Since 1986 Student Sponsor Partners has addressed the high school dropout crisis in New York City by providing low-income students with a high school education. All SSP students are provided sponsors and mentors who provide one-to-one mentoring and make a meaningful impact on their lives. More than 85 percent of SSP students graduate from high school each year, compared to the 64.2 percent graduation rate in New York City public high schools. In 1986 forty-five students started at two partner schools. Since then more than seven thousand have graduated from high school, and in 2014 more than twelve hundred SSPs were in twenty-three partner schools. Further, in the graduating class of 2015, more than 90 percent of SSP graduates were accepted into college. Only 50 percent of New York City's public high school graduates attend college. The Student Sponsor model has been replicated in many other communities around the nation and the world, including Chicago; Boston; New Jersey; Providence; Fort Worth; Bridgeport; St. Clair Shores, Michigan; Washington, D.C.; and Johannesburg, South Africa.

Peter Magnus Flanigan died on July 29, 2013, in Austria, at the age of ninety, surrounded by his family. A decorated carrier pilot in World War II and summa cum laude graduate of Princeton, Peter was a long-time partner at Dillon Read. He was special assistant for international economic affairs to the president of the United States, Richard Nixon, from 1969 to 1974. A fine sportsman and lover of the arts, he was active philanthropically, especially in the area of education reform. Flanigan was the founder of not only Student Sponsor Partners but also the Center for Educational Innovation, and a board member of "I Have a Dream," the Olin Foundation, the Children's Scholarship Fund, St. Ann's School in East Harlem, Catholic University of America, and Portsmouth Abbey School. In June of 2013 he celebrated his ninetieth birthday at the New York Yacht Club in Newport, Rhode Island, and the following night I introduced him at the Portsmouth Institute opening dinner as "an authentic member of the Greatest Generation who remains at the very top of his game today."

In typical fashion, Pete's first line was, "Thank you, Jamie, but if you think this is the top of my game, you're wrong."

I had known him since attending Portsmouth with his nephews in the 1960s, but our friendship was strengthened in 1985 when I went to have lunch with him one day in a private dining room at Dillon Read. Somewhat to my own amazement, I walked out having promised to help him start Student Sponsor Partners. One didn't say no to Pete, and being on that board and mentoring those kids proved to be a deeply rewarding experiences. Later we worked together at the Center for Educational Innovation, where, with Sy Fliegel, I co-wrote *Miracle in East Harlem: The Fight for Choice in Public Education.*

Peter's greatest loves were his family, his faith, and his country. Better than any words of mine, however, were Peter's own remarks, entitled "Lessons in Liberty," as an honoree at the Manhattan Institute's 2004 Alexander Hamilton Award Dinner.

How did I get up here? Perhaps the reason is that I learned well from (prior honorees) Bob Bartley and Bill Buckley about the need to fight for and to defend freedom. The battleground that I chose for myself in this fight for freedom is education. Most of America's children are free, but tragically, many of its most needy and vulnerable children remain in educational bondage.

How can we change that? For twenty years, we have been trying to do it with money. What we have not tried is freedom. Freedom for poor parents to choose the schools that they think are best for their children. Our battle for educational freedom has moved us from New

York City to New York State to the nation at large. We are engaged across the country through the School Choice Alliance, dedicated to the proposition that parents should be free to choose their children's schools.

So perhaps I am before you tonight because I listened well to Bob Bartley and Bill Buckley as they taught the blessings of freedom. And being a dutiful student, I have tried, with the help of so many in this room, to apply their teaching of freedom to education, particularly to the education of our most needy children. I have found that in this endeavor, as in all endeavors, freedom works. So I thank you for this honor, and hope all of you will join with us in this battle for educational freedom.

On his death, Larry Mone, president of the Manhattan Institute, wrote, "Thousands of children benefitted directly from his philanthropy. Many adults were inspired by Peter to devote their lives to providing better educational choices to underprivileged children. His legacy will live on through all those lives he touched. That the number of such lives is incalculable is the true mark of a life well lived."

His son Bob eulogized Peter Flanigan as follows:

Dad believed that politics was the ultimate forum to decide how our society should function. He was personally very committed to Richard Nixon as the best future leader of our country, and in the 1960 campaign he schemed up "New Yorkers for Nixon," which employed the catchy idea of posting lovely young women, including his wife, outside the storefront on Madison Avenue with sashes reading "Vixens for Nixon."

After a high-profile article in the New York Times, Mr. Dillon "suggested" that he take a leave from Dillon Read and dive into politics. We owe Mr. Dillon a huge thanks!

Dad believed deeply in public service and characterized his time in the Nixon White House as "noble and necessary." His advice to legions of younger people, many of whom sought him out as a mentor, was to not count the cost, but dive in and serve our country through public service.

Over the last 30 years, Dad played a legendary role in New York and national education reform and philanthropy. He kept his roots in mind, remembering that his grandfather was "off the boat Irish" and ran a dry goods store in the South Bronx.

So he was an early pioneer of the education movement to bring school choice to low-income kids. Peter and Brigid always looked for what worked, then supported that person or organization to the hilt. Dad was the founder of Student Sponsor Partners, which provided private vouchers and mentors to 6,000 inner-city New York City students. His passion to give a child a great education in the NY Catholic school system was legendary—watch out if you found yourself sitting next to him on the chairlift in Alta or at a dinner party, there's a good chance you'd end up sponsoring a child!

John Kirtley from the American Federation for Children and Alliance for School Choice, where Dad was a longtime board member, said it best, "Few in America have done more over the past two decades to advance educational choice for children than Peter Flanigan. A man most generous of spirit and of heart, Peter believed in the essential dignity and value of every human life and in the fundamental principle that every child—regardless of race, socioeconomic status, or geographic residence—deserves a quality education."

Bob Flanigan closed his eulogy:

Starting in early June, Dad's faith in God and the transcendent was preparing him, I believe, to leave this world with the certainty of where he was going. As the extraordinary birthday of 90 approached, Dad was compelled by his deep and abiding Catholic faith to create the opportunity of a lifetime for his 23 children and grandchildren— to join him in a pilgrimage to the Holy Land. His strength actually seemed to increase during our trip . . .

The funeral at the Church of the Resurrection in Rye could be seen as a final flourish of the Church Triumphant. Both Cardinal Egan and Cardinal Dolan were on the altar, surrounded by several bishops and dozens of priests. In the choir Sister Marie Louise, Peter's daughter, and a group of nuns from her convent in Alabama sang angelically. The large church was packed. Cardinal Egan wiped away tears as he recalled his work with Peter on multiple causes, their evenings attending the Ring Cycle at the Metropolitan Opera, and other memories of friendship. I was not sure how well Cardinal Dolan had gotten to know Flanigan in his relatively few years in New York, but when he said, "Peter wasn't perfect, of course; none of us is, and he had some minor flaws . . . such as a persistence that could verge into pestering . . ." I realized he knew Pete very well!

It was, perhaps, the last of the great *Real Lace* funerals.

Chapter XIII

Assimilation

Leaving the Ghetto

As the seventies and eighties moved into the nineties, a natural process of demographic change continued in America that had consequences for all ethnic categories and classes, including Irish Americans.

Suburban sprawl expanded, and regions such as Florida, the Southwest, and California grew, while there was contraction in once Irish strongholds in New England, New York, Chicago, and the Middle Atlantic states. The Irish who participated in these migrations remained numerous, but their sense of identity was not as monolithic as it had been before. Also, the sense that big families were a social and spiritual good began to break down, as younger families, despite the church's opposition, overwhelmingly employed birth control, and thus had fewer children.

This had an impact on potential vocations as well. Traditionally in Catholic immigrant families, one child would be groomed for the church, but if a family were having two or three children as opposed to eight or nine, that was no longer the case.

As Irish Catholics increasingly intermingled with families of other ethnicities and religions, it was inevitable that assimilation would accelerate. The old conviction that the public schools were repositories of anti-Catholic, Protestant ideology disappeared, and many Irish Catholic families availed themselves of them. This in turn led to an increase in intermarriage among Catholics, Protestants, and Jews, which became a source of concern to many that their particular "identity" was being diluted.

In the world of New England boarding schools, the old St. Grottle-sex schools (Groton, St. Paul's, St. Mark's, Middlesex, St. George's, etc.) began to shed their original identity as Protestant church schools for a more secular program. They also embraced coeducation, and this, along with the loss of Catholic identity, led to many more Catholics attending them (at one time in the 1990s, Groton even had a Catholic chaplain).

At Portsmouth Abbey coeducation was studied in the early 1970s but put off. Canterbury School, by contrast, began an exchange program with Noroton School of the Sacred Heart in 1971 and became fully coeducational several years after that, gaining many Sacred Heart students from several schools in the process. The issue arose again at Portsmouth in the early 1980s, but, again, by only one vote, the monastic council voted against it. The monks trusted that their fourteen-hundred-year-old tradition of educating only boys would prove durable, but they were wrong, and the results were nearly disastrous. The quality and quantity of applicants steadily declined until, in 1990, the school's board of advisors gave the monastery a blunt assessment: go coed or close. A gaping operating deficit was closed by the generosity of Peter Flanigan and others, and a new era began.

The Sacred Heart schools faced a similar challenge. The order withered as many of the nuns laicized and some married. The Madames who remained often went into working for social justice in inner cities rather than educating what they had come to see as an elite group of rich girls. The foundress, Madeleine Sophie's, motto of *noblesse oblige* was deemed anachronistic and replaced by "It is an honor to serve."

Some of the Sacred Heart schools have remained single-sex and thrived. Others have become coed successfully as well.

I wrote, as it happens, the first letter proposing coeducation in the Portsmouth student newspaper in 1969, making arguments that included the financial benefit that would accrue from having a pool of potential applicants twice the size of a single-sex school. At the end I threw in an off-hand proposal calling for a convent to be annexed to the monastery as well. The last, wiseacre line was gratuitous, but mightn't the school today, with the monastery severely depleted and aged, benefit from a few nuns living in the girls' houses and adding to the school's academic, social, and spiritual life?

Needless to say, I was a prophet without honor in my own school at the time, at least to the administration. May 1970 was the month that four protesters at Kent State were gunned down by members of the Ohio National Guard, and I remember the pall that cast over our discussion in our History AP class the morning the news hit the newspaper headlines. It made for a grim finale to the turbulent years of war, racial conflict, and assassinations we had lived through in the late 1960s. The student council that year had offered many proposed changes to school life, including the abolition of morning prayers, one voluntary athletic season, optional attendance at breakfast, extending lights-out for fourth formers to 10:30 p.m., optional attendance at Saturday night movies, foreign study programs, and more places on campus to entertain girls. None was well received, but all came to pass in time. Interestingly, the student council that year did strongly support the continuation of a two-year Latin requirement, and I am glad for today's kids that a one-year requirement was reinstated some years ago. "The only thing more boring than taking Latin I was teaching it," Father Julian once remarked, but the benefits to one's grammatical and vocabulary skills over the long haul are well worth it.

In my lifetime I would have to say that coeducation, along with the design and building of the Belluschi church and campus, have been the two most constructive changes at Portsmouth. They have both in their different ways added beauty, sensitivity, harmony, and a greater ability to experience the love of God and the fellowship of the Holy Spirit. The truth is that the single-sex, 1960s Portsmouth was often a hard-bitten, cold, and sarcastic place. The kindness and genuine care today's students show to each other and everyone else is what most strikes this time traveler to the campus of today. Much credit has to go to all the dedicated faculty members, male and female, monastic and lay, who made the transition to coeducation work so wonderfully well. Portsmouth today is a better, more Benedictine place as a result. Perhaps Father Peter Sidler put it best when he told Dana Robinson '64, "Before coeducation the school may have been more intellectual, but after coeducation it became more intelligent."

CHAPTER XIV

Decay and Falling Away

BY FAR THE MOST DEMORALIZING AND DAMAGING EVENT OF THE YEARS
since *Real Lace* was published in 1973 has been the revelations of
long-standing sexual abuse by priests against young people, mostly young
boys or adolescents. As early as 1962, the distinguished psychiatrist
Father Gerald Fitzgerald, founder of the Paraclete Center to aid troubled priests in Jimenez Springs, New Mexico, met with Cardinal Alfredo
Ottaviani, head of the Holy Office in Rome, to warn him that there was
no cure for pedophile priests. In 1964 Fitzgerald met with the new pope,
Paul VI, to repeat his warnings.

In May of 1985 Dominican Father Thomas Doyle, Father Michael
Peterson, and Ray Mouton presented a ninety-two-page document to
a committee of the U.S. bishops' conference, warning them to handle
pending cases well, defend victims, and, crucially, *be honest with the public.*

In June of that year, the *National Catholic Reporter*, a liberal lay newspaper based in Kansas City, published its first exposé and editorial on the
priestly sex abuse crisis. The story was based on Jason Berry's reporting
of the case of Father Gilbert Gauthe of Lafayette, Louisiana, who ultimately served ten years of a twenty-year sentence for molesting multiple
children. Irish-American priests such as John Geoghan and Kevin Shanley were also accused. Geoghan, by then a former Boston priest accused
of abusing more than 130 children, was convicted of molesting a child
in 1991 and sentenced to nine to ten years in prison. He was killed the
following year by another inmate.

In 1992 U.S. bishops approved guidelines for handling sex abuse cases, but the guidelines were voluntary and not universally applied. They were later viewed as a failure.

In January of 2002, exasperated by the delaying tactics of Chancery lawyers, Judge Constance Sweeney ordered Boston cardinal Bernard Law to turn over ten thousand pages of records. The *Boston Globe* used this evidence to initiate an extensive series on clerical sexual abuse in archdiocese. On April 23 Pope John Paul II called an emergency meeting with U.S. cardinals in Rome to discuss the crisis. The U.S. bishops, meeting in Dallas in June 2002, adopted the "Charter for the Protection of Children and Young People."

Under withering criticism for his and his predecessors' failures to prevent and report these horrendous acts of criminal abuse by priests against innocent children and adolescents, Bernard Cardinal Law resigned as archbishop of Boston on December 13, 2002. In 2003 the Archdiocese of Boston settled 552 claims for eighty-five million dollars.

In 2004 the John Jay College of Criminal Justice released a study sponsored by the U.S. bishops. It reported 10,667 complaints of sexual abuse against 4,392 priests and deacons between 1950 and 2002.

That same year the Diocese of Orange in California settled nearly ninety cases for $100 million.

The first diocese to declare bankruptcy over payments for pedophilia cases was in Portland, Oregon, that year. Since then, other dioceses filing have included Tucson, Arizona; Spokane, Washington; Davenport, Iowa; San Diego; Fairbanks, Alaska; Wilmington, Delaware; and Milwaukee. So, too, has the Society of Jesus' Oregon Province.

In 2007, again after long resistance and calculated legal delay in releasing documents, the Los Angeles archdiocese agreed to pay $660 million to settle abuse claims brought by more than five hundred people. Los Angeles cardinal Roger Mahony said the settlement, along with a sixty-million-dollar abuse settlement in 2006, would compel the archdiocese to reevaluate its ministries and services.

In 2007 the Archdiocese of San Diego reached an agreement with 144 childhood sexual abuse victims for $198.1 million.

The global scope of the scandal came into focus in 2010. Three hundred former Catholic students in Germany declared they were victims of physical or sexual abuse by priests. Brazil investigated allegations that three priests sexually abused altar boys. Investigations in Ireland document child abuse and cover-ups from the 1930s to 1990s, involving more than fifteen thousand children.

In 2011 the Oregon Province of the Society of Jesus, which covers Oregon, Washington, Idaho, Alaska, and Montana, reached a settlement of $166.1 million for more than five hundred cases of clergy sexual abuse.

In 2014 Pope Francis met with victims of sexual abuse. He also established a Pontifical Commission for the Protection of Minors. On June 10, 2015, Pope Francis announced the establishment of a new office at the Congregation for the Doctrine of the Faith to serve as a tribunal to judge bishops who have mishandled abuse cases.

The Associated Press estimated that total settlements from priestly sex abuse from 1950 to 2007 were more than two billion dollars. Bishop-Accountability, a lay watchman's and victims' advocacy group, reported that the figure had reached three billion by 2012.

The church admitted in 2008 that the scandal was a very serious problem but at the same time estimated that it was caused by no more than 1 percent of its priests. However, an analysis of the study the church itself had commissioned from the John Jay College of Criminal Justice indicated that some 11,000 allegations had been made against 4,392 priests in the United States, or approximately 4 percent of the priests who had served during the period covered by the survey.

The church was widely criticized for reassigning known sex abusers, and its rationale that this had also been the practice with public school teachers and Boy Scout troop leaders similarly accused was weak and unconvincing, as if a member of the priesthood of Jesus Christ should not hold himself, and be held, to a higher standard. Legally, many states have now mandated that claims of abuse must be reported to the police, which was not the case previously.

After instituting new procedures, by 2008 the church claimed to have trained 5.8 million children to recognize and report abuse. It had run criminal checks on 1.53 million volunteers and employees, 162,700 educators, 51,000 clerics, and 4,995 candidates for ordination; and it had trained 1.8 million clergy, employees, and volunteers in creating a safe environment for children.

Failure by the hierarchy to recognize the seriousness of the problem, overemphasis on the need to avoid a scandal, use of unqualified treatment centers, a misguided willingness to forgive, and insufficient accountability were all cited as reasons for the scandal by the Pontifical Academy for Life.

Pope Benedict laicized nearly four hundred priests over just two years for sexually molesting children. Eight U.S. Roman Catholic prelates have resigned since 1990 because of their alleged involvement in sex scandals, seven of which involved minors. The best-reported account of the scandal was *The Faithful Departed*, a book by Philip Lawler, a one-time editor of the Boston *Pilot*, the archdiocesan paper, and of *Catholic World Report*. Reviewer Brian Kelly wrote: "What Lawler demonstrates, so convincingly is that the corruption of so many of the clergy is directly related to so many bishops opting to be successful administrators, public relations players, and damage control manipulators, rather than spiritual fathers animated by zeal for souls."

Lawler ended his book on an inspiring call to hope and trust in God, the Holy Spirit, who will not abandon His church. He gives the example of St. Peter Canisius (1521–1597), a Dutch-born Jesuit, the "second apostle to Germany." When he entered Vienna, only 10 percent of the once Catholic city still had the faith. With this 10 percent St. Peter Canisius reconverted the whole city, transforming it into one of the most exemplary Catholic cities of Christendom.

The church was grievously wounded by the sex abuse scandal, and young peoples' attendance at Mass and participation in the work of the church has continued to decline. While the worst of the scandal may be behind us, the shadow cast by the scandal is long and corrosive. A powerful film based on the *Boston Globe*'s dogged reporting in exposing the Boston archdiocese's cover-up of the priest sex abuse scandal, *Spotlight*, won the Academy Awards for best picture and best screenplay in 2015 and will undoubtedly continue to influence the public's perception of the church's integrity and transparency for years to come.

Moreover, in the same week that the Oscars were announced, the *New York Times* reported on March 2, 2016, that a grand jury in the Pennsylvania diocese of Altoona-Johnstown had found that more than fifty priests and other church employees had molested hundreds of children over four decades, and the abuse had been covered up by two different bishops, who, rather than confronting the abuse, had resorted to the now familiar practice of moving the offending sex criminals to new parishes where they could abuse new victims. "They placed their desire to avoid public scandal over the well-being of innocent children," according to the report, written by Laurie Goodstein and Richard Perez-Pena.

Thus, however painful it is for faithful Catholics to acknowledge, thanks to a changing culture and the church's own self-inflicted wounds, the faithful have indeed departed in the last forty years, and it will be for the future to see if they can be evangelized to return.

The consequences of the sex abuse scandal and the broader trend toward secularization in American society have been stark.

Father George Rutler of St. Michael's Church in New York wrote in November of 2014:

The number of people in New York City who currently identify themselves as Catholic is the same as it was 70 years ago. Yet back then weekly Mass attendance in the city was over 70% and today it is about 12%. Most of the decline came in the conflicted time immediately after the Second Vatican Council. In recent years the decline has leveled off, but the numbers have yet to increase. If all Catholics were serious about their response to Christ's call there would be no redundant parishes.

TRENDS IN RELIGIOUS LIFE

If the decline in lay religious observance has been startling, the falloff in vocations to religious life has been even more severe.

According to a 2015 Center for Applied Research into the Apostolate (CARA) report as interpreted by Father Bevil Bramwell, O.M.I., "The total membership among religious institutes of men has decreased dramatically across the last 45 years, from almost 42,000 in 1970 to fewer than 18,000 in 2015." In fact, the number of male religious has declined faster than diocesan clergy declined. Diocesan clergy decreased by 30 percent, while male religious went down 58 percent. This happened as the number of Catholics in the United States increased from forty-eight million to sixty-eight million in the same years.

Bramwell continues: "Among the ten largest institutions, the Jesuits decreased by 70 percent, Benedictines by 47 percent, Maryknoll by 68 percent, Oblates of Mary Immaculate (my order) by 74 percent."

Women religious in the United States grew from 147,310 in 1950 to 181,421 at their peak in 1966. Since then they have declined to 49,883 in 2014, a decline of 72 percent. There are now about as many women in religious life as there were one hundred years ago, although, of course, the population has more than tripled in the interim. Most alarmingly, fewer than 10 percent of women in religious life today are under sixty, a bleak augury for the future of such life.

In cases where there has been an increase in some orders, the report cautioned that this had often come from consolidation, and yet some vibrant orders such as the Nashville Dominicans have experienced a 76 percent growth since 2000, and the Religious Sisters of Mercy of Alma, Michigan, have seen similar growth with Tom Monaghan's financial support, among others.

In male religious orders, the trend toward aging and lack of new vocations is regrettably consistent, although here, too, there are happy exceptions. While the Benedictines have decreased by 47 percent since 1970 (the loss at Portsmouth Abbey has been higher—70 percent), the St. Louis Abbey has experienced rejuvenation, with so many younger monks that they have no place in the monastery to house their aspiring new postulants.

UPDATE: PORTSMOUTH ABBEY AND SCHOOL IN THE TWENTY-FIRST CENTURY

Even as the school and abbey reached their respective pinnacles in the late 1960s and early 1970s, there were signs of social and spiritual fissures (and it should certainly be acknowledged that with institutions it is always dangerous to hearken back to a "golden age"; inevitably there was plenty of tarnish even in the best of times). The breakdown of order and respect for authority occurred throughout American society in the late 1960s as calls for civil rights for African Americans increased and opposition to the Vietnam War grew. The church suffered from an erosion of discipline, and religious orders such as the Society of the Sacred Heart began to question their traditional vocations and works, searching for greater "relevance." This led to large numbers of defections from the sisterhood and a loss of new vocations that persist to this day. Similarly, a growing number of priests sought to escape their vows, and, in a misbegotten desire to maintain numbers of seminarians, too many bishops and seminary rectors were willing to accept candidates who should have been disqualified on emotional, psychological, and, most of all, spiritual grounds.

Although it tried to act responsibly, Portsmouth Abbey was not immune from these societal trends. Several monks with disqualifying disorders left of their own accord or were advised to discern their vocations in the military or in far-off dioceses.

Father Leo van Winkle, whose leadership of the school had been so instrumental in its success in the late 1950s and 1960s, came to feel out of touch with the new era of students and social ferment. He resigned in 1973 in order to resume his studies at Yale and then became head of the chemical engineering department at Catholic University of America, a testimony to his scholarly and administrative reputation. The new headmaster, Dom Gregory Floyd, had been educated after Portsmouth at Brown and Blackfriars, Oxford. He was handsome, glamorous, and progressive in the question of coeducation, which other of Portsmouth's peer schools, such as St. George's, enthusiastically adopted even as the monastery held out for the fourteen-hundred-year-old Benedictine tradition of single-sex education.

The issue came to a head once again in the early 1980s when the monastic council decided by a single vote that the school should remain single sex. Dom Gregory resigned and went on to a successful career as a consultant to the National Association of Independent Schools and, later, with his own schools' executive search firm. In due course he was canonically laicized.

An especially cruel blow was the sudden death due to an aneurysm of Dom Luke Childs in 1976 at the age of thirty-six. Father Luke was a much beloved Harvard- and Oxford-trained alumnus, monk, and teacher who would certainly have gone on in time to be headmaster, abbot, or both. His death deprived the monastery of perhaps its most able, charismatic, and, by many accounts, saintly potential leader. He, Father Gregory, and the now retired Dom Edmund Adams were all members of the Portsmouth class of 1957, and no alumni from later classes since have persevered in the monastery, even as other Benedictine foundations in St. Louis and at Christ in the Desert in New Mexico have experienced a surge in vocations. Inevitably, visitors and friends have asked, "What went wrong at Portsmouth?"

Dom Gregory's successor as headmaster was Dom Anselm Hufstader, a Yale-educated teacher of German and English who was also a talented flutist. Although ambitious to have the job, he soon experienced doubts and entered into a personality crisis that affected the school negatively, and climaxed with his departure from the monastery, uncanonically. He married the woman he had been in love with many years before but had been prevented by his mother from wedding. He subsequently had a daughter and taught English for many years at the University of Connecticut at Storrs.

Upon Dom Anselm's departure in the late 1980s, Dom Leo returned to the monastery and resumed the headmastership, but he was beset by a virulent cancer that had its origins in his work with radiation on the Manhattan Project at Los Alamos during World War II. He struggled on heroically but soon died in the saddle and was replaced by an English monk from Fort Augustus, Dom Francis Williams.

Portsmouth Abbey was not alone among New England boarding schools in experiencing scandal that accompanied changing moral norms. Sexual abuse claims cropped up at many schools, including Exeter, Taft, St. Paul's, Milton, and, most sensationally, at John Byron Diman's first foundation, St. George's, where in the days just before Christmas 2015 the school released its own report on faculty sex abuse of both boys and girls in the 1970s and 1980s. This prompted a rebuttal in early January 2016 by attorney Eric MacLeish that raised the number of victims from twenty-six to more than forty, and the number of abusers from four to nine, including two instances of student-upon-student rape. MacLeish asserted that attempts to report the abuse to administration officials had been stonewalled in 2004, 2006, 2011, 2012, and even as recently as August of 2015, in an attempt to prevent scandal. But, MacLeish said, "The real scandal, unfortunately, was the efforts of the school to silence victims."

One of those who sought to silence victims was former St. George's lawyer and Rhode Island Supreme Court justice William Robinson. MacLeish noted that although the school fired three of the employees concerned after accusations were lodged, it never reported the matter to state authorities, as required by law. He further said that one of the things that made the case unique was that in the state of Rhode Island there was no statute of limitations for such crimes. In mid-January of 2016 a former Massachusetts attorney general was named to oversee a new investigation after a day-long meeting between victims' representatives and the St. George's School's board of trustees.

In May of 2016 a *Boston Globe* "Spotlight" investigation (the same team that had broken the story of the Boston archdiocese's long cover-up of priestly sexual abuse) released a lengthy report detailing faculty sexual abuse of students in dozens of New England private schools over the previous four decades.

Although there were occasional reports of sexual abuse at Portsmouth (including, in 2015, the termination of a senior, married faculty member for a relationship with a student that had begun when she was just fifteen), the school did not experience anything on the scale of the catastrophe at St. George's and elsewhere.

However, its instability in leadership and failure to join almost every other New England boarding school in becoming coed caused other problems. As the 1980s were ending, the school had increasing difficulty attracting applicants in quantity and of high quality, and by 1990 was in danger of closing, so depleted was its enrollment. Peter Flanigan paid the deficit for that year on the understanding that coeducation at last come to Portsmouth. Abbot Matthew Stark had suffered a heart attack and retired after three terms of office, so a younger monk more in tune with the times and the promise of coeducation, Dom Mark Serna, could carry through the coeducation scheme. Years later Abbot Matthew was wont to say ruefully, "This community broke me." He remained a model monk and can be seen praying for hours in the abbey church daily, but he has purposely kept a low profile, apart from the school, in so doing. However, when his turn comes to preach at mass, in the majestic bass the students refer to among themselves as "the voice of God," the congregation listens, rapt.

Coeducation proved popular from the first and opened the school to many daughters and granddaughters of alumni, who were eager to take up the opportunity. Leadership problems persisted, however, and Dom Mark peremptorily dismissed Dom Francis as headmaster without informing the school's board, a move that angered many. The next headmaster was John Wilkinson, former dean of students at Yale. His tenure too proved controversial and short, though he was credited with making necessary cuts in the school's operating budget. An anecdote about Wilkinson that bears repeating regards a meeting he attended at which his colleague deans complained about the dearth of good writers coming out of the Ivy League. "Why can't we any longer produce a Christopher Ogden, an E.J. Dionne, or a Christopher Buckley?" one exclaimed. When Wilkinson smiled, he was asked, "I suppose you are grinning because two of them went to Yale and only one to Harvard?" "No," Wilkinson replied, "I'm smiling because all three went to Portsmouth Abbey."

After John Wilkinson's departure, Abbot Mark assumed the headmastership as well and threw himself into the work of running and representing the school on campus, nationally, and overseas. However, in the process the monastery continued to age and decline. A promising crop of half a dozen novices produced only one professed monk. Some of the departing novices felt they had been "driven away" by the young abbot. Several years later Abbot Mark was forced to resign the headmastership after a series of inappropriate, intense relationships with female students and a writer-in-residence came to light. While not sexual, these did not exhibit the kind of spiritual paternity essential to a mature educator and religious superior. Additional damage was done when the governing body of the school and that of the English Benedictine Congregation were late to intervene.

In fact, even after Abbot Mark's resignation as headmaster, it was hoped by his successor, Abbot Caedmon Holmes, that Abbot Mark would continue in the monastic community; but in the end this proved impossible. Ultimately he too was laicized, married, became a grief counselor at a Providence hospital, and took priestly orders in the Episcopal Church. Today he lives in Portland, Oregon, and in addition to his hospital duties there offers spiritual direction, gratis.

While all these difficulties were going on in the monastery, the school made progress in rebuilding enrollment and building additional housing and an arts center. Dr. James DeVecchi, a faculty member since 1973, was named headmaster in 2000 and presided over a period of stability.

During DeVecchi's headmastership, a capital campaign raised forty-eight million dollars for new residential buildings, several endowed chairs, and increased scholarship funds. College placement to Tier 1 colleges and universities, always a hallmark of Portsmouth, had declined precipitously but now began to improve, though still lagging well behind schools Portsmouth had traditionally considered its peers. And applications, once six for every one student admitted in the 1960s, were now just two or three to one, again far behind Portsmouth's traditional peer schools. An effort to ameliorate this deficit was undertaken in 2008 with Crane Communications, an Atlanta-based marketing firm, but did not materially improve the number of applications. Increasing numbers of Chinese and Korean students provided welcome full tuitions but were not always conducive to building a unified school community. As New England boarding school tuitions continue to rise over and above the ability of an increasingly stretched middle class to pay for them, the financial pressure on parents builds, and Portsmouth, like many schools, struggles to attract the most highly qualified pool of students.

Abbot Mark Serna's successor, Dom Caedmon Holmes, was a retiring classics scholar who had come to the school as lay faculty member in 1965 and entered the monastery in 1970. He had wished to remain as a professed brother but, as monastic numbers declined, was persuaded to seek ordination in 1997. His greatest ambition, he once said, was to be "a good assistant librarian," but in the depleted situation the monastery found itself, he was named prior administrator on Abbot Mark's departure, elected abbot in 2008, and reelected in 2015. He chose as his abbatial motto a verse from Psalm 51: "O Lord, make in me a clean heart."

It had become clear in the mid-1990s that the long-term future of the monastery and thus of the school as a Benedictine monastery school needed to be addressed. A faculty member named Mark John Clark, now at Christendom College in Virginia, broached this subject thoughtfully in 1998 in a white paper calling for a program to manage a transition from a monastic-led religious school to one where the lay faculty would assume more of the responsibility for infusing Benedictine values into the students. "To do so," he wrote, "we will have to absorb to the fullest extent possible the wisdom and the lived faith of the monks."

Clark closed by expressing the hope that the reassertion of an authentically Catholic, authentically Benedictine identity would help the school in raising funds and building a more committed lay faculty. While his plan was not adopted, the monastery did seek to attract new postulants, without success.

From 2009 to 2013 a monastic renewal effort, enthusiastically led by former board of regents chair David Moran '71, of the well-known towing family, identified several candidates, none of whom stayed in their postulancies for more than a few months.

Given these conditions it was perhaps understandable that a national search for a new headmaster went badly from the start (the original search consultant hired, a former headmaster of Brooks, was forced to resign after it was reported he had used his business credit card to procure male prostitutes while traveling on search assignments). The field of candidates ultimately identified was only seventeen, far fewer than the normal search result (former Portsmouth headmaster Gregory Floyd had provided Pomfret with more than fifty full dossiers when he led their headmaster search a year or two earlier). The search committee made the classic mistake of settling on one candidate prematurely, the head of one of the largest private schools in Canada. He indicated he would accept but then asked for another year so that his son could complete his

secondary education in Toronto. At that point a divided committee scut-
tled the search in favor of appointing an interim internal faculty member
who had not applied for the job with whom Abbot Caedmon and most
of his fellow monks felt more at ease. After a year the interim head was
confirmed as the new permanent head, albeit by one vote on a deeply
divided board, several of whom subsequently resigned.

Daniel J. McDonough, an MIT graduate and holder of the Dom
Andrew Jenks Chair in Mathematics, has served on the Portsmouth Abbey
faculty since 1985 in many positions of responsibility and knows the school
intimately. In addition, he and his family are daily communicants at mass
in the front pew of the abbey church, and one of his daughters has entered
religious life. His considerable challenge will be to continue to rebuild the
school's standing in the New England boarding school world and to determine how best to foster the school's Benedictine identity at a time when
monastic presence in the school has drastically diminished. To do it he will
have to reverse a recent decline in total dollars raised each year and find
funds for a twenty-two-million-dollar science building, replacing the one
Father Hilary and Father Leo designed in 1966.

A larger number of faculty than usual resigned after Dan McDonough's
first full year as headmaster. As disheartening as these developments were,
they may give McDonough a freer hand in building the kind of faculty
he envisions.

Meanwhile, while all this was going on at the Portsmouth Abbey
School, its monastery continued to decline. Dom Benedict Lang and
Dom Michael Stafford died. Doms Julian Stead and Christopher Davis
were removed into nearby nursing homes due to declining health, and the
resident monastic community was reduced to ten, including a nonagenar-
ian, two octogenarians, four septuagenarians, and the rest in their sixties.
Then, in March of 2016, Father Ambrose Wolverton, a beloved teacher
of English and music and gifted organist, choirmaster, and pianist, unex-
pectedly died after a brief illness. In September of 2016, Father Damian
Kearney '45, a model monk, teacher and longtime chair of the English
department died at 89 after a brief struggle with liver cancer. Worst of all,
on May 12, the school community was stunned to learn from an e-mail
sent by the headmaster and chair of the board of regents that, after more

than half a century at Portsmouth, "Abbot Caedmon has resigned his positions at the monastery and School and left the campus. This followed his acknowledgement of personal struggles involving conduct inconsistent with our expectations and Benedictine ideals."

The school declined to elaborate on the precise circumstances when queried by the *Providence Journal* and emphasized that the seventy-five-year-old Caedmon's misconduct had not, to anyone's knowledge, affected students but did refer anyone with relevant information to two lawyers at the New York firm of Debevoise & Plimpton who had handled similar cases in the past.

Abbot Emeritus Matthew Stark, as prior, became once again the monastery's temporary superior (doubtless suppressing the words "Lord, let this cup pass from my lips"), until the abbot president of the English Benedictine Congregation could appoint a new superior from outside the monastery.

Only four of the seven monks left today teach in the school, a far cry from the years when every academic department and house was presided over by a member of the monastic community.

Meanwhile, the remaining monks, including such beloved teachers as Father Philip Wilson, though retired, continue to pray the Divine Office patiently and faithfully. Brother Joseph Byron successfully led a project to finance and construct a wind turbine that now produces more than a third of the abbey's and school's electricity. A senior monk, Dom Julian Stead, now residing in a nearby Newport nursing home for the religious, won acclaim from Gregory Wolfe in *Image* magazine for his poetry.

When I came to read There Shines Forth Christ, instead of the somewhat larger-than-life figure I expected, I found a man—a literate and devout man, to be sure, but one troubled by the same daily struggle to be open to God's love and call to holiness that any Christian experiences. Moreover, I found a poet who had mastered his craft and who was able to write of his spiritual life directly, with simplicity and fervor.

"Earth has its heaven, its home," Dom Julian's poem "Maryland" begins, and some of his most moving poems derive from places he has lived or studied in. Raised in England, with youthful years in

Kentucky and Maryland, study in Rome, and half a lifetime in the monastery of Portsmouth Abbey in Rhode Island, the poet has found more than one heaven on earth. His poems of place are also Christian poems because he sees both the createdness of nature, and the stamp of human character on long-hallowed places. Again, is it a coincidence that the poet should be a Benedictine monk with a vow of stability?

Here is a poem of Father Julian's:

Sea Moon

The moon is the landlord of the night
His face impassive and his movement unharried, unhurried
He watches men die and marry and be born
He looks down through lowered eyelids
And watches what he does not see
How can he hear the mouth gasping in the ocean?
Lift up your voice and cry
He cannot hear
Your voice cannot fill the sea and sky
Go down
The way down is the way upward
Darkness down, never to see
The unfeeling starlight
But the sweet salt dark and the brightness
Of the deep height.

Another, younger monk at Portsmouth Abbey, Dom Paschal Scotti, continues the Benedictine's scholarly tradition while also actively teaching in the school. Ignatius Press will publish his latest book, on Galileo, in the summer of 2017.

John Pepper, an alumnus and longtime CEO of Procter & Gamble as well as the nonexecutive chair of Disney, spoke at the school's commencement in 2008 and made these observations to an interviewer to the school newspaper.

BULLETIN: Speaking as a manager, how do you recommend that Portsmouth set its priorities in the educational marketplace of the next two decades?

PEPPER: Recruiting the best possible people for faculty and administrators; pursuing excellence; providing Portsmouth Abbey School students not only with a first class education but also with values for living; continually upgrading your academic, athletic, advancement and other offerings, and constantly assessing your performance. Never say you can't measure!

How to implement, measure, and steward progress at Portsmouth remains a pressing question, especially in the area of Catholic identity.

Competing Visions of the Catholic Future

Two of the country's most respected Catholic intellectuals, George Weigel and Peter Steinfels, spoke on the future of the church at a conference called "Catholicism and the American Tradition" at a recent Portsmouth Institute. Weigel is a conservative but holds an optimistic vision of the future. Steinfels, a liberal long associated with the *New York Times* and *Commonweal* magazine, takes a more data-based view.

George Weigel:

This challenge will not be met by Catholic Lite. Indeed, one of the most powerful indicators that the Catholic Lite project is finished has been the uselessness of "progressive" Catholicism in the battle for religious freedom this past year and a half, a battle the stakes in which Catholic "progressives" manifestly have not grasped.

The challenge won't be met by Catholic Traditionalists retreating into auto-constructed catacombs.

The challenge can only be met by a robustly evangelical Catholicism that can boldly proclaim Jesus Christ as the answer to the question that is every human life because conversion has been deepened by effective preaching, catechesis, and formation; a demanding, full-time, and evangelically passionate Catholicism that models communities of compassion and nobility in sharp contrast to the radical individualism and loneliness of post-modernity; a public Catholicism that articulates in a compelling way the truths on which any civilized society rests, such as the truth of the inalienable right to life from conception until natural death.

That kind of Evangelical Catholicism can help revivify civil society in America.

Weigel's vision is an attractive dream, but how to find the foot soldiers to carry it out remains an immense challenge.

At the same conference Abbot Emeritus Matthew Stark introduced Peter Steinfels, in a brief talk that touched revealingly on the richness of Catholic culture in Abbot Matthew's Baltimore youth.

Some of you might wonder why this monk was asked to introduce Peter Steinfels, a former editor of Commonweal. *You might ask if this monk is a "Commonweal Catholic." While I would not entirely reject that epithet, a better designation would be one I learned from Father Benedict Groeschel. He and I are "Pius XII liberals." If you were a Pius XII liberal and remained such, you are fairly content because you got much of what you wanted. The Mass is in English; The Divine Office is in English; the Index of Forbidden Books is gone; you can eat meat on Friday in normal circumstances, and it is not a mortal sin. No longer in church once a year is the Legion of Decency pledge required. (One could simply stand and repeat the pledge. One could stand and not repeat the words and that was an un-heroic protest. The heroic protest was to sit and say nothing.)*

When in high school and college I read four magazines on a regular basis: Jubilee, Commonweal, Integrity, *and* The Catholic Worker. *Jubilee was remarkable for its essays, artwork, photography, reporting, and for being ahead of the times. There were stories about Mother Therese, Edith Stein, and Hélder Câmara long before the rest of the world heard about them. Integrity embodied its name, and its essays and articles were excellent.* Commonweal *and* The Catholic Worker *were stimulating and thoughtful.* Jubilee *and* Integrity *disappeared in the '60s. There was not sufficient interest.* Commonweal *and* The Catholic Worker *survive. Of the four there was this to be said: Back then they all had in an evident way a great love for the*

Church. It was clear and steady whatever the point of view in other matters might be. Commonweal, *it seems to me, can still show from time to time that love.*

Peter Steinfels's talk focused on the loss of Catholic identity in America as put forth in his recent book, *A People Adrift*:

Many of my conclusions regarding Catholicism in the U.S. could reasonably be located on the moderately liberal part of the conventional spectrum. But behind the whole project was a profoundly conservative concern: the preservation, the renewal, the deepening, of a genuinely life-shaping Catholic identity.

Since I completed A People Adrift, *the bad news about Catholic identity continues to pile up. We are all aware of the Pew findings that one of every three people saying they were raised Catholic no longer see themselves as Catholic, a shocking discovery I never anticipated even in the wake of the sex abuse scandal.*

Does it matter that one-third of Catholics in their youth no longer consider themselves Catholics in their adulthood, most signing off by their early twenties? Does it matter that 80 percent of Catholics, including 70 percent of regularly church-going Catholics, reject papal teaching on contraception? Does it matter that we are ordaining only 30 new priests for every 100 that retire or die? Or that priests' average age has gone from 45 in 1970 to 63 or older now?

Does it matter that perhaps half of marriages involving Catholics are now to a non-Catholic partner, with all the challenges that poses for passing on a strong Catholic identity? Does it matter that a growing percentage are not marrying in the church at all?

Does it matter that 45 percent of Millennial generation Catholics are Hispanic, that the emergence of a plurality or even majority Latino church will introduce new supports for Catholic identity?

The most significant tension is between identity Catholics and inclusion Catholics.

Identity Catholics emphasize adherence to defining beliefs, practices, roles, and structures of authority. Inclusion Catholics worry about extending the church's reach to outsiders, outcasts, the ignored, and the overlooked. The church should be the voice of such people outside its ranks and welcome them within its ranks.

Ideally, identity and inclusion Catholics should recognize and embrace one another's concerns. Inclusion has to be part of identity. Identity has to be the matrix and goal for inclusion. In practice, they appear headed for mutually destructive confrontation.

I am essentially an identity Catholic who thinks Catholic identity probably requires a number of changes that could be considered inclusionist.

In conclusion, Catholic identity is at risk.

Catholic identity cannot be assured by fiat from the top down. It must now be willingly and zealously fostered by a vast network of overwhelmingly lay Catholics.

Catholic identity must incorporate new lessons about the equality and roles of women, about human sexuality, and about bringing faith into a secular world.

Steinfels' analysis is thorough, but, as with Weigel (and they strongly disagree), there is no blueprint for putting his ideas into an actionable plan.

So one is left to ask: Where are the leaders that will implement such ambitious visions?

Epilogue

Endings and New Beginnings

Aedh Wishes for the Cloths of Heaven

Had I the heavens' embroidered cloths,
Enwrought with golden and silver light,
The blue and the dim and the dark cloths
Of night and light and the half light,
I would spread the cloths under your feet:
But I, being poor, have only my dreams;
I have spread my dreams under your feet;
Tread softly because you tread on my dreams.

W.B. YEATS

As DIGBY BALTZELL DEMONSTRATED, SOME ELITES SURVIVE AND OTH-ers fall by the wayside. The *Real Lace* Irish, and the Irish in America as a whole, have done both. The remarkable thing is their ability to rise up again, even after crushing defeats. Daniel Patrick Moynihan's remark on John F. Kennedy's assassination, "I don't think there's any point in being Irish if you don't know that the world is going to break your heart eventually," applies to many of those surveyed in this book, but there are also many heartening stories of perseverance and new triumph.

A 2014 book of photographs by Bill Brett, *Boston Irish*, with text by Carol Belcy, had a foreword by historian David McCullough, who called it "a grand gallery." There were photos of the Boston Police Gaelic Column of Pipes and Drums; Brookline native Conan O'Brien; Sister Evelyn Hurley, S.C.N., in a white wool coat she had knitted for herself;

Carol and Peter Lynch, the hugely successful fund manager at Fidelity; Patriots quarterback Tom Brady; columnist Mike Barnicle; "Nun Day" at Fenway Park in 1968; and, most poignantly given Moynihan's quote, a photo of Bobby and Teddy Kennedy marching on St. Patrick's Day in Boston in 1968, not quite five years after Jack's assassination by Lee Harvey Oswald and less than three months before Bobby Kennedy was killed by Sirhan Sirhan.

The Irish experience in America goes on. Today twenty-two million Americans say their primary ancestry is Irish, while more than thirty-five million say they are partly Irish—more than 11 percent of the population. The heaviest concentrations remain in the Northeast; Miami—at 1 percent—has the least. The Irish have won more Congressional Medals of Honor than any other ethnic group and are justly proud of their record of military service. In Ireland a new form of nativism has grown up as immigration from Poland, Nigeria, and other countries increased in recent decades. This new intolerance held that only those born in Ireland could be called Irish, and there should be no hyphenated terms like Irish-American allowed. Former president Mary Robinson firmly noted, "Irishness is not simply territorial." And the tumultuous welcome given President Obama when he visited in 2011 and revealed that his maternal great-great-great-grandfather, Falmouth Kearney, had emigrated to America from County Offaly effectively made the controversy moot.

REAL LACE TODAY

The *Real Lace* families and their successors have waxed and waned. Over the nearly half century since *Real Lace* appeared, there have been tectonic shifts in business, politics, and religion. The world of the New York Stock Exchange floor where trades were consummated by handshakes, "your word was your bond," and fulfillment was conducted by paper carried by runners is as dead as the dodo. And yet the Exchange still thrives, and my niece, Casey MacGuire, now works there.

Today Wall Street is smaller in terms of people employed, all trading is electronic, and networks are global. While access to capital has thus increased, the potential for destructive insider trading and fraud has also increased, as *The Big Short*, a 2015 film on the 2008 mortgage bubble based on Michael Lewis's book, dramatically depicted. Irish Americans continue to be active in the finance and trading worlds.

For some years, from 1997 to 2007, the "Celtic Tiger" lifted the Irish economy. In 2005, in fact, there were more Americans emigrating to Ireland—forty-three hundred—than there were Irish entering the United States—only seventeen hundred. Until the bubble burst in 2008, immigrants from Ireland to New York in the 1980s and 1990s returned home in hopes of finding a more prosperous life in Eire; but once the Irish economy collapsed, and the bill for the free-spending ways of Irish bankers and politicians came due, there were no more jobs to return to, and the trend reversed itself once again.

In politics there have been a series of seismic shifts, from the New Deal to Eisenhower Republicanism to the New Frontier; the Great Society, Nixon, and Watergate; Carter and the Iran hostages; new economic growth under Reagan; the fall of communism under George H.W. Bush; the Clinton administration's relative prosperity (thanks in large part to a Republican congress); George W. Bush's prosecution of two wars after 9/11; and stalled growth under President Obama. Then came the rise of the Tea Party and the extraordinarily fractious 2016 presidential campaign, leading to the ascendancy of Donald Trump, who, despite a lack of any informed policy, persuaded people he can protect them and create new jobs, even though his record in business would seem to suggest the reverse.

George Marlin pointed out in a 2016 column:

Reagan carried the Catholic vote 49 percent to Carter's 42 percent (Independent candidate John Anderson received 7 percent), and the decade of the 1980s was the highpoint of the voting power of Catholic Reagan Democrats.

Since then there has been a steady decline.

The rapidly declining number of World War II veterans helps explain, in part, why former swing states in presidential elections— New York, Pennsylvania, Illinois, New Jersey—have become deep blue states. Thirty years after Reagan's smashing 1984 reelection (he won 49 states, as had Nixon in '72), many of his Catholic supporters are now in their nineties and have moved to Florida, or have moved on to their heavenly reward.

Catholic Reagan Democrats are simply no longer a significant voting bloc. And many of the children and grandchildren of the "Greatest Generation" are now "cafeteria Catholics," if Catholics at all.

As sociologist Charles Murray pointed out in his trenchant work Coming Apart, *the remaining Catholic blue-collar residents of once vibrant manufacturing towns are no longer "tightly knit, family oriented, hard-working, hard fighting" due to the declining influence of the Church and the triumph of the counter-culture.*

Marlin could have also noted that the Irish-American blue-collar vote is much smaller than it used to be, as indeed is the Irish-American percentage of the electorate overall.

The *Real Lace* families survive and in some cases continue to thrive. Morgan McDonnell is a businessman in Chicago and head of McDonnell International, a sales and distribution firm there. His daughter Martha appeared as a fiddler in Sting's *The Last Ship* on Broadway in 2015 and also performed in Steve Martin's and Edie Brickell's *Bright Star* in 2016.

The eldest of Murray and Peggy McDonnell's children, Pia, married Irish glassblower and entrepreneur Simon Pearce. Their home and company headquarters is in Quechee, Vermont. One of their children, Kevin Pearce, was a champion snowboarder in training for a place on the U.S. Olympic team when he suffered traumatic brain injury in a fall. His life lay in the balance for weeks, but he has made a miraculous recovery and gives motivational talks to others who have suffered similar injuries on behalf of his organization, *Love Your Brain*.

Another daughter of Murray McDonnell, Anna (known as "Pudd'n"' when she was a horsy young girl), has founded a not-for-profit called 5 for 5, which addresses gender inequity on behalf of women around the world. A third daughter, young Peggy, is married to New York district attorney Cyrus Vance Jr. At a recent birthday party in their West Side apartment for her brother, my classmate and close friend Michael McDonnell, I remembered older relatives of my father's generation recounting that the Peter McDonnells and James Butlers had neighboring townhouses on West 86th Street. When my great-grandmother, Mary Butler, died suddenly in 1902, my great-grandfather, James Butler, was so grief-stricken that it was Mr. and Mrs. McDonnell who met the Butler daughters' train at Pennsylvania Station when they returned from Visitation Academy in Washington, D.C. Over a century later it was good to be back on the West Side with the McDonnells again.

And yet another McDonnell, Stephen, has built a successful meat smoking and marketing firm, Applewood Farm. An early financial partner in the venture was Christopher Brady, son of former senator and treasury secretary Nicholas M. Brady, so the Brady, Murray, McDonnell friendships endure as well.

It is a sadness to the McDonnell matriarch, Peggy Flanigan McDonnell Walsh, that her children have fallen away from the faith and seldom go to Mass. It must pain the older generations, living and dead, to see so many present-day Irish Americans indifferent to the faith their ancestors suffered, died, and, in many cases, emigrated to America for.

Of the Bradys, Stephen Birmingham related how Mr. and Mrs. Nicholas F. Brady (an uncle of the present-day former secretary of the treasury Nicholas F. Brady) used their Roman villa on the Janiculum Hill, with its breathtaking panorama of the Eternal City, to entertain the Vatican's most prominent prelates and the future Cardinal Spellman. They also kept a great estate on the part of the North Shore of Long Island called the Irish Channel, where the Graces also maintained an impressive country place. It was there at Inisfada that the now widowed Duchess Brady gave a lavish reception for her friend Cardinal Pacelli, the future Pope Pius XII, when he stayed with her there in October of 1936. A year later Duchess Brady married William Babbington Macauley, a trawler captain and, later, the minister to the Vatican from the Irish Free State. When Mrs. Brady died the following year from complications of a dental procedure, Macauley inherited the bulk of her estate and traveled between Rome, New York, and Florida with his chef-butler, later private secretary, a man named Woods. When Macauley died, he left all of his money to Mr. Woods. Thus, a great portion of Anthony Brady's fortune passed out of the Brady family, to their intense dismay. Inisfada, however, had been left by the duchess to the Jesuits to use as a retreat house. They did so until it was sold by them in 2013. Today's Nicholas Brady was philosophical, commenting to the *New York Times*, "Changing times bring with them changing solutions."

The Bradys have retained equine interests. After leaving government and organizing a successful Latin American investment fund, Nick Brady reentered horse racing in a modest way. On a sentimental trip back to Ireland in 2015, he was persuaded by John Magnier of Coolmore Farms to reengage in Thoroughbred breeding as well. His daughter Kim now leads the venerable Myopia Hunt north of Boston, and several nephews, including Jockey Club steward Ian Highet, own TIC Stables. TIC, Ian says, stands for "Three Idiot Cousins."

Of the younger Buckleys the most politically active are Brent Bozell Jr., who runs Accuracy in Media, a conservative watchdog organization, and William Buckley O'Reilly, a political consultant. After endorsing Barack Obama for president in 2008 and subsequently resigning from *National Review*, Christopher Buckley retired from writing about politics, which he calls "sufficiently self-satirizing" without his further intervention. He remarried to Dr. Katy Close of the South Carolina textile family in September 2012. Buckley's latest novel, *The Relic Master*, a satire set in the sixteenth century centered on the sale of religious relics, was published in December of 2015. Henry and Nancy Kissinger cohosted the book party with Katy Close at the Council for Foreign Relations building on Park Avenue.

Chris Ward '55, son of Jane Wyatt and grandson of Euphemia van Rensselaer Wyatt, died in 2010. He had worked as an aeronautical engineer in California and been a quiet, though generous, philanthropist.

In late February of 2016, Stonor Lodge, the former house of Noreen Drexel on Bellevue Avenue in Newport, burnt to the ground while under renovation. Only a single workman was on the site near the close of the day. Just the chimneys remained standing. Mrs. Drexel's daughter, Nonie, now living in Scotland, wrote me, "I'm glad my mother didn't live to see it."

Jake Murray, author of the Southampton novel *The Devil Walks on Water*, developed bipolar personality disorder and "pathological drinking." He was found drowned off Staten Island; whether he was pushed from the Battery or was a suicide is still debated.

Father D. Bradley Murray, S.J., whom Birmingham mentioned as the holder of a patent, echoing his father's and grandfather's scientific achievements, was an illustrious and beloved teacher at Georgetown Prep until his death in 2010.

Michael J. Meehan, a scion of the Wall Street Meehans, considered scrappy Irish up-and-comers in the 1920s, is today president of the Brook, one of New York's WASPiest private clubs.

Robert J. Ryan is a prominent Republican political consultant who, under Governor George Pataki, became chairman of the Roosevelt Island Authority. He now advises John Catsimatidis, a Greek-American billionaire listed at number 182 on the Forbes 500 list of wealthiest Americans. Catsimatidis has already run for mayor in New York and lost once, but may entertain further political ambitions. In addition to an oil refinery and hundreds of gas stations, Catsimatidis controls the Red Apple and Gristede Foods, the successor to the Butler grocery store chain.

Speaking of the Butlers, Marymount College in Tarrytown, confronting declining enrollment, consolidated with Fordham University in 2002 and then closed in 2008, though there is still a residence for retired nuns there. Marymount Manhattan College and the Marymount School on Fifth Avenue, by contrast, are thriving institutions. A seventy-fifth-anniversary history of the school was published in 2002. Its title, *Educating the Heart and Mind*, was taken directly from foundress Mother Marie Joseph Butler's original prospectus.

The Mara family is one that has stayed close to the church, and today one of the Mara granddaughters, Erin, is teaching first grade at Loyola School. In a recent parish publication, she wrote:

> *I like to think that Saint Ignatius Loyola School chose me, not solely because of a job opportunity; it had chosen me long before I was*

born. In 1952, at a Sunday morning Mass in the Church of St. Ignatius Loyola, a parishioner fainted. Two people rushed to her aid—Ann Mumm and Wellington Mara. These two met for the first time at that Sunday Mass. They were soon married, had eleven children and forty-three grandchildren. I am number sixteen of the forty-three grandchildren. This parish holds many special memories for my family.

Yet another old-line patriarch, Walter J.P. Curley Jr., former ambassador to Ireland under Gerald Ford and to France under George H.W. Bush, died in June of 2016 at ninety-four. An oil executive in India and Italy after decorated service in World War II, in later life he became a venture capitalist at J.H. Whitney and with his own firm. The Church of St. Vincent Ferrer was crowded. "Treat your family as friends, and your friends as family" was one of the favorite expressions of his daughter Peggy Curley Bacon, and it was evident that had been the case as he and his wife Mary, both Pittsburgh-born (she being a Mellon cousin), had made their way around the world in business and public service. The Marine Corps honor guard played "Taps" for this highly decorated combat infantry officer who had fought bravely on Iwo Jima, Okinawa, Guam, and in northern China. Curley never forgot his roots and maintained a farm in the west of Ireland in addition to the family homes in New York City and Bedford. Hugh Hildesley, Anglican priest and Sotheby's auctioneer, recalled being taken to the golf club there by Curley two summers ago, where the golf pro apologetically told them they would have to start on the back nine.

"Why is that?" the former ambassador asked.

"Because the Taoiseach ("prime minister" in Gaelic) has just teed off on number one, and he has a rather large security contingent with him."

"Well, alright," the then ninety-two-year-old feistily replied. "But tell him to get a move on, or else Curley will be playing through."

PORTSMOUTH: ENDURING MEMORIES

Over a recent September I read *The Schoolmaster*, by that eminent Edwardian Etonian Arthur Christopher Benson. The same month I took my younger son up for his last year at Portsmouth, and the two experiences caused a flood of memories of my own boarding school days, now over 50 years ago on the shores of Narragansett Bay.

September brings with it ambrosial associations of still-warm weather in Rhode Island; swimmable water; grass still growing green; and the peach, pear, plum, and apple orchards bringing forth their abundant fruit. Then there was the sweat and pain of early football and, too soon, the onslaught of classes and crushing homework assignments. Dr. Schehl, the Austrian classics department chair, enjoyed insisting, "You should have at least two hours of homework in *every* subject."

I came to boarding school from a small village on Long Island that still had dirt roads and horses. My roommate arrived from Madrid via Carnaby Street with hair that the headmaster swiftly had shorn, psychedelic cufflinks, and a lapel button that blared "Let's Legalize Pot." Nion McEvoy, today the CEO of Chronicle Books in San Francisco, would use his drumsticks to beat out Wilson Pickett's "In the Midnight Hour" after lights-out every night on our cinder block walls until I started bombarding him with my heavier textbooks. The room we shared in St. Bede's House would look microscopic today had it not succumbed to the wrecker's ball several years ago.

September turned into fall, and fall into a very long winter. Winters were colder then. When ice formed on the *inside* of one's window and a mild plea was made to one's housemaster, the reply was not terribly sympathetic: "*My* room isn't cold." So we shivered and persevered.

In a really cold winter, Narragansett Bay would almost completely freeze over, and we could walk several hundred yards out on the ice to smoke cigarettes. This was the setting of the opening scene in Christopher Buckley's first book, *Steaming to Bamboola*.

> *One afternoon as I stood on the edge of the ice, an old Victory ship steamed by, passing so close I felt the vibrations of her propeller under my feet. Her name was Hannibal Victory. She was loaded down and outward bound.*
>
> *Leaning over the taffrail, one of her crewmen was having a smoke. It probably startled him to see a small boy in school uniform*

standing on the edge of the ice a mile out from shore. The seaman's face
creased into a grin. He laughed. And then with a wave of his arm he
beckoned me to jump for it. The seaman laughed again, unaware of the
effect of his gesture on me. I watched him until he was only a speck on
the poop deck of a ship disappearing out to sea.

There were wonderful characters, such as the mad polymath Father Andrew, who never slept and would press on you two-day-old pancakes from deep in his monastic habit if he encountered you on the campus. "Does that pancake taste OK?" he asked one third former who had been too polite to decline the offer. "Yes, Father," the boy lied. "Oh," Father Andrew said, looking relieved. "That's good, because late last night I was sprayed by a skunk and I was afraid it might have ruined the flavor."

A few weeks after Father Andrew's death, the school doctor was working in the infirmary office. He glanced out into the central corridor of the infirmary. There was Father Andrew, looking at him with a lit cigarette in his fingers. The doctor smiled and waved without thinking, and the apparition smiled and nodded back. Then the doctor did a double take. Impossible! He's dead! When he looked again, there was no one there. He rushed out into the corridor, and there was no one. But a wisp of cigarette smoke was vanishing into the air.

Then there was Brother Basil, the gnome-like librarian with hair sprouting out of his ears who could recite all the members of Europe's royal families going back centuries but was so deathly afraid of thunder and lightning that he would call a taxi from seven miles away in Newport to transport him the two hundred yards to the monastery when bad weather threatened.

Or Father Wilfried, who had danced with Pavlova and was a Dragon Rouge of heraldry. He enjoyed sharing his rather racy limericks:

There was once a lass from Aberystwyth
Who took grain to the miller to make grist with
The miller's boy Jack laid her flat on her back
And they mingled the things that they pissed with

And my own housemaster, Father Hilary Martin, whose photograph leaving La Grenouille after lunch with Amanda Burden made the front page of *Women's Wear Daily*, a copy of which mysteriously ended up in front of the abbot's chair at recreation one evening. Father Hilary was unfazed. "I was in New York fund raising, and, after all, you have to eat *somewhere*."

Winter eventually gave way to spring, Sunday morning softball games after mass with the Grateful Dead blaring from the dorm speakers, walks in the woods, and a rare sighting of females on prom weekend in early May (when, romantically enough, in my first year it snowed). Most of the year the closest we got to girls was receiving an occasional letter (yes, once upon a time people really did write letters) from Farmington or Dana Hall, with a wax seal that read "SWAK," for "sealed with a kiss."

That was then. Today the world of boarding schools is very different. When I took Rhoads, the younger of my two boys, up to Portsmouth for his sixth form year, the influence of coeducation was stunningly apparent. The lucky sods are now surrounded by gorgeous and incredibly sweet young ladies with whom to explore the two miles of shoreline down by the bay. The beautiful campus, designed by Pietro Belluschi and only half built in my day, has now been completed. The food is edible now, sort of; vacations are longer; weekend passes—once forbidden—are ubiquitous; pizzas and take-out Chinese are constantly being delivered to the dorms; and every common room has a large TV screen. Yet somehow work is still being done, the masterpieces of the Western canon are still studied, and the monks, fewer and ever so much older now, still sing melodious Gregorian chant. Despite setbacks in recent years, the monastery is once more seeking renewal under a new religious superior and has much to celebrate in what has been achieved as it enters its second century. The three imperatives of *Reverence*, *Respect*, and *Responsibility* remain words for the entire monastic and school community to live by.

The woods where we used to grill steaks over a fire and monastic farm of old have become Carnegie Abbey, a global golf destination. "Where do we take our vow of affluence?" Father Julian, my old Latin master, asked when he saw it. It was Father Julian who wrote on my report card (truly, alas), "Only the occasional yawn would reassure me he had not fallen asleep altogether." To judge from Rhoads's report cards, this may be an inheritable trait.

In almost every way boarding school is a much kinder, gentler, and more joyous experience than it was in the turbulent and decidedly single-sex sixties, and when I left Rhoads, it was with real regret and the sense this really was a place that, for all its challenges, one could come home to again.

Meanwhile, Canterbury School celebrated its centennial year in 2015–16. At a gala in November of 2015 at Gotham Hall in New York, it announced the public phase of a seventy-five-million-dollar capital campaign, forty-five million of which had already been committed, a tremendous achievement for this lay-run Catholic school.

The church in recent years lost several of its most eloquent voices, including *First Things* editor Father Richard John Neuhaus, Cardinal Avery Dulles, and novelist/sociologist Father Andrew Greeley, who died after a long and prolific life. His 1974 book *A Most Distressful Nation* argued that the Irish in America had abandoned their identity and become WASPified. Though he prided himself on his social science objectivity, Greeley could be hilariously churlish and curmudgeonly. My classmate Michael Garvey could quote many of his aperçus but liked this one from one of Greeley's novels best: "He was so stupid even the other bishops noticed."

The election of Argentinian Pope Francis, the first "American" pope, has caused an outpouring of enthusiasm.

Pope Francis expressed longing for a church "that is poor and for the poor." A church, that is, that exists to serve and sometimes to suffer. "A healthy Church sees the contempt of the world as a sign of spiritual progress, another welcome opportunity to conform ourselves to the image of Christ." His thinking is in this sense very much in synch with Dorothy Day's.

Pope Francis's proclamation of a Year of Mercy in 2015–16 and his emphasis on forgiveness and inclusion touched a sympathetic chord worldwide. His welcome in the United States in September of 2015 was tumultuous in New York, Philadelphia, and Washington.

Order of the Sacred Heart

In Stephen Birmingham's *Real Lace*, there is a chapter entitled "Sons of the Priory, Daughters of the Sacred Heart."

It reads in part:

> *For the girls, the right schools are those operated by the order of the Sacred Heart. If a Catholic girl from a good family decided to become a nun, the most fashionable order was the Sacred Heart. In every city the Sacred Heart school is usually considered the "snob Catholic school . . . Their schools, in addition to academic subjects, teach upper class values, morals and manners . . .*
>
> *The Sacred Heart girl is taught how to hold a fork, how to pierce the breast of a chicken Kiev with the tip of a knife, how to fold a napkin, how to speak to servants, how to sit and how to rise from a chair, how to turn the dinner conversation at the conclusion of a course and how to curtsy. She is taught, in other words, how to be an elegant lady, a gracious hostess and a proper guest. . . . A Sacred Heart girl should sit erect with her knees together and her feet flat on the floor, or else crossed gracefully at the ankles—never with knees crossed. When asked what is wrong with knee crossing the Sacred Heart nun will reply, "My dear, nothing is wrong with it. It is just something that a Sacred Heart girl does not do."*

Oh dear, when was the last time anyone saw chicken Kiev on a menu? One hopes today's Sacred Heart girls are being taught how to eat ramen and BBQ. Perhaps Lady Gaga, this generation's best-known alumna of the Sacred Heart School at 91st Street in Manhattan, will lead the conversation on etiquette.

But probably not. Today's Sacred Heart school at 91st Street and Fifth Avenue, housed in the Italian Renaissance building originally built by Otto Kahn, is more concerned with emphasizing academics and the honor of service than finishing young ladies in the gentler arts of society. To judge by my grand-niece Lily MacGuire's progress, it is doing its job well.

Worldwide, the Order of the Sacred Heart, still rooted in prayer, identified five priorities at its general chapter in 2008: (1) dialogue, relationships, communication, and networks; (2) contemplation; (3) community life; (4) justice, peace, and integrity of creation in solidarity with those who are most vulnerable; and (5) focus on young people.

The order now comprises some twenty-five hundred sisters in forty-one countries in its mission to deepen the understanding of God's love and reveal it to the world through the service of education. There are 125 schools in 29 countries around the world and 22 in the United States. Vocations have declined in Europe and North America but have grown in Africa, Latin America, and Indonesia. This is, in part, says Sister Suzanne Cook, "because the Order of the Sacred Heart prizes openness to other religious traditions."

Although still primarily operating schools for young women, the order now has boys' and coed schools. It continues to provide a classical education but one that "looks forward" to the world its students will be entering. "For example, we practice silence for five minutes a day, which may sound almost silly to older people, but where in today's world do children and young men and women ever get a chance to be silent?" asks Sister Suzanne. "This is not about nostalgia," she emphasizes, "but about knowing God with a view to the future."

Knights of Malta

The Sovereign Military Hospitaller Order of St. John of Jerusalem of Rhodes and of Malta (Knights of Malta) continues to attract well-to-do Irish Catholics committed to good works, among them several members of the Carter and Carroll families and J. Barry Donahue of Palm Beach. Robert Shafer, formerly the senior public relations executive of Pfizer, is the order's representative to the United Nations. A recent book, *Secret Places, Hidden Sanctuaries*, by Stephen Klimczuck and Gerald Warner of Craigenmaddie, detailed the Knights of Malta's activities, aristocratic membership, and extensive real estate holdings in Europe and around the world.

Making All Things New: Saving St. Thomas More

After the death of the more reserved Cardinal Edward Egan, his ebullient successor in New York, Timothy Cardinal Dolan, had the unenviable task of continuing to restructure the archdiocese's pastoral, educational, and charitable activities to account for a reduced number of priests, fewer religious and practicing Catholics in the city, and a growing population in the archdiocese's upstate counties. There are still 2.6 million Catholics to serve in the archdiocese.

Under the title of Making All Things New, a plan was put forward to reduce parishes and close some schools. One of these, the beautiful Church of St. Thomas More on East 89th Street off Madison Avenue, created a firestorm of criticism from parishioners who were passionate about retaining their spiritual home. Unlike other parishes suggested for closure, St. Thomas More was financially sound.

Thanks to the impassioned outpouring of support from its parishioners, neighbors in the "village" of Carnegie Hill, and admirers throughout the City and beyond, however, the lovely little church continues to minister to the spiritual and secular needs of the Upper East Side communities it serves in so many generous ways.

Outside consultants had lobbied the cardinal that the pastors of St. Thomas More and the Church of St. Ignatius Loyola on Park Avenue—six blocks south—should be instructed to explore the benefits of a "merger," albeit one that would result in St. Thomas More being closed and, possibly, redeveloped commercially.

The church was built in 1870 as an Episcopal church, and the original congregation merged with the Church of the Heavenly Rest when it moved uptown to Fifth Avenue and 90th Street. The church was then bought by the Dutch Reformed Church of Harlem, which, founded in 1660, is the second-oldest church in Manhattan, and rededicated on October 6, 1929. Sadly, however, that congregation experienced a steady decline in numbers. By 1949 the ecclesiastical complex at 89th Street had fallen into its second period of disuse and plans were made to sell it.

The Roman Catholic Archdiocese of New York, under Cardinal Spellman, bought the property and on July 9, 1950, consecrated a new parish as the Church of St. Thomas More, in honor of the great martyr under Henry VIII who as lord chancellor of England declined to bend to the sovereign's will and went to his death proclaiming himself "the King's good servant, but God's first."

In the ensuing six decades the Church of St. Thomas More has thrived and grown, though successive pastors have paid careful attention to preserving and restoring what is best about its singular Gothic Revival character. At the same time, St. Thomas More has provided abundant ministries. It houses one of the finest and most sought-after preschool programs on the East Side. It is the "parish" church of St. David's School down the block, the Convent of the Sacred Heart at 91st Street, and other schools in the neighborhood. The rectory provides meeting spaces for Alcoholics Anonymous and many other community and parish groups. Furthermore, St. Ignatius Loyola is one of the busiest parishes in the city, with many schools and ministries of its own to attend to. There is no way St. Ignatius Loyola could do justice to the needs of an additional thousand families from St. Thomas More.

As emotions rose in the dispute, Peggy Noonan wrote a piece in the *Wall Street Journal* entitled "Cardinal, Please Spare This Church." She quoted the speculations of others that the church would be torn down and developed to help fund sexual abuse victim payments and the cost of renovating St. Patrick's Cathedral. Although many church closings, Catholic and otherwise, have led to redevelopment in the past, this theory was fiercely contested in a response by auxiliary bishop John O'Hara, the head of Making All Things New. Bishop O'Hara saved his most withering criticism, however, for the idea that Peggy passed along from another that the cardinal might solve any financial problems the archdiocese has by following Boston cardinal O'Malley's example and selling off his large residence in the back of the cathedral in favor of more humble digs. O'Hara pointed out that, unlike in Boston, the cardinal's residence in New York is actually *attached* to the cathedral.

Charles Scribner III, a Catholic convert and art historian, described St. Thomas More as "the parish jewel of New York" and called upon the cardinal "to do what King Henry would not: reverse the capital sentence." Letters poured in for the cardinal, parish and community meetings were held to protest the closure, and social media postings grew exponentially.

To his credit, Cardinal Dolan, though a bit hurt by what he regarded as "insulting" insinuations, retained his abundant good cheer and thanked his correspondents for providing information that would help him make his final decision.

Bishop O'Hara came to two Sunday masses at St. Thomas More just before Christmas and met personally with the parishioners afterwards. He was received cordially and was apparently impressed by what he learned about the special family nature of the parish. A proposal put forth by one of the parishioners at St. Thomas More to merge the parish with that of Our Lady of Good Counsel on 90th Street between Third and Second Avenues was approved. In that scheme, unlike the proposed "merger" with St. Ignatius Loyola, both churches would remain open, albeit sharing a pastor. The pastor of St. Thomas More, Father Kevin Madigan, a personable and veteran priest, previously had simultaneously led two parishes downtown and said he would be glad to do so again. Thus, one of the most precious parishes on what Stephen Birmingham referred to as the "Irish Gold Coast" of the Upper East Side has been preserved.

Cardinal Dolan then capably moved on to complete the fund-raising for the spectacular renovation of St. Patrick's Cathedral and to launch a successful new capital campaign of several hundred million dollars to secure the archdiocese's future ministries, strengthening each of its 297 parishes as well as St. Joseph's Seminary, which in 2016 graduated twenty-four newly ordained priests, its largest number in many years. Thomas Murphy of Cap Cities/ABC, now in his nineties, generously pledged ten million dollars at the outset of this major effort, and thus far it is proceeding ahead of its projected goals.

Another of Cardinal Dolan's initiatives has been the creation of youth ministries, including the Sheen Center for the Arts (named, of course, for Bishop Fulton J. Sheen) in a renovated school in Greenwich Village at Bleecker and Elizabeth Streets. Under the energetic direction of award-winning producer William Spencer Reilly, the center programs cultural events in many different art forms with the hope of leading young people "toward the light." David Mamet was a recent artist in residence who spoke about his faith, and Brian Dennehy is planning an evening of readings from Eugene O'Neill, whose later plays are suffused with religious sensibility. This approach of using "the good, the true, and the beautiful" to attract younger Catholics and potential converts to the arts and to the church is in its own way very Benedictine and consistent with the church's traditional patronage of the arts over many centuries.

It should be noted how dominant Irish Catholic entertainers remain in late-night television. Stephen Colbert, Jimmy Kimmel, Conan O'Brien, and Jim and Jeannie Gaffigan are all highly rated in their time slots, and the Gaffigans, especially, are forthright in presenting, often self-deprecatingly, material about their Catholic faith.

St. Patrick's Day 2016

St. Patrick's Day 2016 was a celebratory event as always, and Jimmy Neary, the Mayor of 57th Street, welcomed an overflowing crowd into his pub near First Avenue, ably assisted by his daughters, Una and Anne Marie, and a loyal longtime staff. He has been doing so since 1968. Before that Jimmy was the lead bartender at a place called P.J. Moriarty's on Third Avenue where Trump Plaza now stands. It had a model railroad that ran around the bar serving food orders and a raucous, loyal customer base. "Sure," Jimmy once assured me. "All your family were in there."

I was afraid of that.

Hugh Carey, Mary Higgins Clark, and even Bill Clinton were frequently in attendance on St. Paddy's Day at Neary's, which still has the best Irish coffee in all of New York.

Al Smith Dinner 2016

The Al Smith dinner remains a highlight of the fall benefit season, especially, as in 2016, during a presidential campaign, when the major party candidates attend in white tie and treat the assembled crowd to a humorous speech at their own and their opponents' expense. The dinner benefits education, health and family services. Cardinal Dolan is the president of the Alfred E. Smith Memorial Foundation, and Al Smith IV is the CEO. A look at attendees from 2000 to 2010 reveals old-line Real Lacers such as J. Peter Grace and Peter Flanigan, joined by such prominent Irish Americans as James Gill, Thomas Joyce, Thomas Moore, Kevin Cahill, John Castle, Mary Higgins Clark, Raymond Kelly, Christopher Quick, Jim MacGilvray, Mary Alice Williams, Jane O'Connell, Bill Bresnan, Denis Hughes, James Burke, Kevin Greaney, Tom Moran, John F. McGillicuddy, Thomas Murphy, Edward Mulloy, Brian Moynihan, Peter Kiernan III, and actor Ed Burns. But Howard Millstein, William Rudin, Jimmy Tisch, and many others have added an ecumenical flair as well.

In 2016 John G. MacFarlane of Zaff in Houston; lawyer Thomas Moore; Thomas M. Joyce of Arxis Capital; John McAvoy, CEO of Con Edison; Lowell McAdam, CEO of Verizon; Tom O'Malley of PBF Refining; William E. Flaherty of Horsehead, the Zinc titan; and Thomas Moran of Mutual of America were on the dais with the cardinal and the presidential candidates of the two major parties.

Maureen Sherry, Mary Callahan Erdoes, and Mary Higgins Clark were among the well-dressed women on the dais along with Hillary Clinton and Melania Trump. Jerry Hall looked glamorous beside her recently betrothed K. Rupert Murdoch and Bill O'Reilly. Jeff and Liz Peek, Steve and Christine Schwarzman, Mark Gilbertson, Bob Devlin, Cy and Peggy Vance, and her brother Stephen Murray McDonnell all adorned the room.

Al Smith V got off the first good line of the evening commending Donald for his civil greeting to Hillary at the beginning of the evening and quoting Hillary's rejoinder. "Thank you, Donald, now do you mind getting out of the Ladies' Room?"

Hillary praised Cardinal Dolan for bringing together two bitter enemies onto the dais in this fiery election season, "Andrew Cuomo and Bill DeBlasio." Trump's best line was, "The media has completely rigged the election. To give you just one example, Michelle Obama gives a speech and everyone says it was terrific. Not long after Melania gives exactly the same speech, and she gets nothing but criticism. I don't get it!"

Hillary shouted out Michael Bloomberg and said, "It's a shame he isn't speaking, because it would be so interesting to hear what a billionaire has to say." She concluded with a stilted but nonetheless occasionally stirring panegyric to Al Smith and the prejudice he had confronted as the first Catholic presidential candidate, calling on all Americans to come together.

Hillary sounded somewhat presidential; Donald sounded sore, an unhappy warrior.

Christopher Buckley emailed me afterwards, "For a moment or two I thought Donald was doing fine. And then . . . it was Aesop's scorpion and the turtle again."

Brideshead Revisited versus Real Lace Revisited

Irish Americans in the twenty-first century have a continuing if somewhat diminished influence in business and politics. Their traditionally strongest sport, horse racing, has been in serious decline for thirty years, though they remain active in football and other athletic pursuits. They continue to be philanthropic. In fact, they remain resilient in many ways. Sadly, their traditionally strong faith has been eroded in recent decades by scandals in the church and a secularizing culture.

According to Vatican journalist John Allen, the church of the future will be distinguished by its globalization, including its shift from Northern Hemisphere countries to the Southern Hemisphere, especially in Africa and Asia, and a lay apostolate to compensate for the lack of religious vocations. "Faith in the church," Allen writes, "has never meant it does everything right; it means never abandoning hope despite all the things it does wrong."

Recall that Evelyn Waugh's novel *Brideshead Revisited* and its masterly TV adaptation, though widely misunderstood, hinged on Charles Ryder's ultimate conversion as he visits the Brideshead chapel after many years, deployed there in wartime:

> *Something quite remote from anything the builders intended has come out of their work, and out of the fierce little human tragedy in which I played; and something none of us thought about at the time: a small red flame—a beaten-copper lamp of deplorable design, relit before the beaten-copper doors of a tabernacle; the flame which the old knights saw from their tombs, which they saw put out; that flame burns again for other soldiers, far from home, farther, in heart, from Acre or Jerusalem. It could not have been lit but for the builders and the tragedians, and there I found it this morning, burning anew among the old stones.*

The renowned philosopher and Catholic convert Alisdair MacIntrye has provocatively asked whether we are waiting for "another St. Benedict for the 21st century?" The idea would be to reimagine prayer, liturgy, contemplation, and ways of living in community, not just for monasteries like Portsmouth Abbey, but as a model for parishes and whole communities worldwide.

For those who have suffered through the noxious atmosphere of our recent politics and culture, the restraint, modesty, and humility involved in such a renewal would be a welcome refresher. And Irish Americans, true to their ancient faith and traditions, could help lead the way.

In June of 2016 Father George Rutler wrote in his St. Michael's parish bulletin:

In these days of transition in the political life of our nation and in cultures East and West, such as we see in the intense growth of Christianity in former Communist lands while the Faith is increasingly suppressed in formerly Christian countries including our own, we are going through a social earthquake not unlike the transition of the Roman Republic into an Imperium.

Our own nation increasingly indulges luxury and selfishness while rejecting its foundational principles, just as decadent Romans from the second century onwards could hardly connect with the virtuous ideals of the former Republic. The Founding Fathers of our country would be bewildered by the ignorance, vulgarity and opulence that permeate politics today.

That said, the opportunities to work for Christ as his stewards are unparalleled, given the fertile minds and astonishing means of communication available to the Church today. It is the nature of a bureaucracy, even in the Church, to promote mediocrity and to perpetuate corruption, but true Christians have unsurpassed means to defy and deny that calcification of the Gospel.

As important as business, politics, philanthropy, and sport are to the life of a country, ultimately man is a spiritual animal, who cannot be made whole without nourishment of the soul. And the Irish, including

Irish Americans, are profoundly spiritual beings, even when they try to ignore that fact. Murray McDonnell learned that, as did, in his later years, Teddy Kennedy. From a young age William F. Buckley Jr. always knew it. Given the social and religious turmoil of the last fifty years, and the diverse challenges facing our culture today, how the next generation of Irish Americans, and all Americans, choose to direct their spiritual energies will be one of the future's great, as yet unwritten, stories.

Bibliography

Aarons, Slim. A Wonderful Time: *An Intimate Portait of the Good Life.* New York: Hearst, 2007.

Alberigo, Giuseppe, and Matthew Sherry. *A Brief History of Vatican II.* New York: Orbis Books, 2006.

Baker, William F., Warren C. Gibson, and Evan Leatherwood. *The World's Your Stage: How Performing Artists Can Make a Living While Still Doing What They Love.* New York: American Management Association, 2016.

Baltzell, E. Digby. *Philadelphia Gentlemen: The Making of a National Upper Class.* New York: Free Press, 1958.

———. *The Protestant Establishment: Aristocracy and Caste in America.* New York: Random House, 1964.

Bayor, Ronald H., and Timothy J. Meagher. *The New York Irish.* Baltimore: Johns Hopkins Press, 1997.

Beebe, Lucius. *The Big Spenders: The Epic Story of the Rich Rich, the Grandees of America and the Magnificoes, and How They Spent Their Fortunes.* Mount Jackson, Va.: Axios, 1966.

Birmingham, Stephen. *Real Lace: America's Irish Rich.* New York: Harper and Row, 1973.

———. *The Right People: The Social Establishment in America.* New York: Little, Brown, 1978.

———. *The Right Places: (For the Right People).* New York: Little, Brown, 1973.

Brett, Bill. *Boston Irish.* Boston: Three Bean Press, 2014.

Bruni, Frank, and Elinor Burkitt. *A Gospel of Shame: Children, Sexual Abuse, and the Catholic Church.* New York: Viking, 1993.

Buckley, Christopher. *Losing Mum and Pup: A Memoir.* New York: Twelve, 2009.

Buckley, William F. Jr. *Nearer, My God: An Autobiography of Faith.* New York: Doubleday, 1997.

———. *The Unmaking of a Mayor.* New York: Encounter, 1966.

Cliff, Brian, and Nicholas Grene. *Synge & Edwardian Ireland.* Oxford: Oxford University Press, 2012.

Corry, John. *Golden Clan: The Murrays, the McDonnells and the Irish American Aristocracy.* Boston: Houghton Mifflin, 1977.

Deyrup, Marta Mestrovic, and Maura Grace Harrington. *The Irish-American Experience in New Jersey and Metropolitan New York: Cultural Identity, Hybridity, and Commemoration.* Plymouth, U.K.: Lexington Books, 2014.

Fitzherbert Family Papers. Swynnerton Park, U.K.

Greeley, Andrew M. *That Most Distressful Nation: The Taming of the American Irish.* Chicago: Quadrangle, 1972.

Hoffman, Ronald. *Princes of Ireland, Planters of Maryland: A Carroll Saga 1500–1782.* Chapel Hill: University of North Carolina Press, 2000.

Klein, Ed. *Ted Kennedy: The Dream That Never Died.* New York: Crown, 2009.

Irvine, Valerie. *The King's Wife: George IV and Mrs. Fitzherbert.* London: Hambledon and London, 2004.

Lardner, James, and Thomas Repetto. *NYPD: A City and Its Police.* New York: Henry Holt, 2000.

Leyburn, James G. *The Scots-Irish: A Social History.* Chapel Hill: University of North Carolina Press, 1962.

MacGuire, James. *The Catholic Shakespeare?* Lanham, Md.: Sheed & Ward, 2013.

———. *The Catholic William F. Buckley Jr.* Lanham, Md.: Sheed & Ward, 2014.

———. *Catholicism and the American Experience.* New York: Sheed & Ward, 2014.

———. *Modern Science/Ancient Faith.* New York: Sheed & Ward, 2013.

———. *Newman and the Intellectual Tradition.* New York: Sheed & Ward, 2013.

Meagher, Timothy J. *The Columbia Guide to Irish American History.* New York: Columbia University Press, 2005.

Munson, James. *Maria Fitzherbert: The Secret Wife of George IV.* London: Constable & Robinson, 2001.

O'Malley, John W. *What Happened at Vatican II.* Cambridge, Mass.: Harvard University Press, 2008.

Ord Family Papers. Washington: Georgetown University Library.

Quinlan, Michael. *Irish Boston: A Lively Look at Boston's Colorful Irish Past.* Guilford, Conn.: Globe Pequot Press, 2013.

Safian, Joanne, R.H.S.M. *Educating the Heart and Mind: A History of Marymount School 1926–2001.* Marymount, N.Y.: Marymount School, 2002.

Sandburg, Carl. *Abraham Lincoln: The Prairie Years.* New York: Dell, 1960.

Shannon, William V. *The American Irish: A Political and Social Portrait.* Amherst: University of Massachusetts Press, 1989.

Short, Edward. *Adventures in the Book Pages: Essays and Reviews.* Leominster, U.K.: Gracewing, 2015.

Stein, Jean. *West of Eden.* New York: Random House, 2016.

Steinfels, Peter. *A People Adrift: The Crisis of the Roman Catholic Church in America.* New York: Simon & Schuster, 2003.

Wakin, Edward. *Enter the Irish-American.* Lincoln, Nebr.: iUniverse, 2002.

Webb, James. *Born Fighting: How the Scots-Irish Shaped America.* New York: Broadway Books, 2004.

Wilson, Edmund. *The Sixties.* New York: Farrar, Straus & Giroux, 1993.

Index

About the Author

James P. MacGuire was born in New York and educated at Johns Hopkins and Cambridge. He has worked at Time Inc., Macmillan, The Health Network, and the Corporation for Public Broadcasting. His poetry, fiction, and journalism have appeared in many national publications.

He is the author or coauthor of ten books and two beloved sons, Pierce and Rhoads.